820
.9
9287
David

David, D.
Intellectual women and
Victorian patriarchy.

KT.

820
.9
9287
David

David, Deirdre, 1934-
  Intellectual women and Victorian patriarchy :
Harriet Martineau, Elizabeth Barrett Browning, George
Eliot / Deirdre David. -- Ithaca, N.Y. : Cornell University
Press, 1987.
  xvi, 273 p. ; 23 cm.

Includes bibliographical references (p. 256-265) and
index.
04620399  LC:86023989  ISBN:0801419654

1. Martineau, Harriet, 1802-1876. 2. Browning,
(SEE NEXT CARD)

3615    91APR11        fc/kc   1-00549831

# INTELLECTUAL WOMEN AND VICTORIAN PATRIARCHY

*By the same author*

FICTIONS OF RESOLUTION IN THREE VICTORIAN NOVELS:
*North and South, Our Mutual Friend* and *Daniel Deronda*

# Intellectual Women and Victorian Patriarchy

Harriet Martineau, Elizabeth Barrett
Browning, George Eliot

Deirdre David

Cornell University Press
Ithaca, New York

© Deirdre David 1987

First published 1987 by Cornell University Press

Printed in Great Britain


**Library of Congress Cataloging-in-Publication Data**
David, Deirdre, 1934–
Intellectual women and Victorian patriarchy.
Bibliography: p.
Includes index.
1. English literature—19th century—History and
criticism.    2. Feminism in literature.    3. English
literature—Women authors—History and
criticism.    4. Martineau, Harriet, 1802–
1876.    5. Browning, Elizabeth Barrett, 1806–
1861.    6. Eliot, George, 1818–1880.    7. Women and
literature—Great Britain.    8. Feminism and literature—
Great Britain.    9. Women authors, English—19th century—
Biography.    10. Women intellectuals—Great Britain—
Biography.    11. Patriarchy—Great Britain.
I. Title.
PR469.F44D38   1987      820'.9'9287      86–23989
ISBN 0–8014–1965–4 (hardcover)
ISBN 0–8014–9414–1 (paperback)

# Contents

# Preface

'Could the intellectual powers of women be given them to be suppressed and cramped by the other sex? If they really are inferior, what danger can accrue from giving them their full exercise?'

*(Desultory Queries and Remarks Proposed to the Whole World, on Behalf of the Female Sex; Designed to Draw Forth An Abler Hand;* anonymous tract, 1828)

One of the more chilling denigrations of female ambition delivered to women in the nineteenth century is contained in these remarks addressed to Charlotte Brontë by Robert Southey in March 1837: 'Literature cannot be the business of a woman's life, and it ought not to be. The more she is engaged in her proper duties, the less leisure will she have for it, even as an accomplishment and a recreation. To those duties you have not yet been called, and when you are you will be less eager for celebrity' (Gaskell, *The Life of Charlotte Brontë*, pp. 102–3). Despite Brontë's chastened admission to Elizabeth Gaskell that she found Southey's remarks 'kind and admirable', if 'a little stringent', they did not inhibit her from going on to create some of the more interesting female minds in Victorian fiction: Rochester fervently breathes in Jane Eyre's ear that her 'mind' is 'his treasure', Lucy Snowe's intellect astonishes in its acid analysis of patriarchal Villette, and Shirley Keeldar's energetic intelligence radically alters her community.

In *Shirley* we also encounter a minor female character, Rose Yorke, whom Brontë situates in the feminist background of a novel dominated by the radiant vitality of its eponymous heroine. Introduced to the reader in her identity as the daughter of an unusually well-educated Yorkshire landowner, Rose possesses a brief history that is given to us in a few paragraphs. We learn all we are ever going to know about her, and it is sadly sufficient. Brontë wishes us to know about Rose's mind. Her mother

wants to make of her such a woman as she is herself – a woman of dark and dreary duties – and Rose has a mind full-set, thick sown

with the germs of ideas her mother never knew. It is agony to her
often to have these ideas trampled on and repressed . . . Rose
loves her father: her father does not rule her with a rod of iron; he
is good to her. He sometimes fears that she will not live, so bright
are the sparks of intelligence which, at moments, flash from her
glance, and gleam in her language.   (*Shirley*, p. 117)

As it turns out, Rose does live, to become 'a lonely emigrant in some
region of the southern hemisphere'.

This book is about three intelligent Victorian women who did not
become exiles from Victorian culture and society and who defied the
patriarchal injunctions against female authorship issued by
Southey. Harriet Martineau, Elizabeth Barrett Browning and
George Eliot made writing the 'business' of their lives; they gained
'celebrity' in their careers; their sparkling intellects flashed out into
their journalism, their poetry and their novels; and their language
'gleamed' with the yield of a mind like Rose Yorke's – a mind 'full-
set' and 'thick sown with the germs of ideas'. These women became
renowned literary figures and emphatically chose not to live the
private, female life of 'dark and dreary duties' partly imposed upon
Rose Yorke's mother and partly chosen by her. Each was strongly
ambitious and each penetrated the male-dominated public world of
Victorian culture.

In that world they were perceived as clever and industrious,
learned and sensitive, sagacious and brilliant, yet they were never
free of a tension inherent in the Victorian subjugation of woman's
mind by male cultural authority. Their writings never cease to
betray a conflict between female intellectual ambition and dominant
Victorian prescriptions for woman's role and function, prescriptions
which, if not as condescendingly dismissive of woman's mind as
Southey's, dictated that female intellect should be placed in the
service of male-dominated systems of discourse. I shall argue that
however dazzling their careers (as prolific journalist, as revered
'poetess', and as the most famous woman intellectual of the Victorian
period), these three writers struggled against an authority which
defended itself against the unsettling conjunction of powerful
intellect and female sex and gender they embodied by labelling
Martineau 'stong-minded' for her forthright ambition, Barrett
Browning 'unchaste' for her choice of eroticised female imagery,
and Eliot 'masculine' for her putative affectation of 'male' modes of
thought.

The high cultural visibility of these three women, the recognition they achieved as working intellectuals that is manifest both in the condemnation and the admiration they invited, is the principal reason for my attention to them. I chose to discuss Martineau rather than, say, Frances Power Cobbe, because while Cobbe, as journalist and public lecturer, was vigorously conspicuous on the cultural and social scene, her writings do not match the rich textual variety of Martineau's outstandingly fertile fifty-year-long career. The transgressive aspects of Barrett Browning's life and work, the provocative combination of sensitive lyricist and indignant political polemicist, make her career as a learned woman poet/intellectual more abundantly suggestive than that, say, of Christina Rossetti, whose identity in her lifetime tended to be submerged by the gothic flamboyance of her brother and his Pre-Raphaelite fraternity. There are many Victorian women novelists who conducted industrious writing lives (Charlotte Brontë and Elizabeth Gaskell come immediately to mind), but Eliot's iconic status as feminine, female *eminence grise* in Victorian culture is unparalleled and remains unusually resonant, despite the large amount of attention paid to it by feminist and non-feminist critics alike.

Let me make it clear that what follows is not a survey of intellectual life for women in the Victorian period. My emphasis is upon the intellectual talent and ambition of three particular women, selected because their careers demonstrate three significant ways in which a woman could *be* a working intellectual in the Victorian period – as a political journalist, as a poet, and as a novelist. I have been interested in the clear choices these women made to advance their careers as intellectuals and I have assessed three cultural performances, so to speak, enacted within the informing contexts of nineteenth-century life. For that reason, I discuss almost all of their texts. The writings about women for which they are best known – the stirring indictments of patriarchal oppression in Martineau's *Society in America*, Barrett Browning's 'novel-poem' about an independent woman poet, *Aurora Leigh*, Eliot's sympathetic explorations of disappointed female lives – will emerge from this study as segments of the larger discussions about Victorian culture and society in which they participated. To isolate the writings about women would be to engineer, in my view, two equally damaging critical enterprises: it would evade discussion of certain political views which need to be understood as expressive of the hegemony of male, middle-class cultural authority in the Victorian period;

and it would render a disservice to these unusual Victorian women.

In analysing almost all of their writings, in discussing all of their politics (sexual and other), I have aimed to achieve two things: one, to disclose the bravery and boldness of their feminist discursions; and two, to show how the career of a woman intellectual in the Victorian period is constituted by an ensemble of discordant, harmonious, and complex relations between different politics, different texts, and different imperatives, all of which sometimes complement each other and also sometimes contend with each other. If one juxtaposes the feminist politics with the sanctions of influential ways of thinking about sex and gender, one sees both the resistance to, and the compliance with, the hegemony of a male-dominated middle-class culture. The conscious resistance to Victorian patriarchy becomes that much more heroic and interesting in the context of the inescapable cooperation with it. That so much of the writing of these three women intellectuals accepts powerful Victorian directives for the proper uses of woman's mind should neither surprise nor offend us. An insistence that we see these writers as both saboteurs and collaborators is essentially what this book is all about.

If we are stirred by Harriet Martineau's peerless indictments of the wretched conditions endured by English governesses, then we must prepare to entertain her sentimental celebrations of family life; if we approve her prescriptions for the achievement of female economic independence, then we must juxtapose those prescriptions with her conservative interpretation of the role of artisans and shopkeepers in the cataclysmic events of 1848, when the Continent was engulfed by revolution but England remained relatively calm. Elizabeth Barrett Browning's daring deployment in *Aurora Leigh* of imagery derived from woman's body must be understood in terms of the ancillary function of woman's art in building a world free of exploitation articulated in that poem; the unambiguous statements in her letters that woman is intellectually inferior to man cannot be conveniently forgotten when we relish *Aurora Leigh*'s invigorating satire of the insulting education offered to provincial upper-middle-class girls. And if we suffer with Romola in her frustrated desire to become an 'instructed woman' and in her humiliation at the patriarchal hands of her father and her husband, then we must wonder why Eliot discusses women's writing in seventeenth-century France and has nothing to say about struggling professional women in her own time; we must also attempt disentanglement of the discordant ideas in *The Mill on the Floss* where radical sexual politics get mingled with conservative social theories in a flood of contending ideologies.

If we understand Martineau, Barrett Browning, and Eliot as both resistant to and complicit with the culture that both encouraged and demeaned them, then it will also become very clear that they did not feel themselves to be part of a 'separatist' female intellectual life. In fact, their careers implicitly refute that myth of autonomous womanhood which is always the insidious ideological core of partriarchy, and sometimes the sentimental fantasy of certain feminist critics – woman, deracinated from history and society, is untainted by 'male' desires for cultural power. For example, in 1848 Charles Kingsley, in his newly invested capacity as Professor of English at Queen's College, invoked 'woman' to his female audience in this way: 'Would to God that she would in these days claim and fulfil to the uttermost her vocation as priestess of charity! that woman's heart would help to deliver man from bondage to his own tyrannous and all-too-exclusive brain' (*The Works of Charles Kingsley*, 20:258). In a representative instance of recent 'separatist' thinking about women, Wendy Martin paradoxically seems to echo Kingsley. Her study of three American woman poets (Anne Bradstreet, Emily Dickinson, Adrienne Rich) claims that their poetry 'celebrates the life of this earth and demonstrates their commitment to nurturance rather than dominance . . . their work elaborates their vision of a loving community of women that forms the basis of a counter tradition to the androcentric society in which they lived' (*An American Triptych*, p. 3). For Kingsley, women signify charity, the 'heart', and for Martin women signify life, love, and community. One makes a neat division between the emotions and the 'brain' and the other between nurturance and dominance. And by implication, of course, men equal unfeeling aggression, death, competition, and alienating individualism. To understand women intellectuals from the dualistic perspective articulated both by Victorian patriarchy and the 'separatist' tradition in feminist thought is to concur in the elevation of male over female in the valuation of intellectual ability and wishfully to believe that women do not desire cultural and social power. My readings of Martineau, Barrett Browning, and Eliot will show that they do.

In many ways, this book could only have been written after the important, pioneering work in feminist literary criticism dealing with the Victorian period undertaken in the last fifteen years or so. Without Elaine Showalter's study of the 'feminine', 'feminist', and 'female' stages in British women's writing, we would not see how Martineau, Eliot, and Barrett Browning are working within and against these emerging classifications. I must emphasise, however, that I do not share Showalter's preference for 'gynocriticism' (the study of women writers) over the 'feminist critique'. In arguing that 'If we study stereotypes of women, the sexism of male critics, and the limited roles women play in literary history, we are not learning what women have felt and experienced, but only what men have thought women should be', she implies that texts written by women yield unmediated expression of female lives, and that they are uninfluenced by culturally dominant ideas about aesthetic form and about women's 'feeling and experience' ('Towards a Feminist Poetics', p. 27). 'Gynocriticism' posits a mythological women's writing based on an essentialist view of women's lives. From a more dialectical position, I see Martineau, Barrett Browning, and Eliot as actively producing and reproducing many male-dominated Victorian ideas about women, while at the same time being actively engaged by Showalter's concern – 'What women have felt and experienced'.

In their ground-breaking, expansive examination of the anxieties of female authorship in the nineteenth century, Sandra Gilbert and Susan Gubar cleared the critical way so that we might see clearly the degree to which so much writing by women in the Victorian period is thick with rebellion, madness, and resentment generated by their ancillary situation. The work of Nina Auerbach and Mary Ellmann, the former disclosing the constraints and pleasures endemic in communities of women and the demonic female power that is disguised by myths of angelic Victorian womanhood, and the latter doing some fundamental and witty 'thinking about women', made it possible for me to elucidate the attitudes of Martineau, Barrett Browning, and Eliot to Victorian myths of sex and gender, and to begin my own work of thinking about these 'thinking women'. This work is revisionist in the sense that from the perspective of resistance to and complicity with the hegemony of male-dominated culture, it takes a new look at the writings of women who have already been the subject of much important feminist criticism.

To investigate the matrix of complex ideas and events that created the lives and careers of these women, I have placed their work within several contexts which can be diagrammed as three concentric circles: the outer circle is formed by the theory of intellectual practice that has proved most useful to my analysis (Antonio Gramsci's writings about the social function of intellectuals); the next circle is formed by theoretical and contemporary views of Victorian intellectual activity; the third is the context of contemporary views of woman's mind and her higher education in the Victorian period. At the heart of these concentric circles rest three careers spanning the years from 1832 to 1879 – from Harriet Martineau's *Illustrations of Political Economy* to George Eliot's *Impressions of Theophrastus Such* – almost half a century of changing attitudes towards women as 'thinking' members of society.

# Acknowledgements

I am grateful to the Graduate Research Board of the University of Maryland, College Park for generous support and also to Annabel Patterson who arranged time for me to complete this project. I have been fortunate in having the encouragement of my colleagues in the English Department at Maryland, especially Theresa Coletti, Richard Cross, Leopold Damrosch, Carla Peterson, William Peterson, and Joseph Wittreich. Edward Said offered helpful advice about the discussion of intellectuals; Barry Qualls generously read and reread and provided many discerning comments; Nina Auerbach's suggestions for revision made this a better book than it was when she first read it. My greatest debt is to John Richetti, an unswerving admirer of intellectual women, who listened patiently to the early development of ideas and in reading final drafts did his best to save me from clumsy argument and infelicitous prose. This book is dedicated to him.

# List of Abbreviations

The following abbreviations appear in the text and in the Notes. Full details of these works are given in 'Works Cited', pp. 256–65.

| | |
|---|---|
| A. | *Autobiography* (Martineau) |
| A.B. | *Adam Bede* (Eliot) |
| B.R. | *British Rule in India* (Martineau) |
| B.S. | *Biographical Sketches* (Martineau) |
| C.H. | *George Eliot: The Critical Heritage* (ed. Carroll) |
| C.P. | *Complete Poems* (Eliot) |
| D. | *Deerbrook* (Martineau) |
| E. | *Essays* (Eliot) |
| E.L. | *Eastern Life, Present and Past* (Martineau) |
| F.H. | *Felix Holt, the Radical* (Eliot) |
| H. | *The History of England . . .* (Martineau) |
| H.E. | *Household Education* (Martineau) |
| H.H.H. | *Health, Husbandry, and Handicraft* (Martineau) |
| H.O. | *How to Observe Manners and Morals* (Martineau) |
| L. | *Letters* (Eliot) |
| L.EBB | *The Letters of Elizabeth Barrett Browning* |
| L.EBB/DO | *The Letters of Elizabeth Barrett Browning to Mrs David Ogilvy* |
| L.EBB/M | *The Letters of Elizabeth Barrett Browning to Mary Russell Mitford* |
| L.EBB/RHH | *The Letters of Elizabeth Barrett Browning to Richard Hengist Horne* |
| L.RB/EBB | *The Letters of Robert Browning to Elizabeth Barrett Barrett* |
| L.M. | *Letters on Mesmerism* (Martineau) |
| L.S. | *'Life in the Sick-Room'* (Martineau) |
| M. | *Middlemarch* (Eliot) |
| M.F. | *The Mill on the Floss* (Eliot) |
| MS. | *Miscellanies* (Martineau) |
| P.E. | *Illustrations of Political Economy* (Martineau) |
| R. | *Romola* (Eliot) |
| S.A. | *Society in America* (Martineau) |
| S.C.L. | *Scenes of Clerical Life* (Eliot) |
| S.M. | *Silas Marner* (Eliot) |

# Introduction:
# Thinking Women and
# Victorian Ideas

'A thinking woman sleeps with monsters'
(Adrienne Rich, *Snapshots of a Daughter-in-Law*, no. 3)

As a social group virtually always of the male sex and masculine gender, intellectuals have been characterised by cultural historians and sociologists in two important ways. From the time of their origin in the universities of medieval Europe and the concomitant growth of their class with the rise of humanism, intellectuals are perceived either as alienated from dominant beliefs and practices in a particular culture or as legitimating those beliefs and practices. A brief summary of the views of four representative theorists of intellectual life, Julien Benda, Karl Mannheim, Edward Shils, and Alvin Gouldner, will outline the central issues and indicate the problematical task of defining women's intellectual work.

The title of Benda's 1928 tract, *The Treason of the Intellectuals* (*La Trahison des clercs*), signalises his polemical position. Writing at a time when European intellectuals were hotly implicated in ideological warfare, Benda asserts that they have betrayed their proper function by selling themselves to politics, by allowing themselves to be swept away by 'political passion'. Implying the corruption of an idealised cultural life in which intellectuals maintained a coolly detached and morally instructive relationship to their society, he charges them with 'betraying their spiritual ministry, their disinterested activity, which should be theirs by the mere fact of their being historians, psychologists, moralists' (p. 75). Tending to rely upon a dualism that sees man either as a thinking, rational human being or as a creature swept away by the 'characteristics of passion' which demand immediate results and deal in 'excess . . . hatred . . . fixed ideas' (p. 46), Benda laments the betrayal of 'disinterested' reason and the selling-out of the solitary, spiritual intellectual to the materialism of the majority.

Exploring what he terms 'The Sociological Problem of the

1

Intelligentsia', Karl Mannheim, in *Ideology and Utopia* (first published in Germany in 1929 and translated by Edward Shils in collaboration with Louis Wirth in 1954), presents an idealistic vision of intellectuals unfettered by class affiliation. Mannheim strongly refutes the belief that highly differentiated intellectuals are members of a social class or are an 'appendage' to a class. For Mannheim, there is 'one unifying sociological bond between all groups of intellectuals, namely education, which binds them together in a striking way. Participation in a common educational heritage progressively tends to suppress differences of birth, status, profession, and wealth, and to unite the individual educated people on the basis of the education they have received' (p. 138). The 'predicament' of the modern intellectual is to avoid 'direct affiliation with classes and parties', and Mannheim believes that there are two possible ways in which the intellectual might be on the way to achieving such a goal: one is by lifting the conflict of interests between political parties to 'a spiritual plane', in a sense by intellectualising politics, and the other is by intellectuals becoming aware of 'their own social position and the mission implicit in it' (p. 142). Essentially, Mannheim wishfully theorises intellectual practice as vocation, almost as if the intellectual, in his 'free-floating' condition, is returned to a secularised version of the traditionally religious affiliation.

The political and historical pressures on intellectual activity denounced by Benda as a corruption of intellectual vocation are assessed more neutrally by Edward Shils. Tracing the history of intellectual work from its origins in religious 'preoccupations' to its secularisation in modern cultures, Shils observes that what was once a search for religious truth has become in modern life a search for 'principles embedded in events and actions, or for the establishment of a relationship between the self and the essential, whether the relationship be cognitive, appreciative, or expressive' (*The Intellectuals and the Powers*, p. 16). Shils pays close attention to the historical and cultural changes which occur when intellectuals cease to be 'solely bearers of religiosity'; their very act of separating themselves from a traditionally religious function, however slow and unmeditated, must lead to a tension 'between the intellectuals and the religious authority of their society' (p. 17). But while Shils confirms Benda's theory of corrosive separation between social, cultural, and religious authority, he does not see this in moral terms: nothing is betrayed and no one is guilty of treason or treachery.

Writing in the 1970s, Alvin Gouldner argues that intellectuals, together with the technical intelligentsia, are actively forming themselves into a 'New Class', always 'in contention with the groups already in control of the society's economy, whether these are businessmen or party leaders' (*The Future of Intellectuals and the Rise of the New Class*, p. 1). Gouldner's theory of this 'New Class' (which exists both in late capitalism and in authoritarian state socialism) insists that intellectuals are not 'priests *manqués*' (a reference to Shils); the 'New Class' is, above all else, *new* and reproducing itself at a faster rate than any other through enormous increases in the number of people becoming technologically literate. Possessing its own 'technical ambitions' which confront communist societies as much as capitalist ones, it advances itself as a 'new élite' (p. 32). According to Gouldner, intellectuals are neither passionately alienated from dominant beliefs and practices in a particular society, nor do they egregiously legitimate them. In a chilling manner suggestive of science fiction, intellectuals reproduce themselves from the pods of their own technologically focused minds.

Unquestionably subjugated by the culture in which they worked and writing in a less developed technological society than that described by Gouldner, women intellectuals such as Martineau, Barrett Browning, and Eliot can hardly be said to be part of his 'new élite', or even part of an old one for that matter. In fact, if one considers the principal ways in which cultural historians and sociologists characterise intellectuals, it becomes difficult to find a satisfactory theoretical place for intellectual women writing in the Victorian period. How, then, can we define their work? If we bear in mind their ancillary status and their putative preference for the emotional over the rational, can we say that they betrayed, as Benda would have it, a world of 'disinterested' reason, a world to which they were thought not to belong in the first place and in which they were, at best, second-class citizens? Did they, in a graceful Mannheim-like motion, float themselves free to a 'spiritual plane' of non-partisan writing, taking their sexual politics with them? Or did they, through their interrogations of androcentric values, perform Shils's pedagogic functions for a society badly in need of moral guidance in an increasingly secularised world?

Of the four representative theories of intellectual life mentioned to this point, that of Shils is, perhaps, most relevant to the work of Victorian women writers. I have found, however, that even if Antonio Gramsci makes no room for women in his writings about intellectuals, the emphasis he places upon the passive, elaborative nature of intellectual work in highly developed societies most usefully illuminates the careers of intelligent women working in the Victorian public sphere. Whether these women accept the passive, elaborative nature of their intellectual work, or whether, because of their ancillary cultural status, they subversively resist particular ideologies (particularly those relegating their sex to a subordinate position) has been the primary methodological impetus of this study.

Gramsci, of course, makes the strongest argument against the imputation of treachery on the part of intellectuals: intellectuals can betray no ideals for the only ideals to which they might be committed are those in whose construction and dissemination they play a constitutive part. As a Marxist whose activities led to his imprisonment in Italian gaols from 1926 until his death in 1937, Gramsci's strong interest in the function of intellectuals in culture and society centres upon their role in changing that culture and society, and, once that change has been effected, the role they might play in a nation transformed by revolution. His best-known writings about intellectuals appear in the *Prison Notebooks*, which are indeed that – the notebook writings of a man expressing the enforced interaction of a prisoner and his readings, and, as Walter Adamson puts it, writings which are both 'enormously diverse in content' and 'shot through with a desire to free Italy from fascism' (*Hegemony and Revolution*, p. 1).

In examining the social meaning of intellectuals, Gramsci distinguishes between two types, the 'organic' and the 'traditional'. Organic intellectuals generally accompany any social group in its rise to power: 'coming into existence on the original terrain of an essential function in the world of economic production, [the ascendent social group] creates together with itself, organically, one or more strata of intellectuals which give it homogeneity and an awareness of its own function not only in the economic but also in the social and political fields' ('The Intellectuals', p. 5). This broad definition includes the scholar, the writer, the man of letters, and may be extended to include all those who participate in the transmission of ideas. It is also a definition that covers the writings of Harriet Martineau, Elizabeth Barrett Browning, and George Eliot, each of whom, from different political perspectives ranging from Martineau's enthusiastic Radicalism, through Barrett Browning's excoriations of middle-class materialism, to Eliot's residual Toryism, gives 'awareness' and 'homogeneity' to the English middle class, and participates in the transmission of influential Victorian ideas. Establishing the category of organic intellectual so that he might have a theoretical framework within which he can refute the notion of the intellectual as above and beyond the realm of class affiliation, as untainted by history, Gramsci implicitly dislodges this figure from that mythical position of disinterest which, according to Julien Benda, he betrays by his involvement in the passions of politics and history.[1]

'Traditional' intellectuals are already in existence when the emerging social class and its accompanying cadres of intellectuals rise to prominence. These intellectuals, Gramsci says, *seem* 'to represent an historical continuity uninterrupted even by the most complicated and radical changes in political and social forms . . . they thus put themselves forward as autonomous and independent of the dominant social group' (p. 7). As a typical example, Gramsci gives the priest; however, any intellectual not tied to a rising social class, unaffiliated by the function of giving awareness and homogeneity to that class, may be considered as belonging to the category of traditional intellectual. Traditional intellectuals are usually opposed to an emergent social class, tending, as Adamson points out, 'at best to be aloof from, and at worst antagonistic toward, its interests' (*Hegemony and Revolution*, p. 144). Unlike the affiliated organic intellectual who performs the key functions of 'elaboration' and 'legitimation' in Gramsci's framework, the traditional intellectual belongs to a different historical time from the organic intellectuals created by the new class; the traditional intellectual believes himself – or herself – to serve no party and to transmit no ideology. However, despite and because of the fact that traditional intellectuals put themselves forward as immune to historical change, they have a history of being organic at one time to one class, and they must be seen as implicated in history and ideology. How might a study of three Victorian women writers benefit from deployment of these two categories of intellectual practice?

The Victorian woman intellectual was a burdened and conflictive figure. Even if popularly successful like Harriet Martineau, beloved like Elizabeth Barrett Browning, or worshipped like George Eliot, she was weighed down by her ancillary identity: as a woman, she was subordinate in a robust middle-class society which, however much it needed its intellectuals for secular guidance, regarded them as marginal and effete (as I shall argue later in this chapter). In terms of Gramsci's categories, these three women were organic intellectuals by virtue of their daughterly intellectual affiliation with the English middle class. With their male contemporaries, they were part of that large social group which proliferated in the nineteenth-century, giving 'awareness' and 'homogeneity' to an increasingly powerful social class and performing functions of 'legitimation' and 'elaboration' for the influential ideologies of that class. But at the same time, Martineau, Barrett Browning, and Eliot were in some sense second-rate intellectual citizens. Sometimes, therefore, they resisted their 'organic' function, sought to escape their ancillary status, by locating themselves and the intellectual women they wrote about in an ahistorical realm where the restraints of a male-dominated middle-class society were transcended. Barrett Browning and Eliot, in particular, deliberately affiliated themselves with the values of an entrenched land-owning class and mythologised themselves as 'traditional' intellectuals unfettered by the contingencies of history as a way of resisting the discipline of their male-dominated society. I have examined the degree to which these three Victorian 'thinking' women do, and do not, resist their culture, and the ways in which they performed on the stage of Victorian intellectual life.

The second of the concentric circles with which I have surrounded the careers of Martineau, Barrett Browning, and Eliot is that of theoretical and contemporary views of Victorian intellectual life. Writers about Victorian culture tend to favour the second of the two models which, as I have already suggested, dominate thinking about intellectuals in general (they are seen either as alienated from society or as deeply implicated in the production and reproduction of culture). Even if they do not share the explicitly revolutionary ideas of Gramsci, writers about Victorian culture usually perceive the intellectual as a vital, enfolded force in the creation and transmission of important ideas and moral values. The beliefs of the intellectual historian Gertrude Himmelfarb, however, are in many ways an exception to this view. Her analyses of Victorian Mind incline more to the idealism found, for example, in Julian Benda's theories of betrayal than to the recognition of intellectuals as complicitly affiliated with the social class holding political power.

Since it is the romantic vision of intellectual life articulated by Himmelfarb against which most theorists of Victorian culture implicitly position themselves, her views require a brief outline.

In Himmelfarb's collection of essays about the Victorian Mind, Leslie Stephen is divested of his intellectual status. Too privileged, entering upon their 'man-of-letters' inheritance as a birthright, Stephen and his fellow-gentleman scholars do not warrant the designation of intellectual. They lack that invigorating alienation from ruling-class ideas which makes for a vocation:

> For if to be an intellectual is as natural as breathing, it can be no more remarkable than breathing. If it has the status of an ordinary occupation, it does not enjoy the extraordinary status of a calling. If it is no special distinction which the individual must laboriously earn, if it comes to him as a right rather than a reward, if it is an incidental by-product of birth rather than the result of application and dedication, then the much-acclaimed Victorian intellectual may have been not an intellectual at all, but rather a cultured gentleman whose occupation happened to be writing. (*Victorian Minds*, pp. 201–2)

The implications of Himmelfarb's negative argument constitute a positive definition of intellectual life as she understands it.

To be an authentic intellectual a man must feel himself to be a foreigner in some way (there are no women in her pantheon of Victorian Minds). What Himmelfarb terms 'recent foreign descent' gives the American intellectual a certain racy alienation. Having no genesis in that awesome set of 'interlocking genealogies that tie together, by birth and marriage, the great names of nineteenth- and twentieth-century English culture', the American intellectual happily possesses 'the typical stigmata of intellectuals everywhere – the academism, bohemianism, or preciosity of the Herr Professor, the feuilletoniste, or the esthete' (p. 201). Graced by his calling, the authentic intellectual writes in ways that are romantically associated with myths of 'genius' – impulsively, irregularly, and with inspiration: 'the sense of writing as a regular occupation, not beholden to inspiration or creative impulse, was and still is typical among English intellectuals . . . This was the sportsmanlike way of writing: no fuss, no anguish, the game played at the appointed time' (p. 211). For Himmelfarb, then, the Victorian man-of-letters is a professional writer rather than an inspired thinker; relishing his

gentlemanly, urbane, relaxed way of being, the English intellectual
regarded his Continental counterparts (especially the German ones)
as somewhat 'unsporting' in their strained cultivation of difficult
ideas. Himmelfarb seems to prefer the mythically bohemian mind of
the Continent to the prosaic intellect of Victorian England.

To be sure, the disposition of Victorian intellectuals to cherish
amateurism rather than aspire to professionalism is acknowledged
by most cultural historians. R. K. Webb, for example, characterises
early Victorian culture as 'resolutely amateur', and he describes it as
disdaining specialisation and cultivating the local review and
quixotic magazine, as encouraging every gentleman to be 'his own
historian and scientist and doctor and philosopher and poet' (*Harriet
Martineau*, p. 245). But Webb and others have pointed out that as the
century progressed, as the natural sciences became a discipline, and
the reformed universities an orderly focus of intellectual life, so
intellectual life itself became a profession where before it had been
a gentlemanly hobby. Those idiosyncratic, even slightly dotty,
amateur intellectuals were replaced by what has been termed the
'urban gentry', men who became members of statistical societies,
Royal Commissioners, and methodical directors of charitable
organisations. In negatively emphasising the upper-class
affiliations of many Victorian intellectuals and in articulating the
myth of disaffected genius constrained by bohemian contingency,
Himmelfarb betrays her preference for intellectuals graced by
vocation to join the fraternity. Just as she seems unwilling to
recognise the presence of Woman's Victorian Mind, she is also
unwilling to recognise the transformations in Victorian intellectual
life that occur along with the transformation of everything else in
Victorian England.

Himmelfarb's relegation of English intellectuals to the status of
sportsmanlike men of letters makes its case primarily through the
life of Leslie Stephen; the glittering career of this intellectual
patriarch, stern coach of his Cambridge undergraduates and bleak
ruler of his domestic territories, reveals the androcentric
impenetrability of the higher reaches of Victorian culture. Noel
Annan's recently revised study of Stephen presents a highly
privileged and extremely well-connected 'man of letters'. Educated
at Cambridge, destined for the church, matching the toughness of
his curious mind with the physical challenge of sixteen mile walks
for tea around Cambridge and daunting feats of Swiss
mountaineering, Stephen emerges from Annan's study as an

astonishing figure. The male world in which he lived, and by this I mean a world of Cambridge tripos, of cricket and rowing, of London clubs and households devoted to his needs, gives a hint of the radical separation between male and female intellectual life in the Victorian period.

Annan traces the emergence of an intellectual élite in nineteenth-century England that found its genesis and authority in the successful families who sent their male children to be fellows at Oxford and Cambridge, headmasters of public schools, and public officials in Whitehall. Rising in social power 'by time-honoured methods' of mercantile expansion, these brewing, banking, and chocolate-making families formed a professional élite class. In this class, mothers, wives, daughters, and sisters were charming, subordinate figures, expected to be well-read and in graceful possession of more interesting 'accomplishments' than the drawing and music acquired by ordinary Victorian middle-class girls. But intellectual life, like so much else in Victorian culture and society, was divided into 'public' and 'private' spheres: the public sphere was male and signified intellectual leadership of the nation and the empire; the private sphere was female and signified intellectual cultivation of civilised discourse. Virginia Woolf confirms this division of the Victorian mind by sex and gender in her remarks about her father's behaviour. Speculating that the disparity between Stephen's 'critical and creative powers' explains his insensitivity to his daughters, she declares, 'Give him a thought to analyse, the thought of Mill, Bentham, Hobbes; and his [his thought] is . . . acute, clear, concise: an admirable model of the Cambridge analytical spirit. But give him life, a character, and he is so crude, so elementary, so conventional' (*Moments of Being*, p. 126). Woolf attributes her father's deficiencies to the narrow, unbalanced, and intense nature of a nineteenth-century Cambridge education, which was unusually restricted in scope at the time he was there, first as an undergraduate reading mathematics in the early 1850s and then as a tutor and Fellow of Trinity until he left the University in 1862. It was an education that crammed students for brilliant performance in competitive examinations, and, as T. W. Heyck points out in his study of the transformations of intellectual life in the Victorian period, an education considered impractical by the end of the century.

Heyck offers three causes for the emergence of intellectuals as a social class in the nineteenth century: the rise of natural science, the

reform of universities, and the emergence of social criticism oriented
to cultural judgments. Two important conditions accounted for the
growth of intellectuals as a social class: an immense expansion of the
economy due to the industrial and commercial revolutions, and the
growth of the middle class and the professions – Heyck observes
that in Georgian England three occupations were regarded as
professions (the clergy, law, and medicine) and that by the end of
the century the professions included also architects, engineers, civil
servants, and solicitors (*The Transformation of Intellectual Life in
Victorian England*, p. 21). In addition, what Heyck terms 'the
triumph of science over theology' led to increasingly secularised
modes of thought and the establishment of various institutions
in which intellectual activity proliferated. And, as Heyck
demonstrates through his meticulous documentation of the impact
of science upon Victorian culture, the importance of science was felt
in the universities. Victorian scientists compelled universities to
focus less upon teaching and more upon research, and the mere
existence of an enlarged number of professional scientists altered
the constitution, curricula, and emphasis of university life.
Moreover, science affected many other fields of intellectual activity;
these fields were converted into professional disciplines through
science, and, in turn, the intellectuals in those fields entered
universities 'and so redoubled the impact of science on university
life' (p. 120).

The universities, then, underwent radical alteration in the
nineteenth century. The Oxford and Cambridge humanistic liberal
education based on classics and mathematics designed to prepare
sons of the governing classes to take their ruling places at home and
abroad gave way to a programme based more on the demand for
science, modern languages, and political economy, and on an
education for the sons of the middle class (a demand that in 1836 had
led to the founding of London University). By the end of the century
the 'Classical Ideal' had lost its monopoly on the higher education of
privileged young men.[2]

Moreover, something else had changed by the end of the century.
After several decades of agitation for women's higher education, the
women's colleges at Cambridge were training women to become
professionals, if not as the architects, engineers, civil servants, and
solicitors that the sons of the middle class were rapidly becoming,
then almost certainly as teachers and headmistresses. Regarded
with amusement or ridicule as an anomalous blue-stocking at the

end of the eighteenth century, the woman intellectual had gained a degree of professional independence by the end of the nineteenth.[3]

As intelligent and ambitious women began to experience significant changes in the opportunities for education and work that were available to them, the powerful middle class developed two related attitudes towards Victorian intellectual life: this class began to regard intellectuals as 'service' figures and to perceive the intellectual's function as a combination of the roles of instructive sage and moral counsellor. As social thought became increasingly secularised, the mercantile middle class, getting commercially richer by the minute but feeling spiritually poorer by the week (especially on Sundays) needed moral guidance. It came to regard the intellectual as it had once regarded the vicar – as a marginal but necessary figure.

Producing only a minimally valuable commodity, the disseminated knowledge of new ideas, the intellectual is frequently associated by the Victorian middle class with unprofitably utilised leisure, with amateurish pursuit of knowledge for its own sake rather than with professional appropriation of knowledge for the economic advancement of society. From the popular perspective, the intellectual life is not an heroic one. That cheery Victorian booster of self-help, Samuel Smiles, makes this comforting distinction: 'It is to be borne in mind that the experience gathered from books, though often valuable, is but of the nature of *learning*; whereas the experience gained from actual life is of the nature of *wisdom*: and a small store of the latter is worth vastly more than any stock of the former' (*Workmen's Earnings, Strikes and Savings*, p. 359). Speaking to his working-class and lower-middle-class readers, Smiles dispels any shame felt about lack of education: long before a reading public came into being, says Smiles, there were 'wise, valiant, and true-hearted men in England': these men were 'altogether unskilled in the art of deciphering literary signs'. They knew what they wanted, how to get it, and how to make England strong.[4]

The powerful, mercantile middle class which Samuel Smiles paraded before his readers so that they might learn 'self-help' and join that social group, expected its intellectuals to perform the functions traditionally performed by the clergy. Where the clergyman might have counselled his congregation in matters of faith, now the intellectual was expected to counsel the middle class in matters of economic, social and religious change. Guidance and support were in strong demand and the men of letters enacted didactic roles. This transformation of intellectual practice by the increased secularisation of public discourse raises an important issue in consideration of the role of women intellectuals in culture and society. If the man of letters became a cultural leader who articulated and diffused new, often disruptive ideas to a middle-class readership, then that man of letters began to lose his mythologised isolation; he became less the privileged, distracted scholar and more an efficient auxiliary assistant to the troubled middle class. What I am beginning to suggest here is that the Victorian intellectual began to perform functions traditionally associated with women's lives. He becomes an ancillary moral lieutenant, an instructive articulating figure. 'He', in fact, loses his predominantly male identification and intellectual work becomes feminised – in the eyes of one twentieth-century cultural historian, not for the better.

Looking back in 1936 to paint his Portrait of an Age, G. M. Young expresses a rueful fear that the Victorian period lost its virility as it lost its 'disinterested intelligence'. The 'function of the nineteenth century' was to disengage this ideologically free intelligence from 'entanglements of party and sect – one might almost add, of sex – and to set it operating over the whole range of human life and circumstance'. As the nineteenth century moved to increased sexual equality, according to Young, 'what failed in the late Victorian age and its flash Edwardian epilogue, was the Victorian public, once so alert, so masculine, and so responsible. Compared with their fathers, the men of that time were ceasing to be a ruling or a reasoning stock; the English mind sank towards that easily excited, easily satisfied, state of barbarism and childhood which press and politics for their own ends fostered, and on which in turn they fed' (*Portrait of an Age*, p. 187). Implicitly echoing Julien Benda's lament for that vanished 'disinterested' reason, Young shows the Victorian age degenerating as it is emasculated by partisan interests: the language of his elegy dualistically equates the 'masculine' with freedom from allegiance to party, sect and sex, with responsible regnancy and with reason; the 'feminine' is implicitly aligned with partisan politics, with irresponsible irrationality, superficial passions 'easily excited, easily satisfied'. Barbarism and childish passions characterise an age no longer 'alert', 'masculine', or 'responsible'. The betrayal of the intellectual through his involvement in politics that amounted to the organisation of class 'passion' mourned by Benda is given a negative feminine cast in Young's elegy for the lost age.[5]

The masculine meanings of a rigorous intellectual life thought to be losing its manly alertness as the nineteenth century progressed take on rich sexist weight when Noel Annan describes the fondness of Leslie Stephen and his friends for mountain-climbing. To be sure, Annan evokes the commonplace connection between a secluded life of the mind and a yearning for the great outdoors, but his imagery is invested with significant Victorian notions about sex and gender. Annan does not evoke the vision of an urban, couch-bound poet gently dreaming of the daffodils. The 'charms of mountaineering resemble those of a great courtesan; in addition to her physical attractions, and the raptures she inspires, she possesses that indefinable quality of mystery which, once felt, binds her devotees to her helplessly for life. It is a power which is exerted with peculiar poignancy over intellectuals' (*Leslie Stephen*, p. 91). In conquering this female mystery and thereby divesting it of its power to inspire awe in men, these male intellectuals (for they can be no other sex in Annan's quaint narrative of female nature and male victory), can experience things which would be otherwise closed to them by virtue of a profession fast losing its virile pleasures: 'danger, intense comradeship, manliness, physical pain in pursuit of a tangible objective' (p. 91). It is in the rare atmosphere of the Alps that Annan's intellectual recovers his sense of 'manliness' diminished by the press of society. Alienated and bored by the worldliness of the city, perhaps even importuned by aggressive women demanding work and the vote, Annan's male intellectual is liberated for a virile symbolic conquest of that dangerous courtesan Nature.

To return now to the Gramscian categories of intellectual function that I have described, it seems to me very clear that the Victorian intellectual, by virtue of the instructive and articulating functions ascribed to him by social historians such as Heyck, must be categorized as an 'organic' figure, however much he – or she – may have resisted an affiliative relationship to the most powerful social class in Victorian England. The function of this intellectual was, indeed, to give 'homogeneity' and 'awareness' to the social class whose political power was secured by the material wealth of the nation and the empire, but whose uncertainty about scientific change, about the meaning (perhaps even the usefulness) of art in a society founded upon immense economic expansion, demanded some dispelling. The figures of the Gramscian organic intellectual, the Victorian intellectual who was subordinate to systems of power founded on material wealth, and the woman intellectual whose presence and identity in Victorian culture I shall soon discuss – all seem to coalesce in a reticular configuration.

It seems to me entirely possible that the emergence of intellectuals as secular prophets and moral teachers legitimated the presence and identity of the woman intellectual; that is to say, she gained a cultural respectability as her conventional function of moral guidance became the property of a social group desired by the powerful middle class. And as the role of intellectual as moral teacher aligns itself with the role of Victorian woman as instructive angel in the house, then the third circle in that concentric diagram of determining influences upon the careers of Martineau, Barrett Browning, and Eliot becomes that much more clearly defined – this circle reveals the Victorian hegemony of male decrees for the uses of woman's mind. We have already seen why the middle class might have needed the services of the intellectual. It is now time to see how that same social class dictated the proper purposes to which woman's mind should be put.


One of the most conservative and influential treatises on the correct employment of woman's mind issued from the bastions of Victorian patriarchy is John Ruskin's well-known 'Of Queens' Gardens', the second of two public lectures delivered in 1864 and appearing in book form with the publication of *Sesame and Lilies* in 1865. The patriarchal attitudes of 'Of Queens' Gardens' were strongly resisted by the advocates of a decent education for girls and women in the Victorian period, but at the same time, as we shall see, these ludicrously pernicious ideas penetrated even the vocabulary and arguments of the women who valiantly fought for improvements in women's higher education in the last quarter of the nineteenth century. 'Of Queens' Gardens' addresses itself to what degree women may enjoy the 'royal authority' of knowing oneself in a 'stronger moral state, and a truer thoughtful state, than that of others'.

It is a very small degree indeed. Ruskin begins by refuting claims for the 'mission and of the rights of Woman' by declaring that just as it is wrong to believe woman is the servile attendant upon man, so too, is it wrong to believe that woman 'who was made to be the helpmate of man' should be seen as a slave. Her function is to guide, rather than to direct, and the division between male and female intellectual functions is prescribed as follows: 'The man's power is active, progressive, defensive. He is eminently the doer, the creator, the discoverer, the defender. His intellect is for speculation and invention; his energy for adventure, for war, and for conquest, wherever war is just, wherever conquest necessary. But the woman's power is for rule, not for battle, – and her intellect is not for invention or creation, but for sweet ordering, arrangement and decision' (pp. 146–7). The lecture continues in this vein. Man does rough work in the open world, woman is protected in the home from all danger and temptation. Home is the 'place of Peace; the shelter, not only from all injury, but from all terror, doubt, and division'. To be sure, this prevalent separation of Victorian men and women into public and private spheres has become a virtual commonplace in Victorian studies. But Harriet Martineau, Elizabeth Barrett Browning, and George Eliot so often betray in their writing a conflict between resistance to and sanction of this separation, that I think it important we not lose sight of the dominant ideologies of sex and gender against which so many Victorian women positioned themselves. In bringing together critical essays about the injunctions to women to 'suffer and be still', Martha Vicinus illuminated these ideologies, and it does not hurt for us to look at them again. And, as Kate Millet reminds us, *Sesame and Lilies* was Ruskin's most popular volume.[6]

Ruskin urges equal education for women so that they may know as much as their husbands and therefore be educated partners rather than frivolous drones. A girl's education should be the same as a boy's, 'but quite differently directed. A woman in any rank of life, ought to know whatever her husband is likely to know, but to know it in a different way. His command of it should be foundational and progressive, hers, general and accomplished for daily and helpful use' (pp. 160–1). Husbands build the foundations of culture and society; wives keep the structures in sound working order. No limits should be placed on man's intellectual ambition; woman's desire for learning should be curbed by the necessity of service to her husband. Ruskin's justification for keeping 'the modern magazine and novel out of your girl's way' and turning her 'loose into the old library every wet day' (like some kind of eager spaniel, one assumes) rests upon an essential difference between 'the making of a girl's character and a boy's': 'you may chisel a boy

into shape, as you would a rock, or hammer him into it, if he be of a
better kind, as you would a piece of bronze. But you cannot hammer
a girl into anything. She grows as a flower does, – she will wither
without sun; she will decay in her sheath, as the narcissus does, if
you do not give her air enough; she may fall, and defile her head in
dust, if you leave her without help at some moments of her life'
(p. 164). The imagery promotes an ideology of superior male sex and
gender by relegating woman to a topos of immanence: you can
chisel and hammer boys, and they in turn become the chiselers and
hammerers of culture and society, whereas girls are rooted in
nature, which is the cause of their delightful blooming but also
the cause of their tendencies to 'fall' – an image resonant with the
iconography of the 'fallen woman' who is everywhere in the
Pre-Raphaelite paintings admired by Ruskin. He may argue that
girls must receive the same educational advantages as their
brothers, but at the same time he also argues that they are utterly
different by virtue of their essentialist qualities.

Ruskin's impassioned exhortation to man to fill and temper
woman's mind 'with all knowledge and thoughts which tend to
confirm its natural instincts of justice, and refine its natural tact of
love', his plea for woman that 'All such knowledge should be given
her as may enable her to understand, and even to aid, the work of
men' are the essence of patriarchal thought. The hegemonic power
of this thought is borne out by evidence that the dominant Victorian
ideologies dividing male and female experience into public and
private spheres did not make themselves felt only in middle-class
life. That the English working class absorbed these ideologies,
paraded them in fact as badges of respectability, is witness to the
infiltrating power of such ideas. Victorian working-class women
were not only enslaved to the contingencies of work in the home, in
the shop, or the factory: they were also enslaved to middle-class
infatuation with a domestic ideal. If the middle-class home was a
sanctuary presided over by a domestic angel, the refuge from a
commercial world given over to materialistic accumulation, the
working-class home was no less devoted to such an ideal.
Unfortunately for the working-class wife, the ideal was rather less
attainable for her than it was for the middle-class woman. From the
time of testimony given before the Parliamentary Commissioners in
the 1840s investigating working conditions in the mines and
factories, to the oral histories of working-class women living in the
fifty years between 1890 and 1940, recently gathered and introduced

by Elizabeth Roberts, the English working-class wife has struggled to keep her home a decent, private place in a dirty, encroaching world, to counter the putative emasculation of her husband caused by her employment outside the home, and to keep the family respectable. In general, the Victorian working-class family thoroughly absorbed middle-class ideologies of sex and gender.[7]

As the force of feminist movements reverberated throughout society and the woman intellectual emerged as an identifiable cultural figure, the patriarchal discourse articulated by Ruskin became shrilly defensive in the essays and lectures of an entrenched male intellectual establishment. For example, the notorious opposition of the *Saturday Review* to feminism and intellectual women reveals itself in the snide tone of a representative selection of articles published in 1868 for American readers. Self-righteously declaring that they 'have nothing whatever to say against the professional self-support of women who have no men to work for them', the anonymous authors of these articles go on to talk about the 'horrid nuisance' of 'inky Minervas' who create 'an intellectual Tower of Pisa under the shadow of which it is not pleasant to live' (*Modern Women and What is Said of Them*, p. 371).

A more desperate defence against intelligent and aggressive women appears in a meditation entitled *The Intellectual Life* by P. G. Hamerton, the author of numerous works of art appreciation in the last quarter of the nineteenth century. From his serene perspective, intellectual women quite simply do not exist because the female sex is incapable of conducting any form of authentic intellectual life. Intelligent conversation with women is a 'dangerous' territory for men to enter: women are so preoccupied with sentimental feeling that they are incapable of accuracy in 'matters of fact, which they neither have nor care for' (p. 272). According to Hamerton, a 'clever woman' is the best of pupils because she is naturally inclined to submit to guidance by a teacher, but she is 'the worst of solitary learners' (p. 236). Hamerton derives his appalling views of marriage from Ruskin; the ideal marriage is one in which wives 'renew' themselves intellectually for their husbands: 'There is hardly any task too hard for them, if they believe it essential to the conjugal life . . . Their remarkable incapacity for independent mental labour is accompanied by an equally remarkable capacity for labour under an accepted masculine guidance' (p. 240). Lacking the 'motive powers' to propel an 'intellectual advance', they dwell in pretty ignorance. Hamerton tops off his sexist disquisition by announcing that if a woman, rather than Archimedes, had perceived an overflowing bathtub, she 'would have noticed it only as a cause of disorder or inconvenience' (p. 247).

The Ruskinian attitude held sway for many decades, restricting woman to her proper sphere of domestic duties and prohibiting her from achievement of her intellectual ambition. To be sure, she was able to write novels, to translate, and to edit, but she did all this in a society which denied her, if she was a middle-class girl, any education beyond that to be gleaned from her governesses, her brothers' tutors, or from the teachers at provincial boarding schools which did a lot for deportment but little for the mind.

In one sense Victorian middle-class girls were more discriminated against than those of the working class. Elementary education for both sexes had been available from the 1830s; the Education Act of 1870 established rate-financed schools, mainly for lower-class children of both sexes, but it was the middle-class girl who had few opportunities for serious secondary education, a loss of little consequence to a working-class girl, for she felt no other urgency than to be employed when she left elementary school. Attending a very small boarding school which taught French, music, drawing, and deportment, catching the educational crumbs from her brother's tutor, or being educated by a governess – these were the choices for a young Victorian female. Until concerted efforts began in the middle of the century for better education for girls, efforts which came from sensible middle-class desires that wives be more than breeders and decorative ornaments, and from what J. A. and Olive Banks term 'an evangelical opposition to frivolity . . . as well as from an Enlightenment concern with human rights and human rationality' (*Feminism and Family Planning in Victorian England*, p. 40), early Victorian middle-class girls, with some rare exceptions, tended to be educated in a similar manner to that enjoyed by Rosamund Vincy, 'the flower of Mrs Lemon's school, the chief school in the county, where the teaching included all that was demanded in the accomplished female – even to extras, such as the getting in and out of a carriage' (Eliot, *M.*, p. 71). With the exception of the pioneering girls' day schools of the 1850s – the North Collegiate School for Girls founded in 1850 and Cheltenham Ladies College founded in 1858 – institutions similar to that attended by Rosamund Vincy were the rule for the daughters of the aspiring middle class. It was not until 1871 that the National Union to promote the education of girls and young women was founded:

sponsoring the establishment of public day schools for girls, the Union raised money by selling shares. The expansion of opportunities is indicated by the fact that in 1864 there were twelve endowed schools and in 1890 there were eighty.[8]

Opponents of serious secondary schooling for girls and higher education for young women almost always adopted three related arguments designed to terrorise their advocates: educated girls have trouble finding husbands, they develop disfiguring masculine traits, and they deplete energy from their reproductive organs through brain work. 'The one thing men do not like is the man-woman', advises the *Quarterly Review* in 1869: woman's duties do not lie 'in the intellectual direction' and it is a sad error for women to squash their 'sprightly intuition' in favour of laboriously cultivating 'the reasoning faculty'.[9] Educated girls become 'strong-minded women' declares Mrs Roe, delivering herself of *A Woman's Thoughts on the Education of Girls*; such girls are 'dogmatic and presumptuous, self-willed and arrogant, eccentric in dress and disagreeable in manner'.[10] 'Strong-minded women' in Victorian usage were often in the unfortunate possession of masculine characteristics, usually in the form of a moustache.[11]

Two public lectures delivered by a physician in the late 1880s constitute a representative summary of the alarming arguments brought against 'brain work' for women during the latter part of the nineteenth century. With the ambitious, career-minded New Woman in mind, T. S. Clouston relies upon an economical model of female physical powers provided by nature; during female adolescence 'body energies of a new kind begin to arise, vast tracts of brain quite unused before are brought into active exercise' (*Female Education from a Medical Point of View*, p. 13). Without explicit reference to menarche, Clouston goes on to argue that adolescent girls are put into a physical and moral turmoil; their sense of right and wrong goes awry, they develop a morbid love of poetry, and the risks to their minds are very great. But more dreadful than this is the risk to the reproductive organs, and to Britain's glorious future: mental cramming upsets the harmony of mind and body, and energy which should be going to perfect the female adult is misused in brain work. What ensues? A danger to the 'future race'. Most great men have had quiet, contented mothers, not highly educated ones; cramming over books and being stimulated by intellectual competition would have created 'small and distorted men'. This crude argument for biology as quiescent, breeding destiny declares that over-stimulation of the brain will result in anaemia, in stunted growth and in 'dwarfish specimens', 'thin and scrawny' types, in nervousness which indicates the brain is over stimulated, in headaches, and in cravings for opiates. The argument climaxes in a dreadful vision of English middle-class mothers producing fewer and puny offspring, and an apocalyptic warning that the English race will be put in danger of extinction if girls are allowed to indulge themselves in 'book-learning'.[12]

The anti-feminism and racial obsession articulated by Clouston and other physicians and anthropologists continued, needless to say, well beyond the end of the century. For example, a series of New Tracts for the Times published by the National Council for Public Morals in 1912 included a fierce polemic against intellectual work for women entitled *Womanhood and Race Regeneration*. The tract argues that the present degeneration of the British race must be reversed by women's dedication of their racially pure, physically sound bodies to the renewal of British power, under unspoken threat from the increasingly restless subjects of the British empire. Another of the tracts, *Problems of Sex*, quite baldly warns that intellectual women may 'have highly developed brains, but most of them die young' (Thomson and Geddes, p. 34).

Delivered from the strongholds of a conservative social order, these polemical stews of patriarchy, racism, and superstition (found in particularly obnoxious form in the 1912 Tracts) had, of course, been scornfully dismissed by feminist activists, both in their words and in their achievements, for at least half a century. Prominent in their number was the moderate feminist Emily Shirreff, pioneer in the cause of women's higher education and founder of Hitchin (later Girton) College at Cambridge in 1869. In 1871 she helped form the National Union for Improving the Education of Women of all Classes; she launched a Teacher Training College named for her sister, Maria Grey; and she was the author of an important text in the history of higher education for women.[13] Published in 1858, *Intellectual Education and its Influence on the Character and Happiness of Women* is, however, an ambiguous work. In the process of making strong claims for the benefits of women's education, it also testifies to the pervasive entrenchment of sexist thought in Victorian culture. Shirreff winds her argument around the ideology of woman as a superior moral creature, and she rehearses the dualistic division by sex and gender into public and private spheres that was so prevalent in the Victorian period.

Where men traffic in partisan, materialistic politics, women are privileged to engage in disinterested intellectual activity: 'In this country, where the struggle for existence is so fierce, where every weapon of successful competition is so valuable, men need perpetually to be reminded that the human intellect, and the knowledge it is able to aspire to and to grasp, are of more worth in themselves than all the worldly purposes for which they are put to daily vulgar use. And how shall they be reminded of this except by the example of those who, owing to gifts of fortune or natural condition, are able to stand aloof from the contest' (p. 24). The clash and tumult of the public world cause men to forget tender feelings, heroic sentiments, lofty ideals; it is woman's cultural duty to remind them of these precious things. Unmolested by the contingent bustle of the market-place, women can cultivate 'love of knowledge for its own sake', and through their feminine offices, pass this knowledge along to men. The argument is fascinating, familiar, and pernicious in the way it elevates woman and justifies her subjugation by male authority.

Shirreff's emphasis upon woman's cultural duty recalls Charles Kingsley's agonised plea ten years earlier for women to become moral teachers in a troubled time. According to Kingsley, women have a 'calling in all ages' but it is an 'especial' one in mid-nineteenth-century society, evoked for the 'ladies' in his audience as 'hunting everywhere for law and organisation, refusing loyalty to anything which cannot range itself under its theories' (*The Works of Charles Kingsley*, 20:259). With the moral elevation of competitive Victorian man as her vocation, the reproof of vulgar employment of the intellect as her mission, educated woman is licensed by the patriarchal thought which invades moderate Victorian feminism as much as it impels the discourse of the male intellectual establishment, to go forth and do her cultural duty. Interestingly, it is a cultural duty that aligns her work with the 'disinterested' function Julien Benda sees as betrayed in his theory of intellectual life: for enlightened Victorian patriarchy, the ideal intellectual woman is loyal to 'disinterested' culture and rejects the vulgar worldliness of partisan politics.[14]

Shirreff outlines a practical course for the education of women, set out in two-year time blocks: from the ages of twelve to fourteen, girls should study arithmetic, geometry and geography; from fourteen to sixteen, natural history, geology, astronomy and composition; and from sixteen to eighteen, history, political economy and ancient history. The impetus for this curriculum is Shirreff's belief that upper-middle-class girls are frittering away their lives in trivial pleasures, and understandably she is less concerned with the employment prospects of this particular social class than she is with uplifting its moral life. If upper-middle-class girls do not act as 'civilizers of men', social barbarism will ensue: 'What society wants from women is not labour, but refinement, elevation of mind, knowledge making its power felt through moral influence and sound opinions. It wants civilizers of men, and educators of the young. And society will suffer in proportion as women are either driven by necessity or tempted by seeming advantages to leave this their natural vocation, and to join the noisy throng in the busy markets of the world' (pp. 417–18). To be sure, Shirreff acknowledges that many unmarried women were forced through economic necessity to seek employment (she labels this necessity 'a social evil' to which 'we must submit'), but she fails to recognise that many women did not believe they were in possession of a 'natural vocation' to 'civilize men' and that others grasped the chance to join the jostling throng in the market-place – an existence far more appealing than the overworked and underpaid life of the governess. In all probability, at the end of the century Emily Shirreff would have spoken differently. A generation of university educated women was coming into existence, moderate feminism was less complicit in patriarchal thought, and Mrs Henry Sidgwick lecturing at Liverpool in 1896 would announce that women should not only have an 'independent career' because they remain unmarried, they should also 'take a share in the work of the world' ('University Education of Women', p. 11).

A measure of Harriet Martineau's exceptional (and almost always unsentimental) view of things emerges when one compares her remarks on women's higher education with those of Shirreff. Looking back in the 1860s to the state of girls' education at the beginning of the century, Martineau finds much to criticise. Employing her impressive mode of popular, intelligent journalism, she addresses the issue of middle-class education for girls and observes that from the period immediately after the cessation of the Napoleonic wars to the present ('a period of high prosperity for certain middle-class interests, while so costly to the country on the whole'), girls' education was at a very low point due to the social ambitions of their parents to 'rise in gentility', an aspiration which takes the form of making sportsmen of their sons and 'fine ladies of their daughters'. From Martineau's refreshingly sensible perspective, these 'fine ladies' were useless creatures, ill-trained to manage a household, ignorant of anything except trivial achievements in music and drawing, and primping before the mirror. The economic depressions of the '20s, however, led in a roundabout way to improvements: their fathers 'ruined', their brothers 'thrown destitute on the world', these young women who had been taught to believe they would always have male protection, were forced into more practical educations which would, at least, prepare them to be governesses – the miserable conditions of which occupation Martineau unflaggingly attacked throughout her life.[15]

With the idealised mandate of enlightened Victorian patriarchy and complicit moderate feminism in mind, it is instructive to compare the arguments advanced for the higher education of women with the function of the intellectual in Victorian culture as it was understood and desired by the English middle class. Just as the Victorian intellectual should offer moral instruction to the middle class in times of rapidly changing values, so the wife should 'civilize' her husband after his forays into the jungles of commerce. Emily Shirreff's arguments for the higher education of women, in particular, resemble the arguments relegating intellectuals to the function of moral servitors to the troubled middle class. It would seem that the ideal and acceptable woman intellectual is the one who seeks no expression for her mind other than that of 'civilizing' men and keeping culture in a healthy condition. Ambitious self has no place in the correct life for intelligent women. It is significant that a woman extolled for the power of her mind in the 1840s and 1850s, Sara Coleridge, is unfailingly congratulated for her lack of ambition.

Elizabeth Barrett Browning extravagantly praised Sara Coleridge for her possession of 'more learning, in the strict sense, than any female writer of the day' (*L.*EBB/RHH, 297–8). From a woman who regularly composed Greek odes for her parents' birthdays from the age of thirteen, who began to write letters to her mother in French from the age of eleven, who certainly had as much Latin and Greek as her brothers, and whose first epic poem was privately printed when she was fourteen, this was high praise. Sara Coleridge was a talented translator, who according to her daughter, by the age of twenty-five 'had made herself acquainted with the leading Greek and Latin classics, and was well-skilled in French, Italian, German, and Spanish' (*Memoir and Letters of Sara Coleridge*, p. 53). Her 'truly feminine authorship' is testified to by the fact that it was not 'prompted by mere literary ambition', and that she dedicated 'the whole of her intellectual existence to the great object of carrying out a husband's wishes – of doing justice to a father's name' (pp. 62–5). The 'feminine' woman intellectual places her mind in the service of husband and father, and Sara Coleridge openly commended other learned women for the qualities she, herself, was said to possess. Describing the apppeal of a certain Miss Fenwick, she observes, 'She is intellectual, but – what is a great excellence – never talks for effect, never *keeps possession of the floor*, as clever women are so apt to do' (p. 278).[16]

Some women intellectuals, however, vigorously interrogated an ideology that mandated the discipline of female mind by male authority. Among that number, Harriet Martineau attacked the confinement of women to ignorance and indolence, even if she also promoted their acceptance of male political and social control. Elizabeth Barrett Browning wrote poetry about the power of female art and female sexuality, even if she made no secret of her belief in woman's intellectual inferiority to man. And George Eliot wrote novels about the struggles of intelligent women for cultural autonomy, despite the equivocations that one finds in her essays and letters.

Let me, then, begin to demonstrate the resistance to and the complicity with hegemonic patriarchy by considering Harriet Martineau, who, with a 'mind full-set' on her intellectual career, could well have inspired Rose Yorke, the intelligent young woman in Charlotte Brontë's *Shirley*. Educated, alert, physically tough, well disciplined, scornful of the confinement of women to angelic ignorance in the house, she was the resilient embodiment of all she believed about the proper life for women. She also possessed a certain unchangeable, unchanging character, defined by a courageous and pioneering spirit to which Matthew Arnold paid homage in his elegy for 'two gifted women' – Charlotte Brontë and Martineau: 'Hail to the steadfast soul / Which, unflinching and keen, / Wrought to erase from its depths / Mist and illusion and fear!'[17] But, as I shall now argue, even when most splendidly in charge of her own experience, climbing Mount Sinai or managing her Lake District household, she was still inescapably influenced by the Victorian mandates for women's lives and minds that dictated a far less aggressive independence of intellect and character than she happily displayed throughout her remarkable career.

# Part One

# Harriet Martineau: a Career of Auxiliary Usefulness

'It was truly *life* that I lived during those days of strong intellectual and moral effort.'
(Harriet Martineau, *Autobiography*, 1:145)

# 1

# Textual Services

In the characteristically self-opinionated fashion that either charmed or antagonised her literary contemporaries, Harriet Martineau tried to have the last say about her life and work. She wrote her own obituary, which appeared in the *Daily News* on 27 June 1876, two days after her death at the age of 74. Some twenty years earlier she had retired to her Lake District home, stricken with the heart disease she believed would very soon end her life, and never one to waste time, she immediately wrote an autobiography that is enjoyably informative about the Victorian literary world she confidently inhabited and surprisingly moving in its revelations of childhood unhappiness. Deploying the cool tone of the obituary writer, she also wrote a short memoir which answers and anticipates almost all past and future criticism of her life and work. It modestly asserts her successes, efficiently articulates her weaknesses, and performs an astute identification of three aspects of her literary production that succinctly sum up the significance of her work as a woman intellectual in early Victorian England.

No complex motives directed 54 years of virtually uninterrupted writing: 'Her stimulus in all she wrote, from first to last, was simply the need of utterance.' Intellectual and expository gifts are assessed as follows: 'Her original power was nothing more than was due to earnestness and intellectual clearness within a certain range. With small imaginative and suggestive powers, and therefore nothing approaching to genius, she could see clearly what she did see, and give a clear expression to what she had to say. In short she could popularize, while she could neither discover or invent.' And of her four volumes of English history, published between 1849 and 1864 and covering the period from the beginning of the peace in 1815 to the outbreak of the Crimean War in 1853, she says this: 'All that can be done with contemporary history is to collect and methodize the greatest amount of reliable facts and distinct impressions, to amass sound material for the veritable historian of a future day, – so consolidating, assimilating, and vivifying the structure as to do for the future writer precisely that which the lapse of time and the oblivion which creeps over all transactions must prevent his doing for himself. This auxiliary usefulness is the aim of Harriet Martineau's history' (*A.*, 3:461–70). Her performance as intellectual, then, is self-characterised as stemming from a need of utterance, as succeeding in popularisation but not in discovery, and as fulfilling an ancillary role. On the stage of English nineteenth-century intellectual history, she cast herself in a supporting part, one that served to highlight the star turns executed by her more luminous, and for the most part male, contemporaries.

The need of utterance she identifies not only drove her as an adult to express herself in virtually every mode available to her (religious tract, essay, newspaper leader, travel narrative, novel, political tale, children's story, translation), it also directed the plaintive grievances of her childhood. The recollections of her early life paint a dismal picture of emotional isolation caused by increasing deafness, a lack of a sense of taste or smell, and chronic dyspepsia. Whether, in actuality, her mother was as coldly indifferent to her as Martineau would have us believe, or whether Martineau was the neglected, plain and sickly child whose tearful, complaining countenance made her the object of family censure, is less important than the image Martineau created of herself. One way she says she dealt with her unhappiness as a child was to voice conspicuous objection to the unjust treatment she felt was meted out to her and to pledge herself (at the age of eight) to a formidable work of moral self-correction that involved tabulating scriptural instructions under the headings of virtues and vices, in order to have, she says, 'encouragement or rebuke always ready at hand' (*A.*, 1:35). She also took enthusiastic advantage of the education and religious training her Unitarian parents provided for her. The need of utterance that began in childhood feelings of exclusion found its first formal and published expression in three articles under the pseudonym 'Discipulus' for the Dissident *Monthly Repository* in 1822 and 1823,[1] got into full and astonishingly popular swing with the *Illustrations of Political Economy* in 1832, and continued unabated through half a century of literary production that even by Victorian standards of self-discipline and dedication to work remains awesome.

Almost every day of her writing life, that is to say when she was not engaged in the travel that invariably became the subject of yet another article or book, she was at her desk from seven-thirty in the morning until two in the afternoon. She claims that before beginning to write she made sure of what she wanted to say and wrote it down 'without care or anxiety'. Always crisply efficient, she was predictably appalled by the sight of Carlyle's extensively revised proofs, 'so irresolute, as well as fastidious, did he seem to be as to the expression of his plainest thoughts' (*A.*, 1:385). A number of her critics have wished, of course, that she had been a little less resolute in her didacticism and rather more fastidious in her own prose. The uncompromising assertion of opinion that she went in for and the sometimes hasty manner of its expression exposed her to charges of rigid dogmatism and journalistic superficiality. Leslie Stephen categorises her as a 'miscellaneous writer' in the *Dictionary of National Biography* and declares that the *Illustrations of Political Economy* are an 'unreadable mixture of fiction, founded on rapid cramming, with raw masses of the dismal science. They certainly show the true journalistic talent of turning hasty acquisitions to account.'[2] In reviewing *Society in America* for *The Times* on 30 May 1837, Disraeli ridicules her 'indifferent grammar', nastily suggests that she was indebted to Cockneys for her use of auxiliary verbs, charges her with 'a morbid love of analysis', and winds up the review by saying there is 'something infinitely ludicrous about her vanity and presumption'. In significant contrast to this élitist tirade, George Eliot declared Martineau to be a 'trump – the only English woman that possesses thoroughly the art of writing'; and despite Eliot's initial distaste for a certain vulgarity she perceived in Martineau's looks and gestures, she admired her industry, intellectual powers, and bustling domestic charm that she encountered when visiting Martineau's Ambleside home in 1852 (Eliot, *L.*, 2:4, 32, 62). But Stephen, Disraeli, and Eliot would have been in agreement about one aspect of Martineau's work: whether viewed from the patronising perspective of Victorian male authority or from the more sympathetic collaborative viewpoint of another woman intellectual, Martineau's writing undeniably gratifies that 'need of utterance' she believed had originated in the isolation of her childhood.

What she uttered was made possible, she herself admits, by an 'earnestness and clearness within a certain range'. In her own words, she 'could see clearly what she did see' and this preoccupation with both the narrowness and the clarity of observation is, I would suggest, the second important aspect of her life and work. On her journey to America in August 1834, determined never to squander time or energy, she set herself up on deck every morning to write a book about how to be an expert traveller. *How to Observe Manners and Morals* is the result. Surrounded by multiple, confusing signs of social organisation and culture, the traveller must be trained in what we might term the 'semiotics of travel'. Vowing to remain efficiently alert, he or she must learn to look closely at such things as gravestones, church architecture, and prisons, must cultivate an informed perspective on what is being observed the better to decipher its meaning and thus become a skilful reader of the social and cultural panorama. Imaginatively and literally, Martineau's most favoured perspective is from high up and far away. Mystifying this perspective into one of knowledgeable disinterest, she imaginatively places herself on an Indian plateau so that she may take an historical look at the Indian plains and the primitive agriculture conducted thereon before the 'millions of natives' began to 'dream of white faces among them as their masters'; she sits on the top of a Catskill mountain so she may take a philosophical look at the landscape that is 'an epitome of the human universe' below her; she engages in distanced, retrospective ordering of her travel journals into narrative and of 'reliable facts' into history. She was an enthusiastic and perennial spectator – sometimes of small things like the perfectly smocked waistbands on frocks made by blind children in a New England institution, but more frequently of large facts of nature and momentous events in time such as Niagara Falls, the Pyramids, the teleological movement of English history in the first half of the nineteenth century, and the large sweep of religious practices from Egyptian temples to the Dissenting chapels of her native Norwich.

Watching, reading, and deciphering the social, cultural, and political signs of her time constitute the foundation of her career. What she says of her work in writing the volumes of English history, that she had engaged in 'consolidating, assimilating, and vivifying' so as to perform a work of 'auxiliary usefulness', may be said about almost all her writing. Just as 'a need of utterance' and a talent for powerful popularisation are generative marks of her career, so, too, is a mode of ancillary elaboration. In a manner that is both passive and active, her 'need of utterance' found its expression in energetic, vivifying analysis of what she quiescently, if alertly, observed: what she observed was ordered into an extensive literary production that legitimated in one form or another many of the influential political and social ideas of her time. This is not to say she was an officially empowered and self-proclaimed propagandist for the English middle-class values and manners with which she found herself most comfortable. Her elaborative 'auxiliary usefulness' was diffused and unannounced, part of the complex cultural processes whereby hegemonic ideologies are disseminated through institutions such as the press, the church, schools and universities rather than coercively imposed upon society. As she was the first to admit, she popularised and did not discover or invent the social and political theories that frame almost all her writing. Yet in a contradictory pattern I see as central to her significance as a woman intellectual, she lived an extraordinarily active, constructive life devoted to passive observation of a rapidly changing society in whose 'making' she believed she had no part. Either she could not see, or was compelled to disguise such knowledge, that her female work of journalistic popularisation 'made' Victorian England as much as did the male work of banking, business, and politics. This was an England she described as being in a constant state of positive alteration, following a sequence of development that she retrospectively imposed upon her own experience.

In what follows I shall argue that Harriet Martineau's career is defined by her auxiliary usefulness to a male-dominated culture. What is interesting about her is that she embraces her subordinate status, while at the same time aligning it with her forthright, courageous, and life-long feminism. She may be said to feminise the function of Gramsci's category of organic intellectual production by intensifying its defining mark of acquiescent labour, a quality conventionally associated with Victorian women in the separation by sex and gender into public and private spheres. The role of organic intellectual is, of course, not imagined by Gramsci in anything other than male terms, yet the function of legitimation which defines that role in his theory bears significant resemblance to the function performed by the Victorian woman in her own private sphere, that of consensual elaboration of the influential beliefs moulded by Victorian man in his own public sphere of political and cultural authority.

At first it might seem that Martineau's uncompromising feminism would mark her career as following the more conventional model of alienation from dominant values, a model proffered by Gertrude Himmelfarb, for example, in *Victorian Minds* where she denies Leslie Stephen authentic intellectual status by virtue of his membership in the English upper classes. However, close analysis of Martineau's feminist writings shows them to be coherent with what one might call her textual services to the English middle class.

This is not to diminish the admirable firmness and sanity of her feminism; if anything, her spirited confrontation of male privilege becomes that much more heroic when understood from a perspective that encompasses all of her writings. In emphasising that Martineau's sexual politics cannot be dislodged from examination within the context of all her politics, my aim will be to foreground her brave feminism, not to assume in dispiriting fashion, that *all* is neatly subject to hegemonic patriarchy. But neither do I want to indulge in unexamined celebration of certain aspects of her work which, for the sake of sentimental feminist convenience, may be dismembered from the entire body of her writings: the feminism both creates and is created by the intricate matrix of ideologies influencing Martineau's life and work. Within that matrix, conventionally feminine qualities of passivity and acquiescence are both facilitated and reinforced by her writings.

What is so engaging about reading Martineau is the challenge of deciphering the ensemble of sex, gender, and social class which influences, indeed constructs, a career. Undaunted by sexist criticism, she manages to reconcile her legitimating functions for the English middle class with her strong-minded sexual politics. As well as feminising the role of organic intellectual, she engineers her feminism so that it serves the ideological aims of that same social class for whom she performs her legitimating role. Her call is for women to be educated so they might clear-headedly, rationally assent to their subjugated condition.

Taking, then, a model of auxiliary usefulness as the governing structure for Martineau's career, I shall first argue that she was almost obsessively fascinated with observation and decipherment from her early childhood. The passive textual recording of an actively ameliorative world becomes a key to her adult intellectual life and in the latter chapters of my discussion I shall emphasise two related points: first, that the model of auxiliary usefulness always informs Martineau's popular writing about women, political economy, slavery, English history and Eastern travel; and, second, that the model also hampers Martineau from a coherent integration of her sexual politics with the writing of fiction.

Martineau's accounts of her life deflate all myths of the privileged consciousness of childhood. No shades of the prison-house close in upon her as she grows older – rather the world becomes an inviting place full of possibilities for independence and liberation: 'My own experience in childhood was of a painful and incessant longing for the future – a longing which enhanced all its innumerable pains, and embittered many of its pleasures – a longing for strength of body and of mind, for independence of action – for an escape in short from the conditions of childhood' (*L.S.*, 177–8). As she represents it in the *Autobiography*, this childhood was such that her first notion of escape from its debilitating constraints was through suicide, and in a rare moment of wryly comic self-analysis, she describes running to the kitchen in search of a carving knife to cut her throat and then losing her nerve because the servants were at dinner (*A.*, 1:18–19). Charlotte Brontë, after reading about Martineau's tormented childhood in *Household Education*, said to her, as Martineau recounts their meeting, that it 'was like meeting her own fetch, – so precisely were the fears and miseries there described the same as her own, told or not told in "Jane Eyre"' (*A.*, 2:324). Considering that Jane Eyre is a penniless and abused orphan (to say nothing of the dissimilarity between Brontë's dramatically unstable family life at Haworth and the more conventionally sober Martineau household at Norwich), the similiarity to Martineau seems somewhat melodramatic, but there is a way in which the Jane Eyre created by Charlotte Brontë may be seen as similar to the Harriet Martineau created by the autobiographer. Novelist and 'miscellaneous writer' chronicle lives that progress from misery to happiness, from humiliating dependence to liberating independence, from turbulent rage to serene rationality.

Obviously, narrative transfiguration of a life governs much writing about the self. However, such transfiguration is especially resonant in the case of Martineau's work (in the *Autobiography* and elsewhere) because of a correspondence between the ameliorative interpretation she places on her own experiences and the ameliorative readings of English social and political life that so thoroughly invest her various works. It is not so much that Martineau's *Autobiography* is an expression of her philosophy, as it is that both the philosophy and the text are directed by the progressivist beliefs central in her culture.[3]

Enlightenment is a conventional image of progress, both in the psychological mythologisation of an individual life and in the political mythologisation of a nation. The individual moves from the darkness of infant ignorance and terror to the light of rational understanding and control, and, in the broadest sense, a nation moves from the darkness of incoherent and instinctive response to the determinants of existence to a management and manipulation

of those determinants. Yet as a child Martineau was almost
preternaturally terrified of the light that is imaginatively suggestive
of mature control and understanding, and as an adult the only time
light ceased to make her uneasy was in her experience of mesmeric
trances.[4] In her straight-talking guide to the management and
education of children, *Household Education*, she emphasises the
importance of literal and moral light in the life of a child. Bracing air,
lots of light, make for a happy child: so, too, does a light of
truthfulness which banishes the prudish euphemisms mouthed by
Victorian parents. But, she confesses, 'my worst fears in infancy
were from lights and shadows'. A magic-lantern show, with 'its
circle of yellow light' drenched her in 'a cold perspiration from head
to foot'; the lamp-lighter's torch cast a gleam that reflected the
shadows of the window frames upon the ceiling and her blood 'ran
cold' at the sight; when the sun shone on the glass lustres on the
mantelpiece the fragments of colour cast on the wall seemed to her
like menacing dancing imps (*H.E.*, 58–63). She feared that the 'light
sky' would fall on her, that the 'dim light' of the dawn would
ceaselessly press upon her eyeballs, and at the age of 53 recalls that
the most terrible of her childhood dreams was to do with light. In the
dream, which she says she had at the age of four, she returns home
at dusk, goes up the front door steps in the dark, and then into the
kitchen where in the 'bright sunshine' her mother lifts her up and
sets her in the sun: 'Such was the dream that froze me with horror!'
(*A.*, 1:15).

   In Martineau's recollections of her family we learn very little about
her father; she describes him as understandably distracted by the
economic fluctuations of the first quarter of the nineteenth century
affecting his bombazine manufacturing business. Her mother's
stern presence dominates the household, radiating the light of
truthfulness in all things, and disciplining the most difficult of her
children to overcome melodramatic, lachrymose indulgence in
feelings of unjust treatment. Although Elizabeth Martineau was not
a particularly well educated or intellectually inclined woman, she
strongly favoured an education for her daughters that surpassed the
prevalent provincial training in sewing and music. In common with
many intelligent girls of her generation, Harriet Martineau was
instructed by her brothers in Latin and arithmetic, in French by her
sister, and that 'desperately methodical' mind she says she
possessed at the age of eight was trained into life-long habits of
systematic application. She was allowed to read all the newspapers

in the house, studied Shakespeare on her own, attended a local school from the age of 11 to 13, and at the age of 16 spent a year at a school in Bristol run by her maternal uncle, Lant Carpenter, a prominent Unitarian.

When she was eight years old she read Milton for the first time and related that 'in a few months, I believe there was hardly a line in Paradise Lost that I could not have instantly turned to. I sent myself to sleep by repeating it: and when my curtains were drawn back in the morning, descriptions of heavenly light rushed into my memory. I think this must have been my first experience of moral relief through intellectual resource' (*A.*, 1:42–3). Martineau's recollection of this experience signalises a recurrent pattern in her intellectual life. As the terrifying morning light is transformed through association with Milton's poetry, as monstrous luminosity becomes the heavenly resplendence of epic literature, in that process all of Martineau's Jane Eyre terrors are mastered through the light of intellectual application. However, this paradigmatic transformation from irrational terror to confident control, effected through what Martineau terms 'intellectual resource', is shadowed with contradiction. As Martineau progresses to intellectual enlightenment, as she becomes vibrantly independent and mobile, she paradoxically becomes increasingly involved in her work of auxiliary usefulness, and the liberation from turbulent feelings of dependence achieved through intellectual success leads to another form of dependence. Martineau's career is primarily devoted to a kind of safe elaboration, repeating in its fully developed form the repetition of received text that she performed as a child when she recited Milton's poetry. Political theory replaces poetry, yet Martineau remains a dutiful intellectual daughter, repeating, in one way or another, the words of her intellectual fathers. She may have rejected the dark stasis of childhood fears and the sequestered life of a provincial blue stocking so that she might open her curtains, let in the 'heavenly light' of Milton, and sit down at her desk every day at seven-thirty to produce the extraordinary amount of writing that she did, yet she retained her affiliation to patriarchal modes of thought.

As Martineau's work chronicles the narrative of English social, historical, and political progress, so, too, her career parallels that chronicle, and as her intellectual practice broadens through political journalism, that practice increasingly becomes the place for justification of the most powerful ideologies of her time. The more she published, the more she was solicited by politicians for a pamphlet to advance a particular cause or courted by prominent hostesses as a somewhat eccentric but always spirited guest, the more Martineau's writings express and create, even in their antagonistic aspects, powerful ideologies of middle-class supremacy, of British imperial power, of competitive individualism, and, most significantly in terms of her status as a woman intellectual, of sex and gender. The constituent conflict between career and gender which most women intellectuals in the Victorian period experienced manifests itself in particularly keen form in Martineau's life and work.[5]

In the essays she wrote while bedridden at Tynemouth, Martineau is understandably preoccupied with an unwelcome aggravation of her role as observer of the social, cultural, and political panorama. When she became ill with a uterine tumour in 1839 she was famous, a fêted figure on the London literary scene and fresh from travels in America. Sequestered upon her sofa and assuming a childhood familiarity with the Bible in her readers as thorough as her own had been, she asks: 'Can we not all remember the time when we conceived the grandest moment of possible existence to be that of a seraph, poised on balanced wings watching the bringing out of a world from chaos . . . To me, this conception was, in my childhood, one of eminent delight; and, when, years afterwards, I was involved in more than the ordinary toil and hurry of existence, I now and then recurred to the old image, with a sort of longing to exchange my function, – my share of the world-building in which we all have to help, for the privilege of the supposed seraph' (*L.S.*, p. 69). Martineau must reluctantly relinquish the image of the seraph, one of balanced, privileged observation of order made from chaos, for the image of a figure actively engaged in the business of 'world-building'. The tension between observation and participation that is inscribed in much of Martineau's prose emerges very strongly from the following long, swelling description of her feelings as she stands under Niagara Falls. That model of auxiliary usefulness characterising her career directs her evocation of the feelings she experienced as a celebrity in America, saluted as far south as New Orleans and as far north as Niagara:

It is an absorbing thing to watch the process of world-making; – both the formation of the natural and the conventional world . . . In its depths, in this noiseless workshop, was Nature employed with her blind and dumb agents, fashioning mysteries which the earthquake of a thousand years hence may bring to light . . . I saw something of the process of world-making behind the fall of Niagara, in the thunder cavern, where the rocks that have stood for ever tremble to their fall amidst the roar of the unexhausted floods. Foot-hold upon foot-hold is destined to be thrown down, till, after more ages than the world has yet known, the last rocky barrier shall be overpowered, and an ocean shall overspread countries which are but just entering upon civilised existence. Niagara itself is but one of the shifting scenes of life, like all of the outward that we hold most permanent. Niagara itself, like the systems of the sky, is one of the hands of Nature's clock, moving, though too slowly to be perceived by the unheeding, – still moving, to mark the lapse of time. Niagara itself is destined to be as the traditionary monsters of the ancient earth – a giant existence, to be spoken of to wondering ears in studious hours and believed in from the sole evidence of its surviving grandeur and beauty. While I stood in the wet whirlwind, with the crystal roof above me, the thundering floor beneath, and the foaming flood before me, I saw those quiet, studious hours of the future world when this cataract shall have become a tradition, and the spot on which I stood shall be the centre of a wide sea, a new region of life. This was seeing world-making.   (*S.A.*, pp. 210–11)

She begins the passage by placing herself in the privileged position of the seraph: the 'natural globe' is created before her eyes as she has previously witnessed the creation of the 'conventional world' in her travels through the towns and villages of America. In the great natural 'workshop', an image which converts nature from an awesomely uncontrollable force to a kind of artisan figure 'fashioning' fall and flood, Martineau's perceptions become sibylline as she divines the future on the basis of theories of geological time probably familiar to her from reading Sir Charles Lyell's *Principles of Geology*, published between 1830 and 1833. That Niagara is understandable as part of a system, likened to a hand in the cosmic clock which moves too slowly for human perception, reveals Martineau's participation in the Victorian discourse that attempts to reconcile contradictory scientific and religious thought. Nature may be fashioning 'mysteries' in her workshop but they are mysteries understandable in the larger geological scheme of things. Martineau places herself at the centre of the workshop, in the actual hub of the natural machine producing natural formations. Paradoxically, she is both the centre and the observer of creation as she stands in the wet whirlwind, a crystal roof above, a thundering floor beneath, and a foaming flood before her – doubly privileged as witness to the present and the future. The observant passivity of the present becomes the sibylline passivity of the future and the writing that Martineau brings out of this cave authorises her work of 'auxiliary usefulness'. The passage implicitly proclaims her as a woman intellectual privileged in the perspective she is allowed, yet at the same time it is a perspective of a world she has not created, in the most obvious literal sense and also in the sense of textual record. As the Cumaean Sibyl writing from the cave, recording, interpreting, and divining a work of nature not of her own making, she executes her share of actual 'world-building' as she records and legitimates the values, manners, and political ideas of her time. This relationship between performing 'world-building' through writing after watching 'world-making' in process frames her participation in the intellectual discourse which 'built' Victorian culture and society.

She was precipitated into a more public, metropolitan life by her father's financial losses in the economic depression of the late 1820s. In a modest way, she had been writing professionally for some seven years, but the family events of 1829 gave her, as she describes it, 'a wholly new freedom': 'I, who had been obliged to write before breakfast, or in some private way, had henceforth liberty to do my own work in my own way: for we had lost our gentility.' Had her father not lost the money that enabled his family's gentility, she goes on to say, she and her sisters would have lived on in the 'ordinary provincial method of ladies with small means, sewing and economizing, and growing narrower every year' (*A.*, 1:142). The failure of the father liberates the daughter from unexamined dependence, forces that critical move from the provincial constraints of Norwich Dissenting circles to the much larger London world of cultural sophistication. For a brief period after her father's financial setbacks, she was engaged to a man named John Worthington, and had she married him it is possible she would have remained an obscure writer of religious tracts and political essays. Judging from her cautious references to the engagement it would have become a disastrous marriage. She was 'very anxious and unhappy' about the attachment and subsequently thankful for not having married at all. Her business in life, she says, was 'to think and learn, and to speak out with absolute freedom what I have thought and learned'. The emotional demands of marriage, the necessary adjustment of habit and disposition, would have hampered that freedom, and Martineau, as it turned out, became happily married to her career: 'My work and I have been fitted to each other' (*A.*, 1:131–3). Lacking the economic support of either father or husband, she possessed the ambition and education that transformed financial reversal into escape from parsimonious provincial life, and she was, in a sense, liberated from one novelistic existence into another. If she may be said to have left behind her the female world of Elizabeth Gaskell's *Cranford* with its emphasis on cooperation and domestic ritual in a community of reduced circumstances, then she arrived in London on a dark and foggy morning in November 1832 much like the hero who inhabits the English novel from *Great Expectations* to *Lucky Jim*, and whose story is the conventionally male one of ambition, struggle, and ambiguous success in the metropolis.[6] The first work she did in London was explicitly undertaken as endorsement of influential economic and political theory, and the textual services which Martineau rendered to the English middle class, sustained until the last autobiographical writings and leaders for the *Daily News*, began with the *Illustrations of Political Economy*.

# 2

# Political Economy and Feminist Politics

The *Illustrations of Political Economy* was published initially in twenty-four phenomenally successful monthly volumes. As the only person who believed that such a work was 'craved by the popular mind', Martineau had some difficulty in finding a publisher, and she was forced to arrive at highly unfavourable terms with Charles Fox, the brother of the Reverend William Johnson Fox, editor of the *Monthly Repository*: publication by subscription, profits to be shared, and the bulk of subscriptions solicited by the author. Discouraged by the conditions and unconvinced she would find any supporters, Martineau characteristically persisted and wrote the first Tale – which turned out to be astonishingly popular. Readers awaited monthly publication of the *Illustrations* with a fervour similar to that displayed in anticipation of the newest number of a serialised novel, and from that time, Martineau recalls, she 'never had any other anxiety about employment than what to choose, nor any real care about money' (*A.*, 1:178). The principal source for the Tales was James Mill's *Elements of Political Economy* and the notion of didactic narratives for the 'popular mind' taken from Jane Marcet's *Conversations on Political Economy* published in 1816. Where Mill intended his work for the educated adult, and Jane Marcet designed her book for young students, Martineau aimed her powerful didactic sights on the social class she consistently saluted as upholders of the best in English culture and society – that composed of artisans and tradesmen.

That the first important book on the 'new science' of Political Economy, Adam Smith's *Wealth of Nations*, should be 'very long; in some parts very difficult . . . and not so clear and precise in its arrangement as it might be' is all to be expected, announces Martineau in her Preface. Smith was not writing for the 'great mass of people', and the lofty male theoretician requires the practical female populariser as translator of abstract thought into vivid application. Believing it appropriate that the difficult theory of political science should be offered in a 'cold, dry form . . . bare of illustration', she declares that once the truths of such a theory are 'laid hold of, it is easy to discover and display its beauty; and this, the last and easiest process, is what remains to be done for Political Economy' (*P.E.*, 1:x–xi). In a self-abnegating gesture of deference to theory, her work is offered as last and easiest. Discovering and displaying the 'beauty' of received ideas, she ratifies political ideas which, if assessed from a more radical and ironic perspective than that available to Martineau, may be seen to have generated many of the social and cultural formations to which she opposed her feminist writings. Moreover, from the writing of the Preface to the completion of the last Tale, from a period of deep discouragement to one of high exhilaration, she followed a precise method of composition particularly apt for the nature of the work she performed in the *Illustrations*. It is a model of production emblematic of almost all her work.

She began by noting the leading ideas on the topics for a particular Tale; she then read up on the subject and restrained herself 'from glancing even in thought' to her story until 'it should be suggested by my collective didactic materials'. She next made the Summary of Principles (found at the end of each monthly number) and incorporated each leading Principle in a fictive character so that 'the mutual operation of these embodied principles supplied the action of the story'. She then outlined the story, reduced her didactic materials to chapters and made a table of contents for each chapter. Having established in the most thorough way the shape of her Tales, she finally filled in a structure dictated entirely by the received Principles it was her mission to illustrate. As the supplier of content for a form determined by received ideas, as the performer of work that was indeed last and easiest, it is no wonder she could say that after having set things up in the fashion described, 'all the rest was easy. I paged my paper; and then the story went off like a letter' (*A.*, 1:194–5).

As a whole, the *Illustrations* propounded a social theory that was an amalgam of Bentham's greatest happiness principle, Smith's *laissez-faire* doctrine, Malthus's *Essay on Population*, and Ricardo's attack on the Corn Laws: as expressed through Martineau's deliberately homespun narratives, it is a social theory predicated on steadfast belief in the benevolent workings of capitalism and of competitive individualism. In 'The Hill and the Valley', for example, the preservation of 'fixed capital' in times of recession is defended on the grounds that capital must be saved to produce more labour. 'Brooke and Brooke Farm' explains that the enclosure of lands by wealthy farmers is in the best economic interest of the community since it brings labourers to a depressed village who, in their turn, rejuvenate the butcher's trade which leads to the purchase of new hats by the butcher's wife, more shopping by the wife's milliner, and the eventual establishment of a new school. The self-interest of one is eventually the best interest of all. In 'A Manchester Strike' Martineau anticipates Samuel Smiles's hortatory addresses to the working class by urging it to husband instead of 'wasting' capital, to save money instead of supporting strikes, and she defends the anti-union position of manufacturers by showing that the working conditions of labour are best improved by 'inventions and discoveries' that create capital.[1] 'The Loom and the Lugger' insists that a regular supply of cheap food will be guaranteed by free trade in corn; embroidered with an exotic setting derived from descriptions of Ceylon given to Martineau by an ex-governor, 'Cinammon and Pearls' sanctions colonisation as essential for the expansion of British markets; and 'Briery Creek' shows the damaging effects of 'unproductive consumption of capital' by teaching that 'an expenditure which avoidably exceeds the revenue is a social crime'. 'The Moral of Many Fables' sums it all up with the sanguine forecast that 'human enjoyment is perpetually on the increase' and that all will become 'intellectual, virtuous, and happy . . . when society shall be wisely arranged'.

The Tales are very heavy going. Characters speak like the embodiment of stiff Principles that they are, the creation of settings is toilsomely mechanical, and even without an awareness of Martineau's method of composition, the reader cannot miss the fitting of doctrinal pieces into a prearranged ideological outline, and must sense that disruptive spontaneity is being banished from the narrative. Allowing for the fact that Martineau produced the *Illustrations* for a particular readership and that by virtue of their didactic nature the Tales necessarily simplify complex economic and political questions into neat formulae, there is still so much naive assertion, so much obsessive rationalisation, that the *Illustrations* are almost embarrassing in their unambiguous ratification of the benignity of the greatest happiness principle. We detect not an atom of the extensive ambivalence and reservation expressed by other Victorian thinkers (Carlyle and Mill come immediately to mind) about the social and cultural consequences of rampant economic expansion – no thundering excoriation of Mammonism here, no cool attack upon the despotism of Custom. The suffering experienced by vast numbers of agricultural and factory workers that became the urgent subject of Parliamentary investigation a decade after Martineau published the *Illustrations* is merely an occasion for pat prescription. We find no recognition of the moral difficulty that impels so much Victorian intellectual discourse, that of reconciling the social actuality of competitive individualism with the ideal of a decent and humane society. Martineau transforms complex problems into happy fables: *laissez-faire* economic systems are the best, and seemingly best popularised in a mechanistic prose analogous to the immutable laws governing the ultimately benevolent workings of such economic systems.

The lesson of her Malthusian tale, 'Weal and Woe in Garveloch', (by 'bringing no more children into the world than there is subsistence for, society may preserve itself from the miseries of want') subjected her to bristling charges that she was writing about matters unsuitable for treatment by a female author.[2] However, 'A Tale of the Tyne', which advocated free circulation of labour and unrestricted commercial competition, brought praise from 'stern Benthamites' who, Martineau records, 'sent round messages . . . that they had met with a faithful expositor at last' (*A.*, 1:254). By the time she was writing the *Illustrations of Taxation* in 1834, the Whig Government had officially acknowledged her expository talents. Knowing that the government had proposed a house-tax unpopular with London shopkeepers who would have to pay increased rents to cover the tax (their landlords having decided it was not in their own self-interest to pay the tax themselves), Martineau felt that 'some good might be done, and no harm, if my Illustrations proceeded *pari passu* with the financial reforms'. Asked whether there was any 'mediated measure' she might perform, the Cabinet provided her with documents facilitating a naked piece of propaganda for the tithe. This is not to suggest that Martineau was an unprincipled political journalist pandering to power. She approved wholeheartedly of the tithe and disdained support of Whig governments. She considered the Whigs a 'remarkably vulgar class of men' tarnished by the 'poverty and perverseness of their ideas' and when she was approached in 1848 by Charles Knight (publisher of texts for the Society for the Diffusion of Useful Knowledge) to write for a proposed new periodical aimed at the working class, she refused on the grounds that the 'Whig touch

perished it at once'. In her view the Whigs 'knew about as much of
the working-classes of England as those of Turkey' (*A.*, 2:298–9).
Her undivided political sympathies were with the social group that,
for her, made up the 'best class of Chartist leaders'. These men did
not require Whigs (or Tories) to speak for them; they were
unequivocal advocates of universal education, strong supporters of
all political measures ensuring the supremacy of English trade, and
would have 'neither the pomp and prancings of Toryism, nor the
incapacity of Whiggism. They were Radical Reformers' (*H.*, 3:557).
Martineau's political discourse identifies Radical Reformers as those
who understand and obey the laws of social progress: strong and
steady development of society originates in immutable evolutionary
laws which man actively implements according to his time and
given place in the causative scheme of things.

Occasionally, Martineau's texts betray implicit uneasiness about
her chosen career of auxiliary usefulness to powerful authority. In
the metaphysical musings that enlace the sociological observations
of *Society in America* (published in 1837), for example, she suggests
that an individual may be seen in two irreconcilable ways: one, 'as a
solitary being, with inherent powers, and an omnipotent will; a
creator, a king, an inscrutable mystery'; and two, 'as a being
infinitely connected with all other beings with none but derived
powers, with a heavenly directed will; a creature, a subject, a
transparent medium through which the workings of principles are
to be eternally revealed' (2:294).[3] Having articulated the familiar
riddle of free will, she flatly asserts that both ways of seeing an
individual are 'true' and leaves it at that. Never relinquishing her
belief in a force outside human control that directs the ameliorative
development of human affairs, she most certainly performed more
as a subject and transparent medium in her intellectual practice than
she did as a solitary and sovereign power. The early Unitarianism
may have been succeeded by Comtean positivism, but Martineau's
Necessitarian belief that the human will is not autonomous
remained unshaken and she adamantly insisted that the
'constitution and action of the human faculty of Will are determined
by influences beyond the control of the possessor of the faculty'
(*A.*, 1:111).

To deny individual sovereignty, however, is not to abdicate from
disciplined self-management. Her rigorous exemplification of
Carlyle's Gospel of Work, her battle with feelings of rage and
inadequacy, her active acquiescence in the laws of positive social

change that can be seen, for example, in her schemes for improving lower-class housing and education while she lived in the Lake District, all testify to the fact that although she accepted the idea of eternal, immutable laws at work in the universe which broach no interference from the human will, she also believed that man (and woman) as *agent* of those laws may choose between active compliance or resigned submission. Martineau chose enthusiastic and vital compliance.

As Martineau embraced her function as explicating agent of theories of political economy and transparent medium of cosmic and social principles, her philosophical and religious beliefs became aligned with her particular position as woman intellectual in Victorian culture. As she achieved that alignment between intellectual function and gender, however, she implicitly undermined the male power that governed her intellectual life. In a subversive process that redeems her from an essentially uninteresting endorsement of dominant ideologies, she denies the omnipotence of man's will (and this is undoubtedly male will, for it is a king whose power is an 'inscrutable mystery') and welcomes the advent of man's highest honour in 'becoming as clear a medium as possible for the revelations which are to be made through him' (*S.A.*, 2:295). Celebrating the dying of superstitious belief in self-originating power and welcoming the birth of a self-dedication of the human will to inscribed laws and principles, she sanctions a structure of instrumentality conjunctive with that of male intellectual authority and female ratification. However, Martineau's thought implicitly subverts male cultural and social power by declaring independence from outmoded beliefs in an omnipotence enjoyed primarily by men and welcoming dependence on certain laws which control the lives of both women *and* men. Martineau's preoccupation with the commonplace problem of free will, which bothered her from the age of six when she asked her brother James to sort it all out for her (he could not), is inextricable from her sexual politics.

For a woman intellectual of Martineau's social class and time, independence often took the literal form of leaving the patriarchal household in the provinces and moving to London. Ironically in the case of Martineau, however, she left the literal world of the father to devote herself to the intellectual needs of new 'fathers' such as Adam Smith, James Mill, Auguste Comte, and, in that later period of her life when she believed she was cured by mesmerism, Henry

Atkinson. In effect, Martineau declares herself independent of patriarchal power and refutes the sovereignty associated with the omnipotent and punitive fathers of the Bible, with the Miltonic fathers of her childhood reading, and with the actual Norwich fathers who prepared their daughters for little more than marriage. Yet her relationship to institutions of power remains fraught with an ambiguity nowhere more arresting than in her polemical attacks upon the subjugation of women.

Harriet Martineau consistently introduced the Woman Question into almost all her writings. Displaying an assertive, vivacious prose and armed with an arsenal of personal observation, her feminist polemics took to the field of sexual politics with a steady aim. Women have risen, she scathingly declares, from a state of slavery (exemplified in the subservience of the Indian squaw which she observed with horrified distaste in America) to the 'highest condition in which they are present seen . . . less than half-educated, precluded from earning a subsistence, except in a very few ill-paid employments, and prohibited from giving or withholding their assent to laws which they are yet bound by penalties to obey . . . the degree of the degradation of women is as good a test as the moralist can adapt for ascertaining the state of domestic morals in any country' (*H.O.* p. 151). However, the feminist politics which Martineau tenaciously inserted into almost all her texts more frequently urge women to educated acceptance rather than angry refutation of their socially inscribed destinies, and the admirable clarity of her splendid indignation is sometimes blurred by the traces of male prescriptions for woman's role and function.

If there was anything more distasteful to Martineau than subjugated and debased womanhood, it was women who whined about their wrongs and rights: she wanted women to be more like herself, or at least as she imagined herself – rational, confident, the intellectual equal of any man, or certainly equal enough to sanction his ideas. Perhaps the most personal statement of her feminism is generated by Mary Wollstonecraft's politics, lamentably based, Martineau believed, on personal misery:

Women who would improve the condition and chances of their sex, must, I am certain, be not only affectionate and devoted, but rational and dispassionate, with the devotedness of benevolence, and not merely of personal love. But Mary Wollstonecraft was, with all her powers, a poor victim of passion, with no control over her own peace, and no calmness or content except when the needs of her individual nature were satisfied. . . . Nobody can be further than I am from being satisfied with the condition of own sex, under the law and custom of my own country; but I decline all fellowship and co-operation with women of genius or otherwise favourable position, who injure the cause by their personal tendencies. . . . The best friends of that cause are women who are morally as well as intellectually competent to the most serious business of life, and who must be clearly seen to speak from conviction of the truth, and not from personal unhappiness . . . women, like men, can obtain whatever they show themselves fit for. Let them be educated, – let their powers be cultivated, to the extent for which the means are already provided, and all that is wanted or ought to be desired will follow of course. Whatever a woman proves herself able to do, society will be thankful to see her do, – just as if she were a man. (*A.*, 1:400–1)[4]

Martineau's feminist programme is dictated by a dualistic perspective on the sexes that unassailably values male over female. It is to Mary Wollstonecraft's detriment that she permitted her conventionally female disposition to get the upper hand and that she behaved just like a woman: a victim of passion, lacking control, obsessed with personal needs and unhappiness, she was essentially unstable when it came to the 'serious business of life' – which, it seems, is conducted best by those who are analytical, dispassionate, capable of subordinating personal need to 'the truth' (which remains undefined in this attack on feminism weakened by femininity). The primary meaning of the sortie against Wollstonecraft is, of course, a distaste for what Martineau perceived as her sexual enslavement to men. Initially it might seem that Martineau slyly advocates renunciation of men as a condition of constructive feminism – from the conventional Victorian perspective on women (and that perspective, together with Martineau's genuinely indignant criticism of sexual injustice, guides this passage), what else could be the source of their 'personal unhappiness' except romantic suffering due to the presence or absence of a man? Martineau here does not speak of women's 'personal unhappiness' being caused by denial of the vote, by the inability to own property in one's own name, or by the lack of freedom to divorce one's husband. A separate sphere founded on feminist isolationism, however, is not Martineau's goal: she seems more concerned with justifying a system of sexual privilege based upon women controlling negative qualities conventionally associated with their sex so that they might, through behaving more like men, become better partners for them – which seems to leave us with one authentic sex and the other performing as emotional and intellectual transvestite.

Martineau urges the opportunity, through education, for all women to acquire the power enjoyed by men so they may perform an equal, but not identical, part in the creation and elaboration of English middle-class values. For this is really the core of Martineau's sexual politics – she wants women to participate in the dominant Victorian discourses of culture and politics, to contribute to the creation and dissemination of the beliefs and practices of the most powerful class in English society. But they have to do all this, as we shall see, in their own female, essentialist fashion.

When she was offered the opportunity to edit a new periodical dealing with political economy, she noted in her journal that an 'awful choice' was before her. If she undertook the editorship she would have to brace herself to the task and suffer like a man: 'undertaking a man's duty, I must brave a man's fate' (*A.*, 2:110). As it turned out, the advice of her brother James persuaded her against such bravery and she chose to write a novel instead, *Deerbrook* published in 1839. Editing a periodical, assuming the authority and responsibility entailed in dealing with other writers – this is man's work in the public world (undertaken with some skill, incidentally, by Mary Ann Evans as unpaid assistant editor of the *Westminster Review*) and in order for a woman to do it she must accept a man's disappointments as well as his rewards. I am not suggesting that Martineau should have rejected the prevailing Victorian equation of leadership and masculinity. Rather, I want to emphasise that Martineau's feminism must be examined within the cultural and social context in which it was articulated, its inconsistencies identified as expressive of the patriarchal values inscribed, revised, and sometimes subverted in that feminism. Obviously unaware that a mode of intellectual activity structured on imitation (suffer like a man, undertake a man's duty, brave a man's fate, and so on) is inferior to its model, Martineau cannot be charged with a conscious belief that women are inferior to men, and to castigate her for flawed feminist politics would be to indulge in self-serving, ahistorical criticism; if anything, my aim is to illuminate the bravery of

Martineau's feminism in the context of her legitimating politics. Moreover, Martineau's unconscious articulation of prevailing patriarchal ideas about sex and gender must testify to the entrenched power of the very beliefs she struggled to revise.

When Martineau travelled to America in August 1834 she received a rude shock. She set out with idealistic expectations based on her understanding of American democratic principles. Practice did not turn out to match principle and the title of the last section of her chapter on Morals and Politics, 'The Political Non-Existence of Women', indicates her displeasure with what she discovered. Significantly, none of her criticism of the social and political status of English women is as vividly compelling as her matchless attack on the condition of women in America. Her polemical emphasis evinces two seemingly disjunctive views of English women, for while implying that they enjoy a higher degree of freedom, *Society in America* seems also to afford Martineau the opportunity for displacement of any uneasiness she may have felt about her acquiescence in the English social and cultural discipline of the female sex. It is as if the criticism of American society is empowered by what Martineau has *not* said about the English treatment of women. The tone of these sections of *Society in America* is pugnaciously interrogative: 'One of the fundamental principles announced in the Declaration of Independence is, that governments derive their just powers from the consent of the governed. How can the political condition of women be reconciled with this? Governments in the United States have power to tax women who hold property; to divorce them from their husbands; to fine, imprison, and execute them for certain offences. Whence do these governments derive their powers? They are not "just", as they are not derived from the consent of the women thus governed' (1:148). Perhaps because Martineau has a text, the Declaration of Independence, by which to measure practice against principle, her rhetorical mode is belligerently analytical, in contrast, say, to the manner adopted in the *Autobiography* for examination of her position as woman intellectual in English society: 'I have no vote at elections, though I am a tax-paying housekeeper and responsible citizen; and I regard the disability as an absurdity, seeing that I have for a long course of years influenced public affairs to an extent not professed or attempted by many men. But I do not see that I could do much good by personal complaints, which always have some suspicion or reality of passion in them. I think the better way is for us all to learn

and to try to the utmost what we can do, and thus to win for
ourselves the consideration which alone can secure us rational
treatment' (1:399). With no institutionalised, inscribed ideal before
her by which to measure performance, she lapses into a mild appeal
for personal action, couched in the vaguest of language suggestive
of sentimental entreaties for people to pull together in time of
adversity. The attack on American political practice in regard to
women, resting upon direct interrogation of the disparity between
inscribed ideal and reality, forces the reader's assent to strongly
stated criticism of injustice. In contrast, the passage delineating the
absurdity inherent in Martineau's own position, that of professional
recognition with no vote, is vapid, delivered in a style matching the
essential powerlessness of her status. Her insipid remedy for sexual
injustice is virtually meaningless – 'I think the better way is for us all
to learn and to try to the utmost what we can do' – and the hope of
women 'winning' for themselves what is, by the standards applied
to American society, only just, indicates propitiation of male
authority, or if not that, a weary resignation to her unjust lot.

   Throughout *Society in America* Martineau is an astute reader and
analyst of the social panorama, at all times concerned with the
'process of formation' of social structures, revising the narratives of
other English travellers to America who 'analyze nothing at all'.[5]
Always alert to the ways in which American morality and
institutions are mutually determinative, she dissects virtually
everything she sees. Despite her polemical appropriation of the
Declaration of Independence for the uncompromising criticism of
American treatment of women, she is characteristically un-
concerned with the origin of morality and institutions, with the
genesis of that 'process of formation' central to her social analysis.
This is not an enquiry into the origins of American culture and
society, nor a search for causes of the lamentable treatment of
women: this is an analysis of the way in which social systems, either
already formed or in a dynamic process of formation, actually work.
As pioneer sociologist, Martineau performs an intellectual function
somewhat similar to that enacted by George Eliot as novelist in
*Middlemarch*. Each figuratively dissects the social web, traces the
fine threads of reticular connection between morality and
institution, and – allowing for the obvious differences between
Martineau's sometimes hasty exposition and Eliot's finely
meditated exploration and between sociological travel narrative and
novel – it is possible to see both women performing a function

characteristic of much women's intellectual practice in the nineteenth century, a function that inclines more to close observation of society than it does to theoretical speculation about its origin. This is not to say that only women writers in the nineteenth century tend more to descriptive than to speculative social analysis. My point is rather that the cultural authority to theorise about society, rather than merely observe the phenomena which is material for theory (an authority demonstrated, for example, in Mill's 'Civilization' and 'On Liberty' or in Carlyle's 'Signs of the Times' and 'Characteristics') is more likely to be exploited by a male than a female writer.

Martineau's declaration that the only 'just' power belonging to a government comes from the consent of the governed is supported by her observations of the Shaker women she encountered in Hancock, Massachusetts. These women are coerced into submission, unjustly ruled by the patriarchal power of their religion, their fathers, and their husbands. As horrifying to her as the Egyptian women she later observed on her Eastern travels, the Shaker wives and daughters are monstrous in their 'frightful costume', disgusting in their aversion to fresh air and exercise, 'pallid and spiritless' in their inertia. Dancing like 'galvanised corpses' they present a spectacle that is 'too shocking for ridicule' (*S.A.*, 1:313–14). Here we have Martineau at her most sensibly persuasive. Who could disagree that women should be healthy and vigorous, that Martineau's contemporaries should have emulated her habit of exercising every day, should have been inspired to energetic travel by her accounts of walking fifteen miles beside her camel when crossing the Egyptian desert, of attacking the ascent of the Pyramids with a determination that astonished her guides, of being the first women to climb Mount Sinai (at least so she claims, and whether she was or not matters little). Her life was the absolute antithesis of the one she describes endured by women subjugated by authoritarian, patriarchal social formations. These Shaker women endure 'the corrosion of unoccupied thought, and the decay of unemployed powers': their lives are one hollow misery from beginning to end, redeemed only in one way – 'by that degree of action that had been permitted to them, in order that they might, in any wise, live' (*S.A.*, 2:296). Occupation, employment, activity create a full and happy life for both men and women, and in a manner that aligns Martineau's sexual politics with her more generalised political and historical writings, she justifies the domination of the British empire over its colonised subjects through her emphasis on Western energy and Eastern inertia.

In writing about the British management of India, Martineau contrasts dynamic European industrialisation with the 'Mussulman pride' and 'Hindoo apathy' that held India in some kind of slothful bondage until imperial power electrified the continent into progressivist movement. In a grammatically murky passage that calls into question the merit of a Hindoo pilgrimage conducted by railway, Martineau celebrates Western technology: 'Immutability, patience, indolence, stagnation, have been the venerable things which the Hindoo mind hated the Mussulmans for invading with their superior energy; and now what is Mussulman energy in comparison with ours, judging by our methods of steaming by sea and land, and flashing our thoughts over 1 000 miles in a second' (*B.R.* p. 341). The passage sarcastically conflates patience with less positive qualities and names them all 'venerable things' to the Hindoo mind: Mussulman 'energy' is superior, but nothing to British industrial power steaming and flashing its way across the Indian continent, spurring the natives into action and freeing them from superstition and cultural backwardness. That colonisation might be seen as a modern form of the patriarchal control that keeps Shaker women in their miserable place does not, in fact could not, occur to Martineau: such a reading would be alien to her imperialistic nineteenth-century historical imagination in which the colonised native stands many steps below the European or American woman on the evolutionary scale of potential development. In a manner that reveals Martineau's auxiliary usefulness to British imperialism and liberal sexual politics, she argues that the native will be released from superstititon and the woman from cultural inertia through acquisition of two qualities cherished by the English middle class in the nineteenth century – rationality and ambition.

In America the confinement of woman's intellect has led to pedantic thought, in itself a hopeful sign because, as Martineau observes, pedantry 'is the result of an intellect which cannot be wholly passive, but must demonstrate some force, and does so through the medium of narrow morals. Pedantry indicates the first struggle of intellect with its restraints' (*S.A.*, 2:227). Favouring imagery of thrust and restraint, Martineau creates a dynamic model in which the intellect struggles through a narrow opening; refusing passivity, it is compelled to express itself where it can (in narrow morality) and is described in the concrete language distinctive in Martineau's prose. Wary of metaphor, critical of ambiguity, and disdainful of words that lost palpable touch with those 'reliable facts' furnishing the work of the historian, she liked language that shocked the reader into a strongly visual understanding of ideas. For example, she describes the women in Egyptian hareems she visited on her Eastern travels as a picture of humanity 'wholly and hopelessly baulked'. The giggling women, all sluggish flesh lolling on silken cushions, are grotesque in their unnatural isolation and enforced companionship of each other. In Martineau's eyes, they have a ludicrous bulk, a deformed physicality, that reinforces her image of them 'baulking' human progress: the bizarre display of ample flesh that is the result of their literal confinement becomes a physical obstacle to their release and a monstrous sign of perverted sexuality.

As may already be apparent, Martineau's writings about workers and women share a central contradiction in the call for them to be educated so that they may rationally assent to their ancillary status. Contradiction is no less apparent in Martineau's participation in the Victorian definition of woman's virtue. According to Martineau, woman possesses an innate moral superiority that must be exercised to check the natural sexual villainy of men: 'Women, especially, should be allowed the use and benefit of whatever native strength their Maker has seen fit to give them. It is essential to the virtue of society that they should be allowed the freest moral action, unfettered by ignorance, and unintimidated by authority: for it is unquestioned, and unquestionable that if women were not weak, men could not be wicked: that if women were bravely pure, there must be an end to the dastardly tyranny of licentiousness' (*S.A.*, 3:130).

In stressing that women must contribute to the 'virtue' of society, Martineau gives precedence to 'moral action'. Certainly this freedom of moral action could take the form Martineau herself enjoyed, the freedom to travel, to write, to publish – indeed, to make money – yet she wants women to exercise their moral muscles, flex that 'native strength' derived from brave purity, so that they might overthrow licentiousness. The force of this unfettered, unflinching woman is somewhat diminished by her dedication to elevating male morality. Martineau, however unconsciously, transforms woman into a kind of vigorous angel with a monopoly on moral probity, an idealising transformation integral to the overall mythologisation of Victorian woman into a creature both inferior and superior to men. Such contradiction is further revealed by the way in which Martineau will also deny woman's emotional leverage: 'I cannot enter upon the commonest order of pleas of all; – those which relate to the virtual influence of woman; her swaying the judgment and will of man through the heart; and so forth. One might as well try to dissect the morning mist' (*S.A.*, 1:205–6). What Martineau did not understand, obviously could not understand, was that the contradictions in her discourse reveal the way in which Victorian woman *was* made the subject of myth, was figured both as morally pure and morally delinquent, as sweetly angelic and aggressively demonic. In locating these inconsistencies in her feminist writings, I do not question the sincerity of her beliefs, but rather want to show how they both expressed and helped to constitute important Victorian prescriptions for woman's role and function. In the enactment of her Gramscian organic role for the English middle class, she necessarily incorporates into her feminist writings the inconsistent views of women held by that class.[6]

At first it might seem that Martineau's auxiliary usefulness to male-governed ideas about sex and gender would have been hampered by the establishment disgust with her inflammatory Malthusian tale of political economy, 'Weal and Woe in Garveloch'. But as Martineau herself points out in the *Autobiography* in 1855, it was already 'too late' for the *Quarterly Review*'s broadside to damage her reputation: 'I had already won my public before Croker [the author of the attack] took up his "tomahawk" . . . all suspicious speculation, in regard to my social doctrines, seems to have died out long ago' (1:208–11). Displaying her splendidly unswerving refusal to be cowed by criticism, Martineau had also very deftly responded to Croker's hysterical attack on her 'unfeminine' tale about population, by publishing an anonymous piece in the *London and Westminster Review* in 1839 in which she defended Queen Victoria from sexist imputations of female inadequacy to rule. Martineau concludes the defence by charging Croker with 'unmanly' conduct in his 'coarse' and 'stupid' attack upon 'Miss Martineau'. Aligning herself with the vulnerable young queen, Martineau cannily ensures that her fitness as spokeswoman for the proper role and function for Victorian woman will remain unimpeachable.[7]

In *Household Education* (1849), Martineau justifies improved education for girls by linking ignorant women and poor housekeepers. But she never explains why, as she claims, women want to be housekeepers. In some essentialist way, they just do: 'I do not see why the natural desire and the natural faculty for housewifery, which I think I see in every girl I meet, should be baffled because her parents are rich enough to have servants' (p. 282). Girls positively relish baking, preserving, clear starching, and ironing; 'natural desire' and 'natural faculty' require rational cultivation, however, and Martineau was a pioneering advocate of what came to be known as domestic science in the curriculum of English schoolgirls. She herself was an enthusiastic, efficient housekeeper, presiding over her Ambleside household of female servants as a benevolent matriarch, and because she seemed to like nothing better than organising a household (except writing a book), she imagines that all women quite naturally feel the same way: 'No true woman, married or single, can be happy without some sort of domestic life: – without having somebody's happiness dependent on her; and my own ideal of an innocent and happy life was a house of my own among poor improvable neighbours, with young servants whom I might train and attach to myself' (*A.*, 2:225). Happy this life may have been, but innocent of the power and authority exercised by Harriet Martineau over her social inferiors it was not. When describing her satisfaction at remaining unmarried, she is thankful for not having had a husband or children dependent on her: here she welcomes the dependence of poor, improvable neighbours and female servants. The Ambleside domesticity which George Eliot found charming embodies Martineau's ideal life for an unmarried woman. In the bracing countryside of the Lake District, she was economically independent by virtue of her own earnings; she exercised woman's innate moral superiority through improvement of her lower-class neighbours by giving them weekly lectures on such matters as intemperance, terrifying her ruffianly audience into compliance by showing them pictures of a drunkard's stomach; and there she had freedom to work and receive visits from her intellectual contemporaries. Living her ideal life of a 'true woman', Martineau broadcast the dogma of self-improvement, education, and hard work for women and the lower classes. Both social groups, if educated according to Martineau's no-nonsense system, become effective members of a middle-class society ruled by consent rather than coercion.

The household order which Martineau celebrates (with herself as intellectual matriarch) may well be seen as a microcosmic ideal of how she believed society at large should function. A disorderly lower class needs education that it might assent rationally (and soberly) to a social system prescribing and defining its place and function: women need to learn more than sewing and music that they might sensibly assent to a system of relationships between the sexes which, however much it values the female study of political philosophy, allots woman a privileged domestic place where the transparent purity and dark sexuality that are a function of her gender may be cultivated and confined. And if Martineau is in charge of this ideal household, then by implication people like herself should be in charge of society, those who actively and intelligently implement progressivist laws of social change remaining outside the control of the individual.

*Household Education* was written for families of the artisan class, a group always admired by Martineau for its dignified self-respect achieved through hard work. The book is aimed at the entire family: all must pull together for the social good, because, as Martineau declares, 'We know very well that we are all, through the whole range of society, like a set of ignorant and wayward children, compared with what we are made capable of being' (p. 4). Her appropriation of a familiar metaphor (society as family) makes us wonder how she views the related issues of authority and obedience: Who is the social father? The social mother? And when does the social child achieve maturity? Employing a rather extreme set of circumstances, Martineau locates the child of an artisan family between the pauper child exposed to the 'noises and sights of vice' (and all Victorian newspaper readers knew what that meant) and the royal child living in habitual solitude and served by palace functionaries: the child in an artisan family lives in an idyllic middle state. The enlightened artisan parent unites book learning with 'hard and imperative labour'; Martineau recounts that having learned the stern lessons of Nature taught by 'the melting fire, the rushing water, the unseen wind, the plastic metal or clay, the variegated wood or marble', he will spend his evenings poring over works of political philosophy. While the nineteenth-century artisans were, as E. J. Hobsbawm observes, 'men of skill, expertise, independence and education' (*Industry and Empire*, p. 90), it is doubtful they were the paragons of muscular and intellectual vigour Martineau wishfully imagines them to be. Joyfully occupying his middle place, happily reconciling in his being competitive individualism and social compliance, Martineau's artisan gives himself over to those immutable laws of progress that have designated the present, the nineteenth century, as transitional – a time of moral difficulty, in which man must balance himself between Christian ethics and what is required in 'the practical management of men's lives' (*H.E.*, p. 17). In Martineau's idealising historical imagination, the future will advance women and the lower orders of the labouring classes to a condition similar to that presently enjoyed by this political paragon, the artisan, where they will happily consent to a belief identifying self-interest with the social good.

# 3

# The Social Parent: Slavery, History, and Reform

Harriet Martineau's attitude towards male cultural and social authority is undeniably ambiguous. Arguably the Victorian feminist who more consistently than any other publicly committed herself to women's causes (from her writings on birth control in 1832 to her active campaigning against the Contagious Diseases Acts in 1871), she never ceased to cast herself in the role of intellectual daughter. The symbolic father who signalises most fully Martineau's equivocal status as lionised intellectual and performer of work of auxiliary usefulness, is the patriarch as 'social parent': this is the liberal father who ordains his intellectual daughters to attack slavery, celebrate the spirit of Reform in nineteenth-century history, and justify Western cultural superiority.

If the uneducated woman makes for an inefficient household, then slavery makes for an inefficient system of production. From her first published attack on slavery in the *Monthly Repository* to the end of her life, Martineau was unambiguously opposed to the ownership of slaves. As one might expect in a Christian journal of Dissent, she couches her argument in persuasive moral terms, stating unequivocally and imperatively that every Christian must be appalled by the practice. However, in 'Demerara', the fourth of the Tales illustrating political economy, she anchors her argument in something more concrete: slaves lose money for their owners. The 'purchase of man' is a poor buy, an unreliable commodity, and the better bargain is to purchase the labour power of the slave: 'Where the labourer is held as capital, the capitalist not only pays a much higher price for an equal quantity of labour, but also for waste, negligence, and theft, on the part of the labourer.' But where the labourer is not owned as capital, 'the capitalist pays for labour only' (*P.E.*, 1:142). The slave-owning system offends Martineau's ideal of sane, efficient management of resources because slave-owners are wasting their capital in human commodities. Instead of capital being reproduced, it is 'sunk', and 'an incalculable amount of human suffering' endured for the sake of 'a wholesale waste of labour and capital' (p. 143).

*Society in America* also contains a persuasively argued attack on slavery. Punctuated by sobering details of oppression and rhetorically varied with summaries of arguments both for and against the system, the attack is chillingly effective through the inclusion of moving personal narratives of slaves wrenched from their families and of shocking accounts of violence, including the sexual abuse of slave children; it is also composed with firm authority and a lucid, uncompromising style which indicates the clarity and thoughtfulness of Martineau's strong feelings. The unwavering courage she displayed in speaking her mind wherever she travelled in America, even in venturing to the South where her Abolitionist sentiments had preceded her, finds a stylistic parallel in the trenchant, stirring language.[1]

Exerting a polemical power similar to that displayed in her sections on the treatment of American women, she refers to her chapter title, 'Morals of Slavery', in this way: 'This title is not written down in a spirit of mockery; though there appears to be a mockery somewhere when we contrast slavery with the principles and the rule which are the test of all American institutions' (*S.A.*, 2:106–7). Practice is measured against principle, as it was in her attack on the oppression of women, and she discovers that the large moral gap is not only uneconomical and irreligious, but also absurd: 'in matters of economy, the pernicious and the absurd are usualy identical'. She advances all possible arguments in favour of slavery that she may demolish them, ridiculing, for example, the slave owner's claim that an 'endearing relation' subsists between master and slave; in her view, it is a relation similar to that pertaining between a man and his horse or a lady and her dog. Always returning to her fundamental position that no man has the right to own another human being and always reiterating her call for 'an immediate and complete surrender of all claims to negro men, women and children as property', Martineau speaks with a confident authority notably absent from the vacillating description of her own unjust English lot.

As long as slaves remain property, rather than being liberated to the economic freedom of selling their labour power, as long as women remain uneducated, rather than being released to the social freedom of exchanging their value as rational wife for economic security, both slave owners and husbands end up with a very poor bargain. Slaves and uneducated women are cheap but worthless commodities. Workers owned as property rather than employed as labour, uneducated women cherished as decoration rather than valued as useful partners, labour treated as capital rather than as a purchasable commodity – all create stagnant economic, cultural, and social systems. Abhorring stasis in any form, Martineau locates the wife of a slave owner in a particularly stagnant position, mired in loathsome privilege. Freed from housework by her husband's status, she is herself a slave to overseeing her house slaves who, owned rather than having freely sold their labour power to domestic service, spend all their time lolling against bedposts and leaning on sofas. The wife of a slave owner exists in a condition of unofficial bondage to her husband, no more than sexual ornament and agent of his pernicious values.

If one considers Martineau's deployment of the metaphor of family for social organisation, then an informing correlative between her calls for women to become rational wives or economically independent employees, for the lower classes to become independent through acquisition of mechanical skills and education, for slaves to become proprietors of their labour as commodity, begins to emerge. The way to social adulthood for women, members of the lower classes, and slaves, is through ambitious individualism. If we recall the bracing lesson of *Household Education* (we are all 'like a set of ignorant and wayward children, compared with what we are made capable of being'), then it is clear that to become a social adult, man must leave the social parent, in a literal sense execute that liberating move from provincial anonymity to metropolitan celebrity enacted by Martineau, and in a symbolic sense reject all social systems that promote patriarchal protection of the individual.

In writing about the 'subordination of the sex' in *Society in America*, Martineau says that the progression or emancipation of any class usually, if not always, takes place through the efforts of individuals in that class. And so it must be for women: 'All women should inform themselves of the condition of their sex, and of their own position. It must necessarily follow that the noblest of them will, sooner or later, put forth a moral power which shall prostrate cant, and burst asunder the bonds (silken to some, but cold iron to others) of feudal prejudices and usages' (2:259). Characteristically employing verbs of action to describe progressivist ideas (the heroic woman will 'put forth a moral power' which will 'prostrate cant', 'burst asunder' degrading bonds), Martineau understands women as a social class, and in more modern terms than she would have employed, sees them as exploited by fathers, husbands and employers. In the most extreme example of female subjugation that she ever saw or could imagine, captive Egyptian women, beyond salvation, hideous in their subjugation, are described as being in a worse position than London slum-dwellers – 'a visit to the worst room in the Rookery of St Giles's would have affected me less painfully. There are there at least the elements of a rational life, however perverted' (*E.L.*, 2:156). The English working class is capable of self-improvement through hard work and thrift, or at least so it goes in Martineau's rehearsal of the myth of a sensible ambition that sunders the social and historical constraints she both acknowledges and denies in her discourse as she simultaneously proclaims freedom through ambition and teaches subjugation to evolutionary laws. In much the same way that English and American women, once they become conscious of themselves as a degraded sex, will collect their moral power and break the bonds of 'feudal prejudices and usages', so the working class can overthrow antiquated social structures modelled on the feudal family of landowner and tenant.

In 1849 Martineau was asked by Charles Knight to take over the writing of a History of the Thirty Years' Peace. Despite the fact that she began her 'great task of the History under much anxiety of mind' due to the illness of her mother, and that she 'sank into a state of dismay' when she laid out her plans for the monthly instalments, Martineau not only found herself 'in full career' in writing the History, she also eventually produced four eminently readable volumes (*A.*, 1:316–18).[2]

R. K. Webb believes that Martineau's *History* 'was not really history; it was a badly proportioned compilation by a tyro, no story of England but a series of review articles partly narrative, partly reflective' (*Harriet Martineau*, p. 278). One might add that she also threw in the odd obituary written for the *Daily News*, yet the *History* is undeniably entertaining, packed with potted biographies of eminent and not so eminent Victorians and succeeding in its aim of popular appeal to the educated but not intellectual reader.[3] George Eliot initially found it edifying, but gave up after reading some hundred pages in the second volume of the 1858 edition, noting in her journal that Martineau 'has a sentimental rhetorical style in this history which is fatiguing and not instructive. But her history of the Reform Movement is very interesting' (Eliot, *L.*, 2:405, 430). Had she read on, Eliot would have encountered Martineau's congratulation of the artisan class as saviours of England in 1848, finding sentiments close to those which she herself expressed through Felix Holt in his 1868 'Address to Working Men'. In a decent society, Felix declares, even though men are poor they can see that social disorder is destructive to all and thousands of artisans have shown 'fine spirit' and 'endured much with patient heroism' (Eliot, *E.*, p. 424).

Martineau's earlier praise of the artisan class had emphasised a high degree 'of knowledge and its results in action'. The knowledge that is as much the privilege of the educated artisan as it is of the scholarly intellectual contributes little to the social good if hoarded by the individual, and Martineau makes an implicit connection between knowledge and capital. Just as capital if not actively reinvested is 'sunk' into sterile stasis where it will not reproduce itself and thereby contribute to the economy, so individual knowledge if not reproduced by active engagement with culture, politics, and society becomes sterile, much like the barren eloquence Martineau attributed to Thomas de Quincey and Samuel Coleridge. She labelled them 'charming discoursers' whose linguistic fluency was 'strangely mistaken for entire intellectual supremacy'. De Quincey, in her view, recklessly spent his intellect in a sterile flow of language: 'Marvellous analytical faculty he had, but it all oozed out in barren words' (*B.S.*, p. 100). Fertile words for Martineau were those that bore as few significations as possible; appalled by what she viewed as the mere use of language for itself, that is to say with no purpose beyond regarding itself as language, she disparaged the curriculum of Moslem schools in India where, she declares, 'a whole generation of boys spend long years and a world of energy on words – a gabble of formulae which does little more than prepare them for a future study of words' (*B.R.*, p. 343). Putting aside for a moment the dubious authority Martineau possessed for discussion of a culture with which she was entirely unacquainted except through the rapid cramming for a timely book in the wake of the Indian Mutiny in 1857, her remarks about wasted words are pertinent in analysing her alignment of cultural, economic, and linguistic sterility. Political economy appropriates an old myth, that of the miser redeemed through fertile engagement with the world, a myth deployed by George Eliot, for example, in *Silas Marner* where Silas lives in 'solitude, his guineas rising in the iron pot, and his life narrowing and hardening itself more and more into a mere pulsation of desire and satisfaction that had no relation to any other being' (*S.M.*,

p. 68). And if Eppie, the golden fairy-child who magically appears on Silas's doorstep, teaches him the fruitlessness of his former life, then Martineau, in her strong-minded fashion, teaches the correct use of knowledge. Proper political action that is the result of knowledge is mandated according to Martineau's ameliorative interpretations of British history: it must perform that work of 'auxiliary usefulness' which is Martineau's self-proclaimed destiny, must actively acquiesce in the laws of progressivist evolution.

In her *History* Martineau describes the economic and political disruptions of 1831 such as rick-burning, machine-breaking, and agitation for Parliamentary reform, and argues that England was saved from revolution by a solid middle class composed of tradesmen and artisans from Leeds, Birmingham, and Manchester. Sending petitions to the House of Commons calling for reform and forming political unions, this class performed the ideal political action, and preserved England from socialistic rupture. These artisans and tradesmen, spurred by a political sagacity born of proper knowledge, 'upheld the patriotic government above them, and repressed the eager, untaught, and impoverished multitude below them . . . When the period of struggle arrived, they did their duty magnificently; and their conduct stands for ever before the world, a model of critical political action' (*H.*, 3:252). Their performance of duty constitutes a model for Felix Holt's action in Eliot's novel, and it is little wonder that Eliot found Martineau's history of the Reform Movement 'very interesting'. Just as Felix intercedes with a riotous mob, places himself between its wrath and the social order in which he believes, so Martineau's artisans and tradesmen function as a kind of sponge for disruptive energies, absorbing the revolutionary force pressing from the class below on behalf of the 'patriotic government' above them.

Martineau was by no means dogmatically unsympathetic to that 'eager, untaught, and impoverished multitude' which must be repressed. Her *History* sensitively describes the sufferings of the working class in the depressions of 1825 and 1826. Yet one finds a recurrent emphasis on ignorance in the workers and little recognition of greed in the manufacturers. Speaking as spectator of an ideal, evolving social system whose manifestation can only be marred by faulty practice on the part of the individual, or at least on the part of the 'eager, untaught, and impoverished' individual, she never opposes her historical discourse to the idea of institutions and betrays none of the distrust of systems we encounter, for example, in Carlyle's thought or in Dickens's invariable juxtaposition of a joyful private life directed by decency and love and a miserable public one governed by barnacled institutions.

Selectively sanctioning one system, however, Martineau supported government supervision of factories in matters of sanitation for it was in the social good, yet she remained opposed to unionisation because of her unshakeable belief in free trade and free sale of labour power. Mingling gentry and lower orders on the village green in the 'amiable and well intended' cricket games organised by the 'Young England' movement of the early 1840s did not work, declares Martineau, because the 'landed proprietor is no longer the social parent of the population on his estates . . . The theory of society now is that the labouring classes are as independent as any others; that their labour is their own disposable property, by which they may make their subsistence in any way that they may think best' (*H.*, 4:311). The implications of Martineau's popularising explanations of social change are provocatively radical: in the English bourgeois revolution, the mercantile class, through purchasing the labour power of its workers, has liberated man from the paternalism of landowners. The social parent has been done away with and the social son, in the form of the middle class, has replaced the feudal father in a social articulation of Freud's paradigm of Oedipal struggle. Fortunately for Martineau and the social class with which she was most strongly allied, the working classes, with their 'disposable property' of labour, did not reproduce the paradigm to attempt wholesale usurpation of the middle class in a struggle for power. That England escaped revolution in 1848 has long been the subject of historical analysis.

Martineau's explanation of England's calm in the face of Continental revolution rests upon the upright behaviour of artisans and shopkeepers and upon the happy assumption that because the worker had been liberated from bondage to a 'social parent', he was earning a living wage and wanted no part of revolution in 1848. If the worker does not profit from the sale of his own labour power, then it is he who is at fault, not the system. Unlike Stephen Blackpool in Dickens's *Hard Times*, Martineau does not find it 'aw a muddle' – quite the contrary, it is all quite coherent. She declares the mills 'fairly wholesome', the owners 'not oppressors' and the pay 'good' (*H.*, 3:335). The working class is poor because it lacks 'knowledge' and it starves because of restrictions on food imports. Here, of course, Martineau does not fault the individual: misguided authority, through restricting free trade, restricts free labour which in turn harms the working-class individual.

A central inconsistency emerges from Martineau's celebration of independence from social parenthood and her sanction of a mythical free market in which, as she puts it, the working classes 'may make their subsistence in any way that they may think best'. Unwilling or unable to recognise that what they thought best may not have accorded with the self-interest of their employers, she fails to see that the worker is both free and not free – a central contradiction of capitalism which, of necessity, remains alien to her understanding. The ambiguities of Martineau's political thinking in these sections of the *History* originate in the ambiguities of the English middle-class politics that it is her apportioned role to sanction as organic intellectual produced by that class, and as the intellectual daughter performing work of auxiliary usefulness for male authority.

On 10 April 1848 the last Chartist meeting was held on Kennington Common in London. It was an event that had been anticipated in an atmosphere of severe uneasiness. Public buildings, banks and bridges over the Thames, all were heavily guarded, yet, as Martineau recounts, there was no violence and peace was kept 'by the citizens themselves re-enforcing the civic police. From that day it was a settled matter, that England was safe from revolution. There were no causes for it, – no elements of it; and there was a steady and cheerful determination on the part of the people, that there should be none' (*H.*, 4:575). England, then, moves forward, cheered on by Martineau's optimism, and expressing through its political upheavals a spirit of ameliorative change that she traces from the end of the Napoleonic wars to the Crimean conflict that lasted from March 1854 to February 1856. For example, she sees the decade preceding the Reform Bill of 1832 in terms of crucial, invigorating change. As the Napoleonic wars unified English national consciousness and instructed her subjects in sacrifice, so discussion of Parliamentary Reform instructs the nation in citizenship. Martineau's unwavering ratification of reform (and Reform) governs her historical imagination.

In describing the Chancery reforms of 1823, which, if we think of *Bleak House*, were obviously insufficient for Dickens, she says that 'no narrative of a process of reform is more instructive than this, in showing how that inexorable Fate – the spirit of reform, evoked by grievance – compasses its end, through all obstructions of human error and ignorance, human will, and even human conscience, when that conscience is deficient in enlightenment' (*H.*, 2:462). The mythologisation of judicial reform as 'inexorable Fate' is paradoxical at the very least. Judicial reform, which is the consequence of dissatisfaction with a system of justice designed and conducted by men, is invested by Martineau with a supernatural power, implicitly outside the control of those who have created the system and those who are dissatisfied with it. Man may 'evoke' that power but it overrides human error, ignorance, will, and faulty conscience. The spirit of reform also empowers such progressive social changes as the establishment of Mechanics Institutes, the founding of London University for the middle-class sons of Dissenting families, and the introduction of lithography that brought art before the 'popular eye'.[4] Moreover, she takes care to document regressive social practices that were, in her readings, particularly prominent in the 1820s: mass hangings, the use of tread mills, rural rituals founded in superstition. Yet what is interesting in this balancing of progressive and regressive events is that the former originate in natural forces beyond the control of man's will and the latter are charged to his malevolence and ignorance. In a perversely negative manner, Martineau seems actually to diminish English cultural, social and political progress by attributing it to fateful omnipotence, and in many ways the *History* can be seen as a transitional text in her writings. Her early Unitarian belief in a benevolent, patriarchal deity is definitively replaced by belief in a benevolent spirit of social progress that will have its Positivist way. And if this benevolent spirit of progress, of reform, determines in omnipotent fashion all human action, then intellectuals such as Harriet Martineau merely work in the service of its laws. The model of agency and auxiliary usefulness continues to govern her work.

Making a suspenseful popular narrative from the events that led to the Reform Bill of 1832, Martineau traces the way in which England 'receives' the idea of political progress and brings it into being. The three readings of the Bill, the mass meetings of the political unions, the resistance of the House of Lords, the royal distaste for such measures, all are deployed as developments in a novelistic plot whose hero is Reform. It is an old-fashioned plot, however, a pleasing fable that stresses a desire for Reform which crosses all classes and invigorates the hero, whose power easily vanquishes every obstacle in his political path. Heroic Reform emerges triumphant and glorious, unscarred by the ambiguous morale and social questions that perplex the heroes of so many nineteenth-century novels.

Martineau's appropriation of heroic motifs is actually quite uncharacteristic as she is, for the most part, reluctant to make heroes out of the social, political and literary figures whose lives she briefly chronicles in her historical narrative. She believed that critical periods in the unfolding history of a nation admit the rule of an individual leader's will: those periods, however, are succeeded by an 'organic state . . . wherein all individual will succumbs to the working of general laws'. The nation may mistakenly demand great political heroes, complain that its leaders have grown 'small and feeble', but this is actually the time when 'the polity is growing visibly organic; and a different order of men is required to administer its affairs' (*H.*, 2:362). This different order of man is the admirable politician who abandons an ideal of consistency at all costs, who will replace an egocentric insistence on the autonomy of the human will with an understanding of those general social laws of which he is the servant. In Martineau's narrative of nineteenth-century English history, this man, of course, is Robert Peel, who emerges as a modest rival to Heroic Reform. Never the preening politician, never the imperial imposer of his own will upon English society, Peel saves England from disaster by perceiving the need for Parliamentary Reform and for repeal of the Corn laws. A Tory but not a Tory Protectionist, Peel saw that the rural aristocracy must give way to the demands of the increasingly powerful commercial class and, from Martineau's perspective, accepted 'the inexorable Fate – the spirit of reform'.[5] His work matches that of Martineau in its auxiliary usefulness to the nation.

Inexorable Fate also took its technological form in the shape of the railway, a phenomenon treated by Dickens in *Dombey and Son* with somewhat less elation than by Martineau who believed it benefited all classes and all regions. Of its 'incalculable blessings', perhaps the most improbable is Martineau's fantasy that peers, manufacturers, and farmers will meet face to face in railway carriages and dissolve class animosity. The factory worker gets a chance to go the seaside and the artisan sees 'unwholesome old streets in London' pulled down, streets much like Staggs's Gardens, the original home of Paul Dombey's nurse, Polly Toodles. Dickens's first description of Staggs's Gardens evokes the scene of excavation for the railway as being like a 'great earthquake' having 'rent the whole neighbourhood to its centre': all is a 'hundred thousand shapes and substances of incompleteness, wildly mingled out of their places, upside down, burrowing in the earth, aspiring in the air, mouldering in the water, and unintelligible as any dream' (Ch. 6). This unintelligibility becomes a brand-new neighbourhood, cleansed of miserable waste ground and rotten houses, boasting railway hotels, railway hackney-coach and cab stands, and, Dickens adds, 'There was even railway time observed in clocks, as if the sun itself had given in' (Ch. 15). Dickens's power to suggest the dubious triumph entailed in man's technological conquest of the sun distinguishes his vivid imagination from Martineau's more prosaic cast of mind. What's more, the recurrent return to the demonic railway in *Dombey and Son* reveals Dickens's participation in the Victorian interrogation of technological progress.

For Martineau, everything is gained and nothing lost through technological development: she remains infatuated with the ideology of amelioration and impatient with the brand of social criticism present in Dickens's novels. For her, Dickens paid far too little attention to the value of suffering in toughening up the individual. Lacking a sound social philosophy, he dwelt too long, she declares, 'On the grosser indulgences' of ordinary life, even though she concedes he was 'a man of genius' (*H.*, 4:608). But Martineau really had little time for genius as it intimated powers that were not easily attributable to the laws of social progress. Genius also signalled the dangerous possibility that ambitious goals are not always realisable through the rigorous discipline Martineau herself adopted. She allowed no space in her literary production for spontaneity, either because she recognised that if she relaxed her practice of assimilating and reproducing received ideas, she might have very little to say, or, perhaps, because what might emerge would be an alarming revelation of a turbulent emotional life kept in check by those highly disciplined methods of work. In my discussion of Martineau's fiction, I shall return to this latter possibility as a way of explaining the peculiar sterility of *Deerbrook*, her novel of love and marriage in economic hard times for the middle classes.

For Martineau, nineteenth-century life is unambiguously improved by technological invention and scientific discoveries. In a deferential appropriation of Adam Smith's image in *The Wealth of Nations* – an 'invisible hand' which 'directs all the private impulses into public benefit' – she describes the pungent process of paper-making as issuing in a 'beautiful substance . . . as if created by invisible hands'. Furthermore, as the railway facilitates positive changes in agriculture, diet, and housing, and broadens the cultural life of all social classes by enabling people to see new and different parts of England, so scientific discovery broadens man's understanding of his place in evolutionary time. The geological discoveries that dislodged early nineteenth-century trust in Biblical myths of the beginning of human life are welcomed with open, popularising arms by Martineau. In *How to Observe* she describes an ancient, swampy earth that resounded with the tramp and splash of monsters 'whom there was no reason present to classify, and no language to name'. The earth dries out, palm groves and tropical thickets flourish in what is now Paris, and then 'savage, animal man appeared, using his physical force like the lower animals, and taught by the experience of its deficiency that he was in possession of another kind of force' (p. 94). It is a good thing, she observes in her *History* that men should know about 'vast spaces of time . . . huge revolutions of nature'.

Attacking slavery, saluting the spirit of Reform, greeting technological change with sanguine forecasts of improvements all round, Martineau does, indeed, enact dutiful, daughterly work for her political fathers. This filial usefulness is further demonstrated in her ratifications of Western cultural superiority in *Eastern Life, Present and Past*. Published in 1848 after she returned from an eight month journey to the Middle East, this compelling travel narrative educates Martineau's Victorian readers in their temporal insignificance. In addition to reminding Victorians that they exist in those 'vast spaces of time . . . huge revolution of nature' evoked in the *History*, *Eastern Life* also contributes to the hegemonic discourse that takes the East as an object of representation, in Edward Said's terms, as 'an idea that has a history and a tradition of thought, imagery, and vocabulary that have given it reality and presence in and for the West' (*Orientalism*, p. 5). *Eastern Life* is an important text in Martineau's sustained celebration of English middle-class values.

The very simple model of temporal evolution structuring Martineau's theory of organic political life and of dynamic social change, set forth in her narrative of reform (the past is reconstructed in terms of ameliorative stages leading to a transitional present which will lead to an even better future), is deployed to govern her narrative of Western superiority. Arguing for an enlightened understanding of cultures and religions far different from the British and the Christian, she goes on to propose that nineteenth-century

Western Christianity is a more mature expression of man's religious impulse than that practised in ancient Egypt. The liberal plea for religious and cultural toleration stems, in fact, from a confident superiority – a culture that does not feel itself to be superior rarely argues for such toleration. Martineau was a vigorous representative in the Middle East of British womanhood, British imperialism, and British intellectual elaboration of the ideology of progress – in sum, a representative of the British representation of the East.

Her book describes a journey made with a party of Liverpool friends that began in Cairo, proceeded up the Nile, covered three months in the Sinai with visits to Petra, Akaba, Damascus, and Jerusalem, and ended in Beirut. Packed with richly distinctive details of daily life on a Nile steamer and nights camping in the Sinai, *Eastern Life* vividly renders the experience of unfamiliar heat, dust, and native life. It offers essential advice to the Eastern traveller, especially to women, who must wear cotton underclothing, brown holland dresses, straw hats, wire goggles, and thick soled boots. A 'lady', Martineau confides in her appendix, 'must not expect health . . . her chief care should be to look to the health of her mind, – to see that she keeps her faculties awake and free, whether she is ill or well; that in the future time she may hope to be at once in possession of her English health, and the stores of knowledge and imagery she is laying up by her Eastern travel' (3:343). Never without her portable writing table, Martineau certainly looked to the health of *her* mind: she made extensive daily entries in her journal, keeping her faculties wide awake and free so that the 'stores of knowledge' docketed in her journal were immediately transformed into three volumes on her return to English soil and English health.

Those three volumes are, of course, more than diverting travel narrative and Martineau intended it that way. *Eastern Life* locates the nineteenth-century dogma and practice of Christianity in a transitional moment in religious history – Christianity, to make a crude paraphrase of Martineau's repetitive formulations, is both better than past religions and inferior to future ones. Martineau, like most Victorian daughters of Dissenting families, was thoroughly familiar with the Scriptures, yet she was not a Biblical scholar and certainly was neither equipped nor inclined to undertake a work of comparative religious scholarship. If she knew anything of the work of the German Biblical scholars, the Higher Criticism that supported historical interpretation of the Scriptures with extensive research, that knowledge is present only in the roughest and broadest form, in generalisations about the 'Human Mind' expressing itself through different stages of religious history.[6]

What is more to the point is an understanding of *Eastern Life* as a segment of Martineau's social and political thought, as one text in the body of her writings which 'make' British culture and society. And Martineau, to her credit, did not attempt to pass herself off as a scholar. Here, as in all her writings, she aimed to popularise, to perform her work of auxiliary usefulness in the service of theories she never claims to have originated, and, also to her credit, she regarded that work as dignified and essential. Without embarrassment she embraced mediation between scholarship and the popular mind: in describing the 'perfection of savage faculty' of an Egyptian boy pulling a boat up the Nile, she contrasts his 'quickness of movement and apprehension . . . strength and suppleness of frame' with the 'bookworm and professional man at home, who can scarcely use their own limbs and senses'. The English scholar manifests intellectual power and little else, and the Egyptian boy, of course, is all native litheness and no mind. She sensibly proclaims a Carlylean gospel of reconciliation of such powers, a reconciliation she herself effected in terms of physical and intellectual vigour as she spent her mornings stamping through the Sinai in her thick-soled boots and her evenings writing in her journal.

For Martineau, the history of ideas is 'the only true history'. However, while 'a great constellation of Ideas' is what holds a people, a nation, a religion together, the great constellation of Victorian ideas is more dazzling than the astral configurations of ancient Egyptian culture: the constellation became 'more noble and more glorious to men's minds as their minds became strengthened by the nourishment and exercise of ages' (1:248). She sees the infant mind of mankind exercised and nourished in a kind of Eastern schoolroom, and Egyptian religion serves as a nursery for the development of Christianity: 'From the lips of this thoughtful people it was that infant nations learned, through a long course of centuries, whatever they held that was most noble . . . We find much that was barbaric, coarse, ignorant and untrue: but the wonder is at the amount of insight, achievement and truth. The ground gained by the human mind was never lost; for out of this Valley of the Nile issued Judaism: and out of Judaism issued in due time, Christianity' (1:335–6).

Fusing imagery of natural and human growth, Martineau constructs a vision of the human mind taking root in the fertile soil of the Valley of the Nile, learning from its Egyptian nurse, repelling entangling weeds of barbarism and ignorance, and finally blossoming forth into Christianity. The entire process is fed by an 'idea' – a spirit, a law, a principle – at work throughout all historical time. Unfortunately this idea remains largely undefined, wandering throughout Martineau's text and religious history from ancient Egypt to Victorian England as something approximating moral good being the highest good and moral evil being the deepest evil. The ostensible purpose of these passages of *Eastern Life* is to instruct Martineau's readers in their duty to apprehend the 'early powers' of the Human Mind manifesting themselves in alien forms. The thoughtful traveller (perhaps one who has studied *How to Observe Morals and Manners*) will look with a clear eye and fresh mind on the 'ecclesiastical sculptures of Egypt', will banish prejudiced notions of 'idolatry, obscenity, folly and ignorance' from his consciousness, so that he may see, with surprised, even startled, vision, 'the elevation and beauty of the first conceptions formed by men of the Beings of the unseen world' (1:201).

Her plea for liberal toleration, for seeing with unprejudiced vision, is undeniably attractive, if hardly revolutionary: who would quarrel with her argument that the ignorant Christian in an Egyptian temple, the proud Mohammedan in a Venetian chapel, and an arrogant Jew in a Quaker meeting house, are all one and the same bigoted thing, or deny that her equation of three forms of religious intolerance seems to imply an equal validity of religious belief and practice? Seeing with Martineau's unprejudiced vision, however, is not quite what it seems. What the Christian sees in Egypt is the 'beauty of the first conceptions formed by men' of religious deities, and while the reader is convinced of Martineau's sincere humanitarianism, there remains the undeniable elevation of nineteenth-century Christianity and British civilisation over all that has preceded it. First is not best in Martineau's thinking. Despite its colourfully documented petition for cultural ecumenism, *Eastern Life* is designed to justify British social, political, and religious systems in the nineteenth century. In discussing Egyptian and Christian faith, Martineau may insist she is not 'claiming parity of value for their objects of faith and ours. It has nothing to do with the comparative elevation, purity and promise of any two faiths' (1:244), yet her evolutionary interpretation of Christianity is in direct contradiction to this claim. Christianity is higher, purer, and holds out more promise than any religion that has preceded it in Martineau's popular narrative of religious history.

On the last night of encampment she gazes at the lights of Beirut and speculates on the future progression of those great ideas manifested in their Eastern forms, ponders the ways in which the Western mind will 'animate and enlighten future generations' through its enrichment by the Eastern mind. She thinks it highly improbable that the destiny of the 'western races' is merely to receive governing ideas of the past, and she concludes her ambiguous examination of the East with a look to the future of 'Human existence'. Assuming the sibylline mode we recall from the Niagara passage, she prophesies that 'the reflective and substantiating powers which characterise the Western Mind [will] be brought into union with the Perceptive, Imaginative, and Aspiring faculty of the East, so as to originate a new order of knowledge and wisdom' (3:332–3). Her adjectives favour the West – reflection implies a sober maturity, and substantiating powers are those which, by verification through material evidence, give weight to ephemeral possibilities merely perceived, imagined, or aspired to by the Eastern mind. Sincerely arguing for an unprejudiced recognition of the 'insight, achievement and truth' in ancient Egyptian culture, and genuinely abhorring the enslavement of women in Syrian hareems, Martineau becomes a compelling feminist representative of the Western representation of the East. *Eastern Life* may be said to display her popularising talents in their least self-aware form.

# 4

# A Novel Liberty: *Deerbrook*

To this point, I have identified the ambiguous nature of Martineau's intellectual practice. This ambiguity, it seems to me, may be attributed to a number of causes: the tensions inherent in her performance as woman intellectual in a male-dominated culture, the contradictions involved in ratifying ideas which in themselves are ruptured by contending values, and the very real, practical urgency of journalistic deadlines. However, Martineau's prose and thought manifest an impetuosity, an eagerness to avoid digressive speculation, which is not entirely the consequence of these related causes. Martineau is deeply uncomfortable with self-analysis. Her professional life is a narrative of discipline of the passionate, feeling self by the rational, intellectual self, and I want to suggest she may have been compelled to ambiguity, haste, and inconsistency by a desire to avoid material which threatened to disrupt her laboriously acquired intellectual authority.

In recalling the writing of her 'Sabbath Musings', a series of occasional pieces which appeared in the *Monthly Repository* early in her literary career, she says they are 'outstanding proof' of an immature self an an immature time. Ponderous refutations of dogmatic belief in man's innately fallen condition, Wordsworthian meditations on reciprocal interfusions of nature and the moral life, turgid explorations of religious doubt – all reveal bathetic thought: 'I had now plunged fairly into the spirit of my time, that of self-analysis, pathetic self-pity, typical interpretations of objective matters, and scheme-making in the name of God and Man' (*A.*, 1:157). The writing is 'morbid, fantastical, and therefore unphilosophical and untrue'. Self-analysis, self-pity, subjective interpretation of objective matters, scheme-making, all amount, from Martineau's pejorative perspective, to an arrogant assertion of the self upon the world. If, for a moment, we share this perspective, then Martineau's unrelenting metamorphosis of an aggressive career into a passive demonstration of objective principles and laws becomes unusually resonant. Insisting on her mere auxiliary usefulness, she does a number of things: she unwittingly defines one function of the organic intellectual, that of legitimation of ideologies favoured by the social class whose political dominance generates a group to which Martineau belonged; in her unwitting definition of this political function, she reveals the unconscious, consensual nature of hegemony itself; and in terms of her own psychological exigency, she negates an aggressive self. Martineau's insistence on a kind of intellectual powerlessness is directed by political and psychological imperatives, and, moreover, reveals her unconscious consent to the power she enjoys as organic intellectual. Denial of self, denial of power – both testify to intense presence of self and power.[1] Martineau's self-confessed inability to write successful fiction may be traced to her conscious or unconscious reluctance to assert a sovereign self upon the world, to her discomfort with the exercise of authorial power.

In admitting her failure as a novelist (in the memoir/obituary), Martineau, as usual, contrives to anticipate criticism of her defects: 'The artistic aim and qualifications were absent; she had no power of dramatic construction; nor the poetic inspiration on the one hand, nor critical cultivation on the other' (*A.*, 3:462). Actually she possessed the artistic aim and that was to achieve the composed clarity of Jane Austen. She may have had the qualifications, but she lacked the power of dramatic construction and of poetic inspiration. Moreover, she seemed to feel that there was something not quite correct about writing novels, something morally suspect in the manipulation of readers to no end other than the excitement of feeling. In her uneasiness about the pernicious ability of fiction to excite the reader with description of things both true and not true, she sounds very much like the nineteen-year-old Mary Ann Evans, who, at her most fiercely Evangelical, condemns the omnivorous reading of novels (Eliot, *L.*, 1:21–3). Mary Ann Evans, however, became George Eliot in February 1857, and despite Eliot's insistence that she did not produce her fiction for the ordinary kind of reader, she became technically adept, in ways that are beyond Martineau's power or inclination, in writing novels that appealed to intellectual and non-intellectual readers alike.

That sovereignty which is essential for the creation of a text of one's own, firmly exercised by George Eliot, eluded Harriet Martineau; or she was so afraid of it that she unconsciously refused to display an assertive, authorial self. When she was producing the *Illustrations of Political Economy* the troublesome nature of creating fictions was clearly not an issue. With a form firmly established in advance, with received principles requiring didactic demonstration already in place, she was merely required to fill in the design. If nothing else, the novelist needs to be a designer, to relish manipulation of events and the arbitrary development of character; in other words, the novelist must be willing to replace the given world governed by 'great ideas', inexorable laws, immutable principles, with a world created by an aggressive, writing self. And this is a world that possesses its own great or not so great ideas, its own laws and principles. In refusing the authority of the novelist, Martineau refuses to become sovereign of her own text.

In the *Illustrations*, Martineau crudely employs narrative to demonstrate political principles, and what may be charitably characterised as plot in her didactic stories is a mechanical unfolding of events designed to show the effects upon society and individuals of deficient understanding of these principles. When recalling the difficulties of 'plotting' the *Illustrations*, Martineau declares that 'creating a plot is a task above human faculties', for no human mind can trace all the antecedents of a single action, which she seems to think is the main business of the novelist: the best one can do is 'to derive the plot from actual life, where the work is achieved for us: and accordingly, it seems that every perfect plot in fiction is taken bodily from real life' (*A.*, 1:238). Either unwilling or unable to acknowledge, as Eliot does in the well-known passage from *Adam Bede*, that the novelist's mind (even if figured as a faithful mirror) necessarily transforms 'real life' as it copies its plots into fiction, Martineau makes writing novels an act of passive agency. Rather than the novelist being the sovereign authoriser of a text, the text is derived from 'actual life, where the work is achieved for us' and once again, Martineau imagines her literary practice in ancillary terms. She naively believes in a virtual correspondence between language and reality, between the plot of life and the plot of the novel, which, as George Levine observes in his study of nineteenth-century realism, was never the faith of serious Victorian novelists.[2]

Martineau began the writing of *Deerbrook*, published in 1839, after being discouraged by her brother James from undertaking that 'man's work' of editing a new periodical dealing with political economy.[3] She records in her journal that 'I was at liberty to ponder my novel'. It was a demanding liberty to which James released her and which she began to enjoy in June 1838. Just as the death of her father released her to literary celebrity, so James set her free to tackle a form in which she fervently wished to succeed, despite her distaste for what she perceived as its immoral stimulation of the emotions, and also despite her lack of confidence in her own imaginative powers. She approached her task with great expectations and a good deal of trepidation: accurately assessing her past writing as 'almost entirely about fact', feeling constrained by the necessity of having to be 'always correct', and longing 'for the liberty of fiction, while occasionally doubting whether I had the power to use that freedom as I could have done ten years before' (*A.*, 2:107–8). Released from the bonds of fidelity to 'facts' and rigid attention to accuracy, she set to work, but as a reading of *Deerbrook* shows, she was correct to doubt her powers of composition. The novel is hampered by infelicitous prose and a strongly conservative narrative voice that endorses many of the unpleasant 'facts' of women's oppression which Martineau so bravely exposed and attacked in *Society in America*.

In January 1838 Martineau finished reading *Pride and Prejudice* (for the second time) and wrote in her diary that she found it 'wonderfully clever . . . I long to try'. She then read *Emma* and found that 'most admirable. The little complexities of the story are beyond my comprehension, and wonderfully beautiful' (*A.*, 3:214, 218). A reading of *Deerbrook* confirms that not only the complexities of Austen's narrative skill remained beyond her understanding or ability, but that Austen's precisely balance prose was equally beyond her faculty. At first, it might seem unfair to compare Martineau's unpolished technique to the finely modulated skill of Austen: why, after all, should we expect a writer who excelled in political journalism and travel narrative to produce fiction comparable to that of arguably the finest novelist of the nineteenth century? But it is precisely because Martineau implicitly models herself on Austen, and because, in my view, Austen possesses the quality markedly absent in Martineau's fiction, the ability to take sovereign command of a text of her own invention, that I focus upon this connection.

'Why is it that love is the chief experience, and almost the only object of a woman's life?' asks the narrator of *Deerbrook*. A naive, modern reader of an Austen novel may well ask this question, but Austen's power lies in the fact that the novel will answer such a question without ever once referring to it. Austen describes a society in which courtship and marriage constitute a woman's destiny and the business of heroines such as Emma Woodhouse and Elizabeth Bennet is to discover an appropriate complement to their own intelligent, witty, and affectionate dispositions. The confident composition of Austen's prose matches the confident approbation of the social values she so cleverly delineates and which require no intrusive affirmation on the part of a narrator. One problem with Martineau's novel, and there are many, is that she ambiguously questions those values unquestioned by Austen, leaves such issues unresolved, and then relapses into a breathless reliance on the 'elaborate, delicate distresses' which she abhorred in the work of sentimental novelists such as Fanny Burney.[4]

*Deerbrook* tells the story of two sisters from the English Midlands, Hester and Margaret Ibbotson, who move to the country village of their cousins, the Grey family. Hester marries a country doctor, Edward Hope, who is hopelessly in love with Margaret, who is hopelessly loved by Philip Enderby, who in his turn, is hopelessly loved by a lame governess, Maria Young. Margaret and Philip eventually marry, leaving Maria Young eccentric to this circle of frustrated courtship, which is where she was in the first place. Invested with little psychological complexity, Martineau's characters function more as psychological and moral emblems than as anything else: Hester stands for destructive jealousy, Margaret for noble renunciation, Edward for moral rectitude, Philip for dignified adherence to his own moral code. And Maria Young, necessarily distanced from the romantic entanglements by virtue of her social position and her intelligence, stands for a sequestered detachment – making her, by far, the most absorbing figure in the novel. She is also the character whose feelings and values most clearly resemble those of Martineau. This is not to say that Martineau identified herself with one character more than another in an unconscious displacement of her own neurotic sexuality, as Robert Lee Wolff declares and as Gaby Weiner implies, but rather to point out that there is more similarity between Maria Young's pronouncements (and characters in *Deerbrook* tend to pronounce rather than engage in reciprocal discourse with each other) and Martineau's beliefs, than there is between the values of other *Deerbrook* characters and those of Martineau as they had become articulated by 1839.[5]

A paragraph from the opening chapter of *Deerbrook*, a laboured echo of the polished opening of *Pride and Prejudice*, demonstrates Martineau's enthusiastic but feeble emulation of Austen's style. Austen's beginning sentences are among the most famous in the history of the English novel, matchless in their compressed irony and richly suggestive of Austen's views of community, greed, ambition, courtship and marriage. They need no repetition here. An abridgement of Martineau's paragraph, describing the appearance in the Grey community of an eligible bachelor, Edward Hope, indicates the extent of her ambition and its faulty realisation:

> It is a fact which few but the despisers of their race like to acknowledge, and which those despisers of their race are therefore apt to interpret wrongly, and are enabled to make too much of – that it is perfectly natural, – so natural as to appear necessary, – that when young people first meet, the possibility of their falling in love should occur to all the minds present. . . . Probably the sisters wondered whether Mr Hope was married, whether he was engaged, whether he was meant for Sophia, in the prospect of her growing old enough. Probably each speculated for half a moment, unconsciously, for her sister, and Sophia for both. Probably Mr Grey might reflect that when young people are in the way of meeting frequently in country excursions, a love affair is no very unnatural result. But Mrs Grey was the only one who fixed the idea in her own mind and another by speaking of it.   (1:20)

Martineau's verbosity virtually destroys the simple information conveyed here: most people imagine that young people will fall in love, including the young people themselves. The repetition of adverbs such as 'probably' to no incremental, significant effect and the jarring diction destroy any pleasing resemblance to the opening of *Pride and Prejudice*: a phrase such as 'despisers of their race' lacks that quality of elegant dismissal which permits Austen to express her finely cultivated hatred of certain values and characters, without ever appearing egregiously hostile. Quite simply, Martineau is gauche where Austen is graceful. Like Austen, Martineau introduces an aggressive female character, but Mrs Grey is only endowed by Martineau with the social pretensions of the interfering and ambitious Mrs Bennet, and given nothing of that paradoxical admixture of vulgarity and faded charm that is an unhappy reminder to her husband, her daughters, and the reader, of the miseries ensuing from a marriage founded on sexual attraction rather than on the fine balance of eroticism and rationality that unites Elizabeth Bennet and Darcy. Martineau also employs the motif of neighbouring and competing families (the Rowlandses are to the Greys as the Lucases are to the Bennets), but Martineau deviates from Austen in the class origin of her characters. It is here that her novel gains interest beyond laboured imitation. She writes about the middle, rather than the upper-middle class: the Ibbotson sisters are the orphaned daughters of Dissenting middle-class Birmingham parents and Mr Grey and Mr Rowland are partners in a coal and timber business. Martineau's ideas about the evolutionary development of literature suggest that she not only wrote about middle-class businessmen because they belonged to a social group with which she was familiar, but also because faithful representation of a rising social class in England in the late 1830s was, for her, a moral and political imperative.

While writing the obituary in 1852 of a now obscure figure, Miss Berry, Martineau reviews the changes in literary taste that had occurred during the first half of the nineteenth century. She proposes a theory of dynamic progress consistent with the general nature of her intellectual discourse. Literary taste is formed and improved through reactionary response: 'Before Miss Burney had exhausted our patience, the practical Maria Edgeworth was growing up. While Godwin would have engaged us wholly with the interior scenery of man's nature, Scott was fitting up his theatre for his mighty procession of costumes, with men in them to set them moving; and Jane Austen, whose name and works will outlive many that were supposed immortal, was steadily putting forth her unmatched delineations of domestic life in the middle classes of our over-living England' (*B.S.*, p. 263). Practical Maria Edgeworth is clearly an improvement over Fanny Burney, whose novels Martineau considered utterly unreadable, devoid of good sense and sincerity; Scott's concern with history and society properly replaces Godwin's morbid psychological obsessions; and Austen's steady hand creates characters more plausible than Scott's actors on the stage of dramatic history.

Scott, however, is accorded high praise by Martineau for his emphasis on the commonality of all human experience, and despite what she sees as a failure to represent accurately the subjugated state of the lower classes and to gloss over the vices of the aristocracy, he performs valuable moral service by satirising the 'eccentricities and follies' of society. Martineau hopefully inserts herself in this ameliorative narrative of English fiction. Where Austen, in Martineau's view, commendably shifts the subject of the novel from the feudal past to the early nineteenth century, from the heroic pageantry of tournaments to the domesticated conflict of the drawing room, she focuses upon a social class and a social scene familiar from her *Illustrations of Political Economy* – merchants and professionals in a small English village. She also introduces a topic never mentioned in Austen's novels, the economic hardship experienced by characters other than those with whom the narrator is directly concerned. Austen's characters experience economic setbacks by virtue of entailed wills or diminished private incomes: Martineau delivers didactic straight-talk about a nationwide inflation that almost destroys the career of a country doctor.

Lacking the technical proficiency to interweave romantic narrative with political analysis displayed by Elizabeth Gaskell in *North and South* and Charlotte Brontë in *Shirley*, Martineau cannot develop an imaginative parallel between the financial difficulties of an individual family and of a nation. The actual hardship endured in rural areas during the 1820s and '30s becomes intensely melodramatic in *Deerbrook*; poachers, 'daring beyond belief', exhort frantic villagers to overturn meat wagons, old people and children trespass for wood, and genteel ladies are frightened on their afternoon walks by ill-looking fellows. Compelled by her politics, Martineau mounts the sermonising soap box to deliver herself of many pages justifying poverty as a teacher of proper values. Poverty provides 'new objects' of labour for the masses, a new perspective on nature for the merchant, and opportunities for people of reduced rank to thaw their frozen hearts 'at the great central fire of humanity'. Perhaps the most unfortunate justification of poverty comes when the narrator describes the changes forced upon an ambitious working-class family by economic recession: 'The father may sigh to see his boy condemned to the toil of the loom, or the gossip and drudgery of the shop, when he would fain have beheld him the ornament of the university; but he knows not whether a more simple integrity, a loftier disinterestedness, may not come out of the humbler discipline than the higher privilege' (2:132). In an effort to justify social inequality, Martineau patronisingly elevates a mythological working-class integrity over the putative narcissism of university life, and Maria Young, in an effort to justify her own unhappy life as a lonely governess, engages in a similar mystification of inequality: why should we demand, she asks herself, 'that one lot should, in this exceedingly small section of our immortality be as happy as another' (2:301). Granted, Maria Young's unhappiness stems from unrequited love and physical

deformity, but had she read Martineau's persuasive indictments of
the exploitation and injustice suffered by English governesses, who
rarely received pensions, endured many indignities, and often
earned the wages of a nursemaid, she would have understood that
her unhappiness was not entirely due to emotional isolation and
lameness.[6]

In her obituary of Charlotte Brontë which appeared in the *Daily
News* in March 1855, Martineau declares that governesses are
warranted in their objections to the Brontë novels in which 'their
share of human conflict is laid open somewhat rudely and
inconsiderately, and with enormous exaggeration' (*B.S.*, p. 46).
Martineau disapproved of 'passion' occupying centre stage in the
melodramatic lives of Brontë's female characters and was uncomfortable with the 'amount of subjective misery' packed into
*Villette*, which she reviewed in the *Daily News* on 3 February 1853.
Criticising Brontë's characters for their damaging preoccupation
with romantic feelings, she finds Jane Eyre and Lucy Snowe victims
of the erotic longing which, in her view, undid Mary Wollstonecraft.
Even if Martineau designed Maria Young as emblem of the material
plight of the governess class, it is ironic that the power of the
character resides in exactly the qualities Martineau found so
distasteful in Lucy Snowe as narrator of *Villette* – a fierce
emotionalism combined with acid detachment from an unhappy
environment.

Maria Young admits she would rather be a scholar than a teacher.
Like many intellectually ambitious young women in Victorian
fiction, she studies German, but unlike Diana and Mary Rivers in
*Jane Eyre*, she studies alone, her only companions the dictionary and
a grammar book. She concedes that teaching has its pleasures but
they are insignificant to what she terms the 'sublime delights of
education'. In an early scene in the novel, she sits by her window to
look out upon the spring landscape, beyond the gardens and
shrubberies to a meadow where almost all the central characters in
the novel are picking cowslips. The positioning of Maria Young to
some extent resembles that of Lucy Snowe as spectator in the
*Villette* art gallery and at the theatre (the angry, yet fascinated,
observer of fetished female sexuality in the shape of a lush
Cleopatra, and a cool, sceptical reader of the Belgian bourgeoisie),
and more precisely that of Fanny Price in *Mansfield Park* as she sits
upon the bench at Sotherton, mismatched and misguided lovers
passing before her as she literally remains the stable centre of a

discontented group, and, of course, the metonymical essence of all that is good in Mansfield Park itself. Maria Young is a solitary, contemplative, female figure, whose dependent yet privileged position suggests something of Martineau's ambivalent feelings about being an intellectual woman in Victorian England. She constructs an interior monologue for her character governed by many of the ideas and feelings articulated in her own non-fictional writings.

As Maria Young watches the running children, she fancies that 'the pleasure is more in the recollection of all such natural enjoyments than at the moment'. If not exactly advocating a Wordsworthian recollection in tranquillity, then Martineau certainly preached retrospection as central to a detached analysis of experience, especially after the excitements of travel which permit no immediate assessment. Maria Young then recalls her pleasure in the opening lines of Book 5 of *Paradise Lost*, 'Now Morn her rosie steps in th' Eastern Clime / Advancing, sow'd the Earth with Orient Pearl', and one remembers Martineau's recollection in the *Autobiography* of the almost swooning delight she felt as an eight-year-old girl when the morning light flooded her room, a delight generated by repeated readings of Milton's poem. 'How I love to overlook people, – to watch them acting unconsciously, and speculate for them!' continues Maria: overlooking people, valleys, historical epochs, Niagara Falls, Chartist demonstrations, and speculating about ancient Egyptian culture and the lives of Shaker women – these are Martineau's pleasures. Privileged perspective is the governess's consolation, a 'post of observation on others' that must not stop at 'mere knowledge': 'Women who have what I am not to have, – a home, an intimate, a perpetual call out of themselves, may go on more safely, perhaps, without any thought for themselves . . . but I, with the blessing of a peremptory vocation, which is to stand me in stead of sympathy, ties, and spontaneous action, – I may find out that it is my proper business to keep an intent eye upon the possible events of other people's lives, that I may use slight occasions of action which might otherwise pass me by' (1:67–8).

Growing up in a large family, becoming a literary celebrity with the publication of the *Illustrations*, entertained and fêted wherever she went in America, solaced by a procession of visitors to her sick bed at Tynemouth, surrounded by friends and relatives in the last twenty years of her life at Ambleside – Martineau was hardly

solitary. Yet the interior monologue of Maria Young suggests some
of the psychological conflict Martineau almost certainly experienced
by virtue of the contending claims of her gender and her intellectual
fame, and by virtue of the tension between that repressed,
passionate, tearful female child and that confident adult who,
through a narrative of discipline, became as famous and as
productive as any male intellectual of her time. For Martineau and
the many other women who actively participated in Victorian
culture and society, to be a woman intellectual is often to be both
powerful and powerless: this figure enjoys the power of intellectual
production and bears the powerlessness of agency in the discourse
to which she contributes. She may, like Martineau, have been
required to prescribe disciplinary medicines for herself, may have
insisted, as does Maria Young, that knowledge originating from
observation must become useful social and moral action. Finding
herself without the conventional comforts and duties of Victorian
womanhood that Maria Young speaks of – a husband, children,
sympathetic ties – a Victorian woman intellectual like Martineau
must rely upon her own formidable powers, and, of course, fashion
her own extensive family of friends and colleagues.

I have no wish to deny the warmly professional homosociability
enjoyed by intellectual and literary women in the Victorian period,
women united by feminist causes, political action, and shared work,
nor do I want to make a reductive psycho-biographical reading of
Martineau's work. What I am suggesting is that the figure of Maria
Young, and the literary figure of the governess as she appears
throughout Victorian fiction, represents some of the conflict
experienced by Harriet Martineau and other women intellectuals in
the nineteenth century.

In conceding that Maria Young, 'of all the *Deerbrook* characters,
was most representative of the novel's author', Valerie Pichanick
contends that the governess is 'far from being a self-portrait'
because she does not bear the physical disability and the solitary
independence experienced by Martineau with her 'sense of duty or
cheerful determination'. Pichanick further suggests that because
Martineau never experienced romantic or sexual passion, the love
scenes are implausible (*Harriet Martineau*, p. 117). It seems to me one
cannot assume that merely because Martineau announced she felt
cheerful, she *was* cheerful, any more than her retrospective
satisfaction in remaining unmarried negates sexual desire. Quite
simply, the love scenes are poor in *Deerbrook* because Martineau

lacked the technical ability to write them, and also because those love scenes are strangely interfused with dominant ideologies of sex and gender that Martineau elsewhere subverts with great verve and vitality.

The strong feminist sentiments of *Society in America* barely find their way into *Deerbrook*, the most provocative statement being a remark by Margaret that if Maria Young were a man her 'sensible' qualities would be labelled 'philosophical'. Married life is so conventionally idealised from a conservative male perspective that the wife performs a kind of refined, cultural service for the husband, and the forthcoming marriage of Hester and Edward celebrates a hierarchy of duties. When the husband 'comes in to rest from his professional toils', he will see 'the books destined to refresh and refine his higher tastes', and will sit down to enjoy 'the music with which the wife will indulge him' (1:263). Whatever the social class of the husband, it is he who is benevolent master: 'the hopeful young artisan' brings home 'his bride from service'; the aristocrat 'enriches his palace with intellectual luxuries for the lady of his adoration'. Where is Martineau's ideal woman, single or married, who exercises daily, eats a sensible diet, keeps herself intellectually alert, supports herself through her own work? Here we have a rapturous contradiction of Martineau's calls for female independence and the descriptions of preparations for the marriage of Hester and Edward are saturated with a pathos alien to Martineau's usual writing, and, needless to say, to that of the woman novelist she most admired, Jane Austen.

The fervent encomium of domestic bliss may, of course, be attributed to an early Victorian taste for sentimental fiction. Assuming, for a moment, Martineau's model of evolutionary literary development, then *Deerbrook* follows the sharp rationality of Austen that was reaction to gothic excess, and accompanies the early comic genius of Dickens that makes us, as modern readers, forgive his procession of domestic angels. Yet Martineau was deeply critical of the early Victorian fictional distortion of women's lives. Offended by Dickens's sexual politics and insipid heroines, in 1849 she refused to contribute some articles on the employment of women to *Household Words*, claiming that in Dickens's prior articles he had 'ignored the fact that nineteen-twentieths of the women of England earn their bread' and that he prescribed woman's destiny 'to dress well and look pretty, as an ornament to the homes of men' (*A.*, 2:419). Martineau cannot seem to effect a satisfactory formal translation of her dynamic indictments of patriarchy into fiction. Apparently so beset by the necessarily unrecognised contradictions diffused throughout her work, she cannot create a female character who is intellectually ambitious, sensibly cognisant of the social and cultural limitations imposed upon her, plausibly independent, and if not as eminently successful as Martineau, then at least functioning reasonably well in the world. The only way Martineau seems able to introduce an intelligent, ambitious woman into her novel is to have her lame, solitary, alienated, and obsessed with unrequited love. Maria Young is a physically and psychologically deformed woman intellectual, seemingly punished for the quality of her mind by a woman who valued mind in women above all their other qualities.

Having ironically accused Scott of doing female emancipation a great service by depicting women as 'passionless, frivolous, uninteresting beings', Martineau called for 'enlighted application' of his powers to the 'achievement of new aims' (*MS.*, p. 55). In writing *Deerbrook*, she gave herself the opportunity to achieve these new aims, to point the way to alteration of women's destiny as it was inscribed in Victorian society. She did not rise to her own self-created occasion. In locking herself so severely into rigid representations of womanhood, she allows no room for the dynamic complexities of character and social change in which she so strongly believed, even if they exist within the larger frame of ungovernable laws. Accustomed by the time she began *Deerbook* to a kind of writing defined by the propagation of received theories and ideas and the justification of influential ideologies, she was strangely powerless when it came to the production of a text of her very own and unable to exercise authorial 'authority' to create a world of her own making, rich with the possibility of ameliorative change that is everywhere the mark of her social thought. The pattern of auxiliary usefulness which facilitates almost all her non-fictional writing about women, political economy, household education, American society, and Egyptian travel, impedes her writing of fictional prose.

Martineau's expressed intolerance of undisciplined thinking and lax modes of behaviour may also partly account for the insipidly conservative nature of *Deerbrook*. According to her prescriptions for developing the art of thinking (predictably, she sees thinking as technique to be acquired by good habits and training), writing novels would very likely impede such development: an 'unchastened imagination' is particularly harmful, inclined to disrupt the smooth operation of Martineau's mechanical model of the intellect in which impressions are classified as they are received and retrieved from their taxonomic order when required.[7] An undisciplined mind is a 'perverted' one, somewhat like that described in her monitory account of a reader of Scott's *Waverley*, a kind of refugee from *Tristram Shandy*, who, when asked to render an account of the novel, digressed so alarmingly by talking about where he was sitting when he read a particular chapter, who called to interrupt his reading, and where he ate his dinner on that particular day, that his eventual version of the novel was horribly disfigured by 'strange disorder' (*MS.*, 1:76).

Perhaps, too, Martineau was so thoroughly subject to the Chistian ethic of truthfulness that, for her, as it was for a number of Victorian novelists, to make a fiction was to make a lie. In *Household Education* she devotes a chapter to the importance of locating and eradicating the 'seat' of the 'moral disease' of lying. Her reassuring words to parents of untruthful children relate the tale of three young people of her acquaintance who mastered a juvenile delight in fantasy to become 'eminently honourable and trustworthy persons' (p. 105). She considers the common linguistic habit of exaggeration damaging for children, advises parents to avoid metaphorical language, and to teach truthfulness as *duty*.

'Duty' is a keyword in Martineau's texts, an abstraction and practice directing her life and work. 'From my youth upwards I have felt that it was one of the duties of my life to write my autobiography' is the beginning sentence of that text, and all her literary production is perceived as dutiful labour:

> Authorship has never been with me a matter of choice. I have not done it for amusement, or for money, or for fame, or for any reason but because I could not help it. Things were pressing to be said; and there was more or less evidence that I was the person to say them. In such a case, it was always impossible to decline the duty for such reasons as that I should like more leisure, or more amusement, or more sleep, or more of any thing whatever. . . . What wanted to be said must be said, for the sake of the many, whatever might be the consequence to the one worker concerned.   (*A.*, 1:189–9)

If the writing of fiction is understood in terms of this sternly defined and disciplinary 'authorship', then the failures of *Deerbrook* can be more readily fathomed. Unauthorised by the need to popularise abstract theory or the moral duty to publicise injustice, Martineau's novel is not directed by the pressure of things that 'must be said'.

Any summarising assessment of Martineau's remarkable career must originate in her *Autobiography*, that narrative of a life which progresses from despair to delight, from shameful dependence to exhilarating independence, from fury to serenity. It is a text impelled by the need to record the optimistic story of self-improvement. The passionate, complaining child becomes the controlled, successful woman, and it is rare amid all this self-legitimation to encounter discursive passages suggesting, even for a moment, that Harriet Martineau, dutiful literary worker, confidante of politicians, honoured traveller, was still in her imagination a confined, rebellious girl. Such passages rupture Martineau's careful self-mythologisation as composed intellectual. In much the same way that the disjunctions in and between many of her other works reveal those texts as engaged in the ratification of ideas themselves fraught with contending beliefs and practices, so, too, the disjunctions in Martineau's *Autobiography* are witness to the way in which she actually created herself as a disciplined intellectual from the inchoate material of her life.[8] The disjunctive breaks in her *Autobiography* reveal the transgressive self which was composed, so to speak, through the writing of that work: the inconsistencies that we sometimes encounter in Martineau's elaborating and popularising texts also betray transgressive, disruptive material.

*Society in America*, we recall, mounts its stirring attack upon the wretched subjugation of American women, while at the same time it records Martineau's triumphs as a woman intellectual privileged to watch 'world-building', but only permitted participation in that enterprise through her work as *recorder* of the natural and social scene. The *Illustrations of Political Economy* didactically tend to gloss over the very real suffering experienced by masses of workers so that Martineau may unambiguously ratify the benignity of the greatest happiness principle. *Eastern Life* pleads for religious toleration, yet elevates Western nineteenth-century culture over all that has preceded it; and *Deerbrook* curiously banishes all the feminist politics so vigorously inserted into *Society in America*: in Martineau's novel about women and marriage, we end up with cloying celebrations of domestic bliss, which, even by the most sentimental of Victorian standards, seem discordantly excessive.

The most resonantly discordant material to be found in the *Autobiography* describes Martineau's relationship with her mother. The composed record of filial duty to political fathers is disturbed by a story of intractable resentment of the mother.

In 1839 Martineau became severely ill while on holiday in Italy and returned home to be cared for by her sister Elizabeth's husband, a Newcastle physician. An enlarged, retroverted, and possibly tumorous, uterus was diagnosed, and she moved to lodgings in Tynemouth where she spent her famous five years in the sick room. R. K. Webb's and Cecil Woodham-Smith's interpretations of this illness as primarily psychosomatic have been sensibly contradicted by Valerie Pichanick, who notes that while 'it is true that Victorians were preoccupied with their health . . . it is less than accurate to ascribe their physical symptoms entirely to psychological causes. Genuine ill-health was common'.[9] Undoubtedly, Martineau was ill, but whether she exaggerated her symptoms or whether the symptoms were partial displacement of psychological malfunction into the body, is of less interest in terms of Martineau's performance as intellectual, that the way she narrates that illness in her text, and how that narration was governed by the contending claims and ideologies which, in my reading of her, direct that intellectual performance.

She records that before she went to Italy she had been laid low for many years as the result of 'excessive anxiety of mind . . . extreme tension of nerves' brought on by having three difficult members of her family on her hands, and in her house – her mother, her aunt, and her brother Henry. It is her mother who creates the most severe anxiety, and I quote the following passage at length as a rare occasion when Martineau allows herself the discursive freedom to reveal psychological vulnerability, realising as I do so that I may be subjecting myself to charges of indulging in the biographical criticism I rejected for a reading of *Deerbrook*. In this instance, however, biographical interpretation is justified as it moves beyond mere identification of fictional character with novelist to demonstrate crucial connections between Martineau's family life and her broader significance as one of many Victorian women intellectuals:

My mother was old, and fast becoming blind; and the irritability caused in her first by my position in society, and next by the wearing trial of her own increasing infirmity, told fearfully upon

my already reduced health. . . . Heaven knows, I never sought
fame; and I would thankfully have given it all away in exchange
for domestic peace and ease: but there it was! and I had to bear the
consequences. I was overworked, fearfully, in addition to the
pain of mind I had to bear. I was not allowed to have a maid, at my
own expense, or even to employ a work-woman: and thus, many
were the hours after midnight when I ought to have been asleep,
when I was sitting up to mend my clothes. Far worse than this, my
mother would not be taken care of. She was daily getting out into
the crowded streets by herself, when she could not see a yard
before her. What the distress from this was to me may be judged
of by the fact that for many months after my retreat to
Tynemouth, I rarely slept without starting from a dream that my
mother had fallen from a precipice, over the bannisters, or from a
cathedral spire; and that it was my fault. . . . A tumour was
forming of a kind which usually originates in mental suffering;
and when at last I broke down completely, and settled myself in a
lodging at Tynemouth, I long felt that the lying down, in solitude
and silence, free from responsibility and domestic care, was a
blessed change from the life I had led since my return from
America.   (*A.*, 2:150–20)

Her mother's irritability is *first* caused by Martineau's success and
next by her own infirmity; Martineau has never sought fame (which
utterly defies the descriptions of intensely ambitious efforts to get
the *Illustrations* published); Martineau, the literary celebrity, is
pettily denied a maid and Martineau, the daughter, is not even
allowed to take care of her own mother. In an astonishing
deformation of the image of an aggresive, active, intellectual woman
who dominates the social, cultural and political scene (*and* the pages
of the *Autobiography*), we receive a dismal picture of a passive,
impotent daughter in the punitive hands of a domineering mother.
It is as if Martineau replays in the writing of her own life what she
does to Maria Young in *Deerbrook*: intelligence brings nothing but
trouble and suffering. What's more, the nightmares of her mother
falling from a high place constitute a telling reversal of the dream to
which I referred in my discussion of Martineau's fear of light. It is a
dream that terrified Martineau when she was four years old.
Coming in from the dark she goes into the kitchen where 'it was
bright sunshine. My mother was standing at the dresser, breaking
sugar; and she lifted me up, and set me in the sun, and gave me a bit

of sugar. Such was the dream which froze me with horror!' (*A.*, 1:15). The child dreams of maternal power in being lifted to a high place, out of the dark into the sunshine: the adult woman dreams of destruction of that maternal power as the mother falls from a high place symbolising the pinnacle of authority – a cathedral spire.

This tortuous sequence of complaints, abnegation of responsibility for success, and nightmares of maternal power, simultaneously affirms and denies the verifiable actuality of a young woman who dislodged her mother's authority by her own intellectual eminence and inserted herself, albeit as passive agent, in social and cultural formations dominated by symbolic fathers. And as a punishment for this usurpation of maternal and paternal power, the daughter believes she became sick in her reproductive organs by virtue of the 'mental suffering' inflicted upon her by her mother. In a female revision of Freud's paradigm of male oedipal struggle, the daughter replaces the mother, not to become sovereign over the father's territory and possessions, but to remain a guilty, dependent daughter.

If, as Nancy Chodorow argues, because 'they are the same gender as their daughters and have been girls, mothers of daughters tend not to experience these infant daughters as separate from them in the same way as do mothers of infant sons' (*The Reproduction of Mothering*, p. 109), then daughters must feel themselves as not separate from their mothers. Martineau's anguish seems to originate in her strong identification with, and dependence on, her mother. In Freud's paradigm, the son's differentiation of himself from his father is culturally and socially expected, indeed encouraged: because culture and society do not expect them to be different from their mothers, because in certain ways they are expected to reproduce their mothers through their own acts of reproduction, daughters tend to remain locked in primary relationships of identification and dependence. Martineau's troubled narrative of illness and nightmares of maternal power suggests how strongly she was bound to her mother, how much she resented that bond, and how highly she paid in psychological terms for cultural and social separation from maternal authority. This is the painful dilemma of a successful woman intellectual in the Victorian period, whether she be a wife and mother, or not: her mind and her ambition propel her into the male-dominated world of cultural production; her sex and her gender bind her in the female world of biological reproduction.

Martineau's filial narrative also suggests the ways in which her public career made her both an emblem of resistance to patriarchy and a figure painfully vulnerable to patriarchal attitudes. The breadwinner for a middle-class household composed of her mother, her aunt, and one brother in the years following her popular and financial success with the *Illustrations,* a *female* intellectual celebrity for whom politicians sent their carriages, she performed the patriarchal function of taking care of dependent members of her family. Unhappily for her, however, Martineau was also made subject to those patriarchal values against which she so fiercely protested. The descriptions of dependency and guilt threading the complex configurations of her family life betray exactly how effective the ideologies against which she struggled were in their power to govern her feelings. It is not only in *Deerbrook* that we encounter legitimations of influential Victorian attitudes towards sex and gender. We discover them also in the way Martineau accounts for her illness.

Her self-characterisation as a Victorian woman intellectual is inescapably accompanied by her ambivalence about that status and is deeply engraved with evidence of her subjection to prevailing myths about women. She is vulnerable to two enduringly powerful Victorian legends of sex and gender: woman's destiny is primarily determined by biology and biology is hampered by an over-stimulated brain. In becoming an intellectual, Martineau dislodged her mother from her 'spire' of maternal power. In describing her illness, Martineau says a tumour originated from the 'mental suffering' inflicted upon her by her mother's complaints – complaints, we recall, stemming from Martineau's eminent 'position in society'. The meaning of Martineau's filial story, then, is that she was incapable of potential motherhood by virtue of the intellectual eminence which originally dislodged her mother from her parental authority.

Martineau's career as woman intellectual may well be understood in terms of filial relationships. She is very much a daughter of the male economists and politicians who constructed the shapes and ideas of her discourse. She welcomed her own agency, elaboration, and legitimation; and there is no better or more accurate characterisation of her professional life than her own – a career of 'auxiliary usefulness'. Had she lived at a later historical moment, she would have delighted in Gramsci's analysis of her intellectual genesis as coeval with the solidifying political power of the English middle class; she would have welcomed the definition of her intellectual function as that of giving 'homogeneity' and 'awareness' of the capitalist's function in the social and political fields. Relishing her enactment of popularising services for middle-class Radical ideas, she performed as an organic intellectual: in her own terms, she performed as a dutiful daughter in her family and in her culture, always explicitly enacting work of auxiliary usefulness and always implicitly expressing the tensions and conflicts inherent in the careers of women intellectuals who succeed in what was, in Martineau's time, a man's world. Through a rational programme of disciplined work, she mastered that transgressive self of childhood and subdued a rebellious, feminist womanhood not amenable to subjugation and service. Whatever else one might say about Martineau, that she was bossy, a rigid and narrow thinker – perhaps as R. K. Webb would have it, 'a second-rate mind' – at least she had a mind that people knew about. She used that mind fearlessly to speak the subjugation of women by Victorian patriarchy. If only for that, she deserves admiring recognition.

When she came back from the Middle East, Carlyle wrote to Robert Browning, 'Miss Martineau has been to Jerusalem and is back; called here yesterday, brown as a berry; full of life, loquacity, dogmatism, and various "gospels of the east wind".'[10] Despite Carlyle's patronising tone, I like this image of her – the intellectual woman, full of life, brown from stomping across the Sinai in her sensible boots, wasting no time in setting Carlyle straight about Eastern life. Martineau may have been an auxiliary intellectual, but she is a splendid Victorian, certainly as intelligent as any of her male contemporaries, and, I daresay, twice as energetic and tough minded.

# Part Two

# Elizabeth Barrett Browning: 'Art's a service'

'Mrs. Browning's "Aurora Leigh" is, as far as I know, the greatest poem which the century has produced in any language.'

(John Ruskin, *Things to be Studied*, 1856)

# 5

# A Clerisy of Poets and the Softer Sex

In the composition of her autobiography, Harriet Martineau calmed the transgressive self of childhood and the angry feminism of her womanhood. Celebrant of the auxiliary usefulness performed through her prolific textual services to Victorian ideologies of politics, history, imperialism, sex and gender, Martineau emerges from the *Autobiography* as a serene figure. It is only in the narration of her filial story that we find traces of the psychological, cultural, and social prices exacted from her as payment for her astonishing success as woman intellectual. The only autobiographical text we have for Elizabeth Barrett Browning is brief, a girlish 'glimpse' into her life written when she was fourteen and expanded and amended when she was in her early twenties. And we have little evidence of prices exacted for intellectual eminence. Precociously learned, allowed access to everything in her father's well-stocked library, critically acclaimed for the scope of her 'intellectual compass', and, until she went off to Marylebone Church at the age of 40 to marry Robert Browning, lovingly supported in her secluded scholarly life by her family, Elizabeth Barrett Browning betrays no unease about her status as famous intellectual poet.

In place of formal autobiography we have a collection of letters which, even by Victorian standards of sustained correspondence, is unusually extensive, and a nine book novel-poem entitled *Aurora Leigh* tracing the struggle and success of a woman poet in the nineteenth century. From these letters, from that novel-poem, and from much of Barrett Browning's other poetry, a self-created myth of the intellectual woman poet emerges. Barrett Browning, the most celebrated and cherished of 'poetesses' in the Victorian period, praised then for her tender evocations of womanly sympathy, and hailed now for her daring deployment of eroticised female imagery of the body, mythologised herself as a member of a privileged élite. Self-tutored in a conventionally male Classical education and feeling the absence of a sustaining female literary tradition, she affiliated herself with a corpus of male poets ministering to a secular, materialistic culture. Her entanglement in the ideological matrix of sex, gender, and intelligence that produces the Victorian woman intellectual seems to have determined a firm identification with male modes of political thought and aesthetic practice, and whatever feminist sympathies she may be said to possess are, in my view, thereby strongly compromised.

If my discussion of Martineau's career tended to return with some structural regularity to the *Autobiography*, my discussion of Barrett Browning will take *Aurora Leigh* as the governing text for analysis of all her work. In recent years, *Aurora Leigh* has become a key poem for feminist critics concerned with nineteenth-century women writers. For some, *Aurora Leigh* is revolutionary – a passionate indictment of patriarchy that speaks the resentment of the Victorian woman poet through a language of bold female imagery. For others, the poem is less explosive, and Barrett Browning's liberal feminism is seen as compromised by Aurora's eventual dedication to a life governed by traditionally male directives. I want to submit, however, that *Aurora Leigh* is neither revolutionary or compromised: rather, it is a coherent expression of Barrett Browning's conservative political views, with which her sexual politics are consistently coherent. I shall argue that in *Aurora Leigh* female imagery is employed to show that the 'art' of the woman poet performs a 'service' for a patriarchal vision of the apocalypse. Woman's talent is made the attendant of conservative male ideals.

In analysing Harriet Martineau's career, I pointed to the combative discordance of some of her feminist writings when they are assessed in the context of her popularising textual services to a male cultural establishment. I find little discordance in Barrett Browning's writings. Sexual politics and more general conservative politics coherently align themselves. To be sure, Barrett Browning's career may be said to resemble Martineau's in the way her texts disclose woman's writing as ancillary to male authority, as an essential (and essentialist) component in a work of 'auxiliary usefulness'. But Barrett Browning was strongly opposed to the values of the social class which generated and sustained Martineau's career and in terms of Gramsci's cultural theory, she differs significantly from Martineau. Martineau's popularising work makes her career an almost perfect example of organic intellectual activity. In sharp contrast, Barrett Browning created a legend for her career that identifies her as a traditional intellectual, or, to be more precise, as an intellectual yearning for a world thought to have existed before the nineteenth-century emergence of the social class generating organic intellectuals like Harriet Martineau.

Consistently opposing her political and poetic values to what she perceived as the debased imperatives of English middle-class life, Barrett Browning aligned herself with the tradition of poetic practice which gained new intensity during the Romantic period and acquired particular social significance for the early Victorians: the poet is an isolated figure, graced by his or her vocation as prophet/sage to witness an ideal order obscured by materialistic incoherence. And as further evidence of profound difference between Martineau and Barrett Browning, Martineau believed everything – English culture, American society, woman's situation, her own life – to be in a dynamic state of ameliorative alteration: Barrett Browning saw her society as in a degenerative state of negative alteration. As a correlative to this perception that Victorian culture and society were going downhill, she mythologised herself as mediating poetic agent between a debased, fallen world and a harmonious, transcendent order. Affiliating herself with those modes of intellectual activity opposed to the organic function, she ministers to a Victorian world lapsed into greed and disorder, and through the poet figures in her work, she discloses an ideology of ideal aesthetic practice.

In 'The Poet's Vow', one of Elizabeth Barrett Browning's early ballads published in 1836, a gloomy Manfred-like figure suffers from self-inflicted poet's block, 'His lips refusing out in words / Their mystic thoughts to dole'. He has vowed to live in solitude away from the 'weights and shows of sensual things / Too closely crossing him' – away, too, from his intended bride, Rosalind. In the inexorable way of mournful ballads, Rosalind pines away and dies but not before having made elaborate arrangements worthy of Clarissa Harlowe for her funeral bier to be transported to the poet's ancestral home. She delivers her symbolically wounded and literally dead self with a scroll recording her injuries. This vicariously produced text, the only one that a poet who refuses to weep for other men *can* in any sense write, is a letter begging him to re-enter the world through grieving for her death. 'The Poet's Vow' is hardly an exciting poem with which to begin discussion of Barrett Browning's career, which until the recent feminist attention to *Aurora Leigh* has tended to be perceived in terms of a revitalised existence in marriage to Robert Browning and the ways she loved him recounted in *Sonnets from the*

*Portuguese*. Yet this early, minor poem tells a parable that informs much of Barrett Browning's life and work, and it anticipates some important features of her later political poetry.

The melancholy poet refuses the world, like Wordsworth's solitary figure in 'Lines Left upon a Seat in a Yew-Tree', the closing lines of which poem form the epigraph for Barrett Browning's ballad. The contemplative figures in both poems deliberately reject action in favour of narcissistic passivity, and in so doing violate Barrett Browning's unswerving dictum that the poet must move and live in the world.[1] Moreover, Barrett Browning's gloomy poet causes the death of a woman through his retreat from poetic action. The wounded woman is a familiar figure in Barrett Browning's poetry, sometimes literally injured like the raped Marian Erle in *Aurora Leigh* and sometimes deployed as a metaphor for a society wounded by class antagonism or a nation injured by imperialism and its own struggles for unification.[2] Barrett Browning's poetry, with the exception of some lyrics and the *Sonnets from the Portuguese*, urgently addresses questions of the place of poetry in a changing culture and the function of the poet in a materialistic society. A poet associated in the popular imagination with the sickroom and romantic love, she is remarkably and paradoxically a vibrant participant in the energetic Victorian discourse attempting to locate and to define the meaning of intellectual and aesthetic life in an increasingly secularised community. In her own strangely vital and sometimes even violent way, she is as much an active figure in this community as Harriet Martineau and George Eliot. Frail, reclusive, highly learned, inhabiting a world of texts by virtue of her seclusion, she was intellectually aggressive and strongly political – in many ways, the most intellectual woman of her time. She was scholarly from an unusually early age, and, as Robert Browning observed in a Prefatory Note to poems he selected and arranged in 1887, 'self taught in almost every respect'.

In the Preface to 'The Battle of Marathon', an ambitious, highly derivative epic paying dutiful homage to her early literary hero, Pope, she announces that now (in 1819 when she was thirteen) 'even the female may drive her Pegasus through the realms of Parnassus'. Vigorously as she attempted to drive her poetic chariot in this poem, it flounders in the sands of convention, encumbered with the epic apparatus she assiduously employs. What we see in 'The Battle of Marathon' is the woman intellectual (or rather the girl intellectual) performing *as* intellectual, displaying her learning in a self-conscious fashion, in a sense showing that despite her gender, to say nothing of her age, she could produce the poetry traditionally associated with male authors.

The poem is primarily notable for the plenitude of classical learning displayed by an adolescent girl, for the parade of reading that constituted her early education, and it may be seen as precocious graduation exercise from the singular university she created for herself. Her library was her father's, replete with Classical literature and works of philosophy and political economy. She studied seven languages, translated Classical and Byzantine Greek, and undertook intense study of English and Greek prosody. As a girl, she relished eighteenth-century biographies and memoirs, and consumed, along with numerous other texts, the work of Samuel Johnson, Horace Walpole, Kant, Berkeley, Hume – plus, and understandably for an ambitious poet, Milton. From 1828 to 1832 she read Classical Greek with H. S. Boyd, usually at the rate of a hundred lines a day, writing to R. H. Horne in 1843 that at Hope End (the comfortable Herefordshire country house where she lived until the age of twenty) she studied Greek 'as hard under the trees as some of your Oxonians in the Bodleian' (*L.*EBB/RHH, p. 127). In 1844 *Blackwoods Magazine* paid tribute to this early industry, judging her powers 'to extend over a wider and profounder range of thought and feeling, than ever before felt within the intellectual compass of the softer sex'.[3]

When depressions in the West Indian sugar trade compelled her father to sell Hope End and she moved to Devon for her health (eventually taking up residence in that darkened room in Wimpole Street for some four years), her reading became even more intensely omnivorous. She consumed travel narratives, the fiction and poetry of her English comtemporaries, and European novels, justifying the reading of such racy figures as Eugene Sue and George Sand by saying she had read so much already nothing could really shock her. As a bookish girl she lived in and through texts, and as an intellectual woman, barely going out, receiving few visitors, seeping herself in all the latest periodicals and daily newspapers, and pursuing a programme of serious study (in 1843, for example, she read the Hebrew Bible from Genesis to Malachi), she is a female version of the male scholar whose life is spent in a library. It is unsurprising, therefore, that almost all her writing is generated by the reading and writing of other texts. If travel and active participation in political life become text in the career of Harriet

Martineau, then in the life of Elizabeth Barrett Browning it is text itself which becomes the source of textual production.[4]

When Barrett Browning looked for female poetic ancestors, she found none, and declared that before the work of Joanna Baillie, the late eighteenth-century Scottish dramatist and poet, there was no such thing in Britain as a 'poetess': 'England has had many learned women, not merely readers, but writers of the learned languages in Elizabeth's time and afterwards – women of deeper acquirements than are common now in the greater diffusion of letters, and yet where were the poetesses. . . . I look everywhere for grandmothers and see none' (*L.EBB*, 1:231–2). She looked, of course, in those places that were available to her, in what we now term the canon. Had she looked in the uncanonised actuality, there were many women whom she could have claimed as female literary ancestors, but the fact that an extremely well-read woman poet could discover so few female poetic ancestors testifies to the canonised dominance of male poets.[5] In her experienced absence of a sustaining female ancestry, in her very real isolation as a woman intellectual denied the regular companionship of other intelligent women, she attached herself to an androcentric line of poetic descent.

Moreover, despite her lyrics and justly famous sonnets, she also affiliated herself with a traditionally masculine genre: the epic. As a consequence of her Classical education, early in her career she apprenticed herself to this genre. In her maturity she revised the genre to write a major poem tracing Aurora Leigh's Odyssean quest for poetic identity and a home in the world and positing the proper political and social function for a poet in national life. In discussing the profession of literature for women, Dinah Craik tellingly praised *Aurora Leigh* for its successful competition with male poetry – women can be 'acute and accurate historians, clear explanators of science, especially successful in imaginative works', she declares, but Barrett Browning's poem proves that 'we can write as great a poem as any man among them all' (*A Woman's Thoughts about Women*, pp. 50–1). Epic poetry is androcentric in its thematic concern with heroes and war, indeed with arms and the man, and with elucidating the ways of God (or gods) to man, rather than with those ways of God to that part of man which is woman. Barrett Browning's self-termed 'novel-poem' *Aurora Leigh* is a formal hybrid that attempts to fit the explosive material more often to be found in the social novels of the 1840s to the traditional, male form of the epic; Barrett Browning chooses as the subject of her epic poem matters more usually represented by the genre dominated by women writers in the nineteenth century, namely the novel.[6]

The plot of *Aurora Leigh* traces the development of its heroine from her Florentine childhood to eventual marriage to her cousin Romney. The orphaned child of an English father and Italian mother, she is sent to England to live with an aunt who trains her in the conventional accomplishments of young ladies and for marriage to her cousin. At the age of twenty Aurora refuses his proposal, inherits a small income on the death of her aunt, and moves to London determined to become a poet. Some ten years later, having achieved a modest recognition for her work, she learns that the Christian socialism favoured by Romney which she had scorned as insufficient to remedy social evil, has taken the form of intended marriage to a working-class girl, Marian Erle. In a stunningly visual depiction that calls to mind Hogarthian London, rich and poor meet at St James's Church where Romney vainly awaits his bride. Marian never arrives having been persuaded to leave for Australia by the woman who wants Romney for herself. Duped by the maid of this voluptuous aristocrat (Lady Waldemar) and drugged in a French brothel, Marian is raped. Aurora learns her story two years later when she spots Marian, now the mother of a baby boy, in a Paris flower market; she takes mother and child to Italy where they live happily together in the countryside of Aurora's childhood. Believing Romney to have married Lady Waldemar, Aurora is astonished to see him arrive on her porch one summer evening. The last two books of the poem are devoted to an extended dialogue between Romney and Aurora about the need to unify spiritual and material remedies for social ills, Aurora having at last realised that Romney has been blinded by an injury received in the fire that destroys his utopian socialist community. The poem is punctuated by Aurora's lengthy meditations upon art; it contains an arresting amount of violent imagery; and by the time of Barrett Browning's death in 1861 it had gone through five editions.[7] In the broadest terms, Barrett Browning attempts a reconciliation of female and male: the poet/heroine is married to her cousin, private art is wedded to public politics, intellectual ambition united with the social good, and novel joined to poem.

The essential subjects of *Aurora Leigh* are Victorian society and the Victorian poet. Addressing itself to the ways in which poetry can remedy such evils as the rape of a working-class girl, the sexual lasciviousness of the aristocracy, and the provincial narrow-mindedness of the gentry, *Aurora Leigh* attempts to find function and meaning for poetry in the modern world. To be sure, a poetic self-consciousness that examines the function and meaning of poetry is hardly new to the nineteenth century, but what is remarkable about Barrett Browning's novel-poem, and her work in general, is an interrogation of whether there is a place and function for the poet at all in a society undergoing rapid alteration in all things. *Aurora Leigh* participates in the aesthetic discourse that examined the function of the artist in society, a discourse formed, for example, by Tennyson's 'Palace of Art', Arnold's 'Resignation' and Browning's 'How it Strikes a Contemporary'. *Aurora Leigh* was also conceived at an interesting moment in literary history, in the 1840s, when the Romantic poets were all dead, Wordsworth in his decline, Tennyson barely known, and the novel a vigorous form that dominated the popular market. The composition of the novel-poem spans a crucial decade of changes in English literary taste: most intensively worked on in the early 1850s (Books I–VI were finished by March 1856), when it was completed in October 1856, Tennyson, Browning, and Longfellow had, at least, revitalised the English appetite for reading poetry, even if the novel remained sovereign with the reading public.

*Aurora Leigh* evokes poetry as balm for the wounds inflicted upon society by the materialistic values represented and questioned by the social novels of the 1840s. Barrett Browning admitted from the start of composition of the poem in 1844 that she wanted to write something of a 'new class', rhetorically asking 'where is the obstacle to making as interesting a story of a poem as of a prose work . . . Conversations and events, why may they not be given as rapidly and passionately and lucidly in verse as in prose' (*L*.EBB/M, 3:49). Robert Browning thought there was no obstacle at all. When she wrote to him some two months after asking the above questions of Mary Russell Mitford, declaring her intention to write a poem that meets 'face to face and without mask the Humanity of the Age', he enthusiastically responded that such a 'fearless fresh living work [is] the *only* Poem to be undertaken now by you or anyone that *is* a Poet at all, the only reality, only effective piece of service to be rendered God and man' (*L*.RB/EBB, 1:32–7).

It is important to remember that when Barrett Browning articulated these plans for *Aurora Leigh*, the poem that was going to upset conventions, take a combative, confrontational stance in the English drawing room, she had barely been out of the house for two years and before that had lived an extremely secluded life at Hope End and Torquay. As I have already suggested, what Barrett Browning knew best was literature: immersed in text from the earliest moments of her writing life, she was spurred to write a confrontational poem in reading about what needed to be confronted. A veritable textual matrix of homage and literary allusion, *Aurora Leigh* is a discourse about society composed from other discourse.[8] It is a novel-poem, a poetic art-novel, written by a woman who had been tutored, literally and figuratively, by patriarchal Classicists, who figured poetic creation through conventionally male, sometimes sexual, imagery, who literally had no experience of the society she set out to represent, and who made the subject of her formal hybrid female intellectual ambition.

What I am emphasising here is that Barrett Browning's literary practice was almost exclusively textual; that is to say, she held no salons, attended no dinners, and until her marriage travelled virtually nowhere. I do not mean this merely in terms of male literary dining out, the sort of activity welcomed by Robert Browning who was always walking backwards and forwards from Camberwell to London as a sought-after dinner guest. Despite their ambiguous social status, George Eliot and George Henry Lewes constantly entertained, dined out, and journeyed on the Continent; if her account is to be trusted, Harriet Martineau was only at home in the mornings, writing about what she did the rest of the time; Elizabeth Gaskell, productive social novelist, ran a busy Manchester household; Barbara Leigh Bodichon, Eliot's close friend, was a highly visible figure on the London intellectual scene. These women and the thousands of others who were active in English intellectual life saw the world in ways that Barrett Browning did not. What she did see was society represented by various forms of writing: what she insisted the poet saw was a privileged vision of a better society than the one she encountered in her extensive reading.

If, then, Barrett Browning, as a highly self-referential writer concerned with the role of the poet, deliberately produces a work she terms a novel-poem, it is certainly relevant to consider why she did not attempt to write a novel. The answer is two-fold: she believed that poetry was privileged over fiction and that the poet was a gifted being, called to the practice of poetry in ways the novelist was not elected to the practice of fiction. Consistently elaborating these values in her poetry, letters, and other writings, she consciously performed as a member of an aesthetically advantaged élite, mythologising herself as a member of that clerisy of poets described by Samuel Coleridge, whose poetic function is redefined in a secular community.[9] That she was, in person, kind, modest, sincerely sensitive to the needs of her friends and remarkably forgiving of her father's tyrannical behaviour, is undeniable. Her personality and her manner do not indicate an unsympathetic élitism. Yet her performance as intellectual poet is strongly governed by explicit and implicit beliefs that the poet works in the highest aesthetic form, that the poet is chosen by, rather than chooses his vocation, and, in the terms of the cultural theory which has informed my readings of nineteenth-century women intellectuals, that the poet is a traditional, rather than organic intellectual. Bearing in mind Gramsci's foremost categories for traditional intellectuals (the clergy and the teaching profession), it is possible to construct a conjunctive paradigm in Barrett Browning's work linking form, vocation, and intellectual definition: the privileged poet produces poetry designed as solace, sometimes cure, for the ills suffered by a materialistic society, and poetry also designed as an education in superior cultural values.[10]

Understood from this perspective, the novel becomes the form of the organic intellectual, embraced by a writer such as Dickens whose work he, himself, would have been the last to characterise as culturally privileged. Dickens's business was to represent the teeming, secular world of the social class that produced him as organic intellectual, and, in ways that we now find thoroughly ambiguous, to present fictive remedies for the social malaise he describes. And bearing in mind the dominance of the genre by women writers in the nineteenth century, one can also define women's intellectual/literary practice primarily in the terms associated with the function of the organic intellectual: ratification of the influential ideas which are consented to by individuals in society, rather than imposed upon them by coercion. As I have shown, Harriet Martineau not only embraced her organic function as populariser of dominant ideologies, she also implicitly aligned that function with the subaltern role of Victorian women as it was designated by her culture.

Barrett Browning may very well have been incapable of writing a novel, but the point I want to emphasise here is that she had absolutely no desire to do so. Her close friend Mary Russell Mitford related that to fool her physician Barrett Browning had a small edition of Plato 'so bound as to resemble a novel' (*Recollections of a*

*Literary Life*, p. 270), a strategy richly suggestive of her views of fiction. By implication, she rejects both the role of organic intellectual and the form that may be associated with it, choosing instead a model of literary production associated more with male than with female authors and, in Gramscian terms, with traditional intellectual function. In her view the novel was an inferior genre, all very well for Dickens whose celebrity was to her a curious marvel and who she believed would 'pass away, with all his "coarse caricatures", in the period of a *lifetime*' (*L*.EBB/RHH, p. 202). If Dickens had any merit at all, she believed he owed it to reading Victor Hugo (and French novels remain exempt from her condemnation of the genre; crafted in ways that English novels were not, their authors possessed superior 'faculty of composition').

'The taste for fiction is a thing distinct from the taste for literature' she wrote to R. H. Horne and reading novels was low on her hierarchy of intellectual tasks, self-indulgence in the pleasure of listening to stories, a gratification which is a 'pleasant accompaniment to one's lonely coffee-cup in the morning. . . . After breakfast we have other matters to do – grave "Business matters", poems to write upon Eden, or essays on Carlyle, or literature in various shapes to be employed seriously upon' (*L*.EBB/ RHH, p. 172).

In Barrett Browning's 1843 poem 'upon Eden', 'A Drama of Exile', she places herself with some trepidation with those poets destined to write about the Fall with the majestic presence of Milton looming over them. While the regal reputation of *Paradise Lost* in English literary history has created numerous anxieties of influence for male poets, for a woman poet to write in the shadows of Milton creates multiple anxiety, rebellion and revision, as Sandra M. Gilbert and Susan Gubar have convincingly demonstrated.[11] For Barrett Browning, it is her first exercise in poetry as witness to a transcendent, instructive order.

Beginning the Preface to 'A Drama of Exile' by saying that 'the subject of the Drama rather fastened on me than was chosen', she ambiguously proceeds to establish herself as both a passive and an active poet. Feeling that Eve's part in the Fall has been 'imperfectly apprehended hitherto' and that it is 'more expressible by a woman than a man', she will now undertake to give Eve a voice. The oscillation between being subjugated agent of a momentous poetic theme and autonomous spokeswoman for Eve becomes clearer as she elaborates her relationship to Milton: 'I had promised my own prudence to shut close the gates of Eden between Milton and myself, so that none might say I dared to walk in his footsteps. He should be within, I thought, with his Adam and Eve unfallen or falling, – and I, without, with my *EXILES*, – I also an exile! It would not do. The subject, and his glory covering it, swept through the gates, and I stood full in it, against my will, and contrary to my vow, – till I shrank back fearing, almost desponding; hesitating to venture even a passing association with our great poet before the face of the public' (2:143–4). She chooses to exile her fallen poetic self from the paradise of patriarchal poetic power, knowing in her dutiful prudence that she cannot walk there, has no licence by virtue of her sex and poetic immaturity to venture on Milton's ground. Yet the force of that power is so strong that it sweeps through the gates so that she stands 'full in it', against her will and against her vow. Electing to place herself in an inferior position to Milton *because* he is so powerful, Barrett Browning is consequently overwhelmed by his power. And the implication here, too, must be that she, the mortal poet outside Eden, is subject to the same power that Milton himself is subject to as he composes *his* epic, the power of God, of divine inspiration, just as, in a sense, Aurora as poet is subject to a power vastly greater than her own.

In 'The Drama of Exile', then, Barrett Browning as poet is made twice passive, by Milton and by God. A significant registration of her difference from Milton (putting aside all questions of qualitative difference between her poem and his) is that she chooses the form of verse drama with no poetic voice, in contrast to Milton's epic which begins with those lines (wanting no repetition here) invoking the poetic muse. Milton speaks as poet, as epic singer: as dramatist, Barrett Browning effaces herself from her text, secreting herself behind the mask of her 'masque'. Unlike Harriet Martineau, for whom Milton's verse was a source of consolation not of emulation and who relished work of auxiliary usefulness not of propitiatory revision, Barrett Browning must hide herself in her poem, shield herself from charges of misplaced ambition. Her own Eve declares herself 'twice fallen' from 'joy of place, and also right of wail'. She is given right of wail by Barrett Browning, who hopes to correct an incorrect emphasis upon Eve that sees her 'first in transgression' but not also '*first* and *deepest* in the sorrow'. Through her Eve, Barrett Browning wanted to voice that 'peculiar anguish [which is] the fate of woman at its root' (*L*.EBB/RHH, p. 286).

Adopting an assertive interrogative style which implies the power

she once possessed, and relishing the asking of questions to which
she obviously knows the answers, Barrett Browning's Eve
forwardly articulates her own sin and guilt:

> . . . The lady of the world, princess of life,
> Mistress of feast and favour? Could I touch
> A rose with my white hand, but it became
> Redder at once? Could I walk leisurely
> Along our swarded garden, but the grass
> Tracked me with greenness? Could I stand aside
> A moment underneath a cornel-tree,
> But all the leaves did tremble as alive,
> With songs of fifty birds who were made glad
> Because I stood there?
>
> (2: lines 1238–47)

The shameful misery she feels is intensified by her knowledge of
having chosen, even willed, such a state: 'And is not this more
shame, / To have made the woe myself, from all that joy? / To have
stretched my hand, and plucked it from the tree, / And chosen it for
fruit?' (lines 1253–6). The woman who emphasises her power in
bewailing her loss, who could redden roses with her touch, who
could improve upon nature and make a tree sing with pleasure for
her presence, continues, in a sense, to dwell upon herself as she
laments her undoing. Where Adam consistently speaks of 'our' fall
and the fate 'we' share, Eve consistently employs the first person
pronoun, and her speeches repeat such typical phrases as 'Alas, me
alas, / Who have undone myself', a linguistic emphasis that does
not escape the notice of Lucifer, always a figure preternaturally alert
to narcissistic preoccupation. 'Boast no more in grief' he tells her,
'your grief is but your sin in rebound.' Taunted by various earth
spirits who resent the post-lapsarian misery they share with Eve
and Adam, Barrett Browning's first parents are consoled by a
phantasmal Christ who instructs Adam in disciplining Eve to her
future role as 'First woman, wife and mother', sanctified to work
and devotion. A poem inspired by Barrett Browning's desire to give
utterance to Eve's (and woman's) 'peculiar anguish', becomes a
silencing of Eve's expressive voice. From a lengthy self-abnegation
that serves to intensify her former power and actually gives her *more*
power as a vital speaker, Eve moves to a dignified, noble acceptance
of her Miltonic destiny. She finally becomes silent and acquiescent

to her suffering – the Marian prototype obedient to Christ's will. Although Eve's eventual destiny is ineradically inscribed for Barrett Browning, the disciplining of Eve by Christ and Adam and the implicit disciplining of the female poet by one of her poetic fathers which Barrett Browning describes in her preface to 'A Drama of Exile', become significant in analysis of her developed ideology of the poet intellectual. Impeded by the absence of a positive female tradition, chastened by the presence of patriarchal power, to have a poetic voice, it would seem that an intellectual woman poet must dedicate her talent to conservative, androcentric ideals.

*Poems of 1844* also included 'A Vision of Poets', a lengthy homage to poets of the far and recent past: 'God's prophets of the Beautiful / These poets were.' More significant in terms of Barrett Browning's ideology of the poet intellectual than this mystical fantasy, consisting of three hundred tercets whose rhyme and metre tax the reader's attention, is Barrett Browning's explanation of the genesis of the poem: it originated in her desire to express 'the mission of the poet', a mission obscured by the materialism of her society as she perceived it. The Victorian poet 'wears better broad-cloth, but speaks no more oracles . . . the evil of this social incrustation over a great idea is eating deeper and more fatally into our literature than either readers or writers may apprehend fully' (2:147). The ideal poet performs oracular functions, is the cultural agent between a troubled society and ideal values which are encrusted, obscured by materialism. The poet's mission is remedial, he is empowered through his vocation to reveal the organic connections between God, man, society and culture obscured in a secular world. And even though Barrett Browning always emphasises the poet's craft, she also believes in the necessity of certain attributes for the poet which cannot be acquired: 'Without the essential thing, the genius, the inspiration, the insight . . . the most accomplished verse-writers had far better write prose, for their own sake's as for the world's' (*L.*EBB, 1:464).

Barrett Browning's belief in 'the essential thing' governs all her aesthetic views, whether articulated in her letters or in her poetry. For example, Aurora Leigh's meditations on the meaning of poetry explore 'the inspiration, the insight' which Barrett Browning believed all poets *must* possess. Aurora insists that the poet unifies 'Natural things / and spiritual, – who separates those two / in art, in morals, or the social drift, / Tears up the bond of nature and brings death, / Paints futile pictures, writes unreal verse, / Leads vulgar days, deals ignorantly with men, / Is wrong, in short, at all points' (VII. 763–9). In linking 'natural things / and spiritual', the poet displays possession of the fourth element of genius which Barrett Browning accorded the finest poets in 'An Essay on Mind': Association follows Invention, Judgment, and Memory. As Aurora Leigh explains it, the poet is enabled to perform this associative function by virtue of a privileged vision: 'Art's the witness of what Is / Behind this show . . . For we stand here, we, / If genuine artists, witnessing, for God's / Complete, consummate, undivided work' (VII. 834–9). The poet, then, by virtue of possessing 'the essential thing, the genius, the inspiration, the insight', links through an associative faculty, the 'natural' and the 'spiritual'.[12]

In itself, Barrett Browning's preoccupation with the function of the poet is hardly noteworthy. Examination of the ways in which poets figure their relationship to God, man, society, and culture has long been a central critical enterprise, and Barrett Browning's beliefs are derived from a wealth of poetic self-examination locating the poet in an inspired, yet subjugated position. However, this well-established examination is given particular meaning by Barrett Browning in two ways: she participates in the well-documented Victorian endeavour that seeks to recover a lost social and cultural unity (which is, of course, mythical), and she adopts for her own career a governing model traditionally associated with male poets. Moreover, she implies, if the poet's visionary power, his special insight, could be enjoyed by all men, then society would transcend its degenerate, materialistic condition:

> . . . If a man could feel,
> Not one day, in the artist's ecstasy,
> But every day, feast, fast, or working-day,
> The spiritual significance burn through
> The hieroglyphic of material shows,
> Henceforward he would paint the globe with wings,
> And reverence fish and fowl, the bull, the tree,
> And even his very body as a man –
> Which now he counts so vile, that all the towns
> Make offal of their daughters for its use.
>
> (VII. 858–66)

It would seem, then, that Barrett Browning's ideal world is one where all men are poets, a concept that has certain revolutionary implications. If all men felt all the time as poets do in their ecstasy, then they would no longer be alienated from society, culture, or work. They would lose that consciousness of self which Carlyle in 'Characteristics' identifies as symptomatic of a diseased society, would no longer be so driven by his 'cash-nexus' that they sell their daughters as 'offal' in the streets (one of the several references to prostitution in *Aurora Leigh* which scandalised the critics). If the poet's mission is to instruct all men to feel and see as he does, then eventually he will no longer *be* privileged, will possess no mission, have no special insight. This is a revolutionary, apocalyptic vision, the 'New Jerusalem' invoked at the end of *Aurora Leigh*, and here figured as an end to self-awareness and an end to art. This view implies, of course, that art is symptomatic of a fallen society in the sense that representation signalises mediation between man and his world. Barrett Browning calls for a direct connection. Instructed by the poet, man will discover his Edenic self, a self lost in the post-lapsarian world of commercial individualism given demonic vitality by Carlyle in *Signs of the Times* – 'We remove mountains, and make seas our smooth highway; nothing can resist us. We war with rude Nature; and, by our resistless engines, come off always victorious, and loaded with spoils' (pp. 34–5). Implying that poets are empowered to save man from destruction by his own creation, those 'resistless engines', Aurora declares that they are 'The only teachers who instruct mankind / From just a shadow on a charnel-wall / To find man's veritable stature out / Erect, sublime' (I. 865–8). The imagery of obfuscation is similar to that employed by Barrett Browning in her Preface to the *Poems of 1844*, where she describes the genesis of 'A Poet's Vow': the 'great idea' of the oracular function of the poet has become encrusted, obscured by a morally and culturally degenerate society. She will strip away the darkening layers.

If one considers, then, the principal motifs of Barrett Browning's definition of poetic function, those of privileged insight, instruction, and consolation, it is clear that to be a poet is to be a traditional intellectual in the sense that Gramsci defines such a function: it is to minister to those members of society who are troubled by the mounting domination of English life by secular, materialistic, middle-class values; it is to elevate oneself as superior to the organic intellectuals generated by the middle class, and to create oneself as the restorer of a legendary, lost unity which not only existed in terms of a coherent society, but also in terms of the relationship between nature and the artist. In common with many other Victorian poets and social thinkers, Barrett Browning constructs a pre-industrial Eden, the topos of benign authority, of joyful obedience, and of poetry, where the artist tends to copy order, rather than to create it. This is not the topos of the novel, which inclines to representation of conflict between authority and the individual and to the imposition of fictive order upon a disjunctive world. Avidly reading in her seclusion, Barrett Browning became intensely familiar with the social incoherence given form and sometimes resolution in the nineteenth-century novel, and she decided to fit the disturbing material of this genre to a revised epic form. Undertaking to instruct fallen man in his possession of that essential sublimity obscured by the ideologies welcomed and elaborated by organic intellectuals such as Harriet Martineau, she implicitly affiliates herself with the land-owning classes whose power was in decline. Through her heroine, Aurora Leigh, she aligns sex, gender and vocation in a female poetics and a sexual politics which dedicate woman's art to the realisation of a conservative ideal.

# 6

# The Social Wound and the Poetics of Healing

The mind that produced *Aurora Leigh* was praised by the *Westminster Review* in 1857 as one remarkable for 'its abundant treasure of well-digested learning, its acute observation of life, its yearning sympathy with multiform human sorrow, its store of personal, domestic love and joy'. This was a rare moment in an avalanche of negative criticism (including the rest of the *Westminster's* review) which roundly condemned Barrett Browning's prolixity, extravagant metaphors, eccentric rhymes, riotous metre, and, most significantly and pervasively, her use of 'unfeminine' poetic language and her choice of poetic subject. She is labelled an 'unchaste poet'. Accused of depicting female types the critics seemed to prefer *not* depicted by a 'poetess' beloved as much for her refined seclusion as she was for her scholarly verse, she had dared to parade before her astonished readers a lascivious aristocrat, a raped working-class girl, and an intellectually independent heroine. She was accused of writing in a 'high fever', of taking the literary field like Britomartis, an assertive, mythological maiden who escaped the sexual advances of Minos by leaping from a rock. Like Britomartis, Barrett Browning takes a Spasmodic leap from her rock, not, however, as frantic escape from male pursuit, but to immerse herself in the representation of subjects more usually treated by the novel: utopian politics, female sexuality, rape, urban misery, and the female struggle for professional recognition. In what follows, however, I shall argue that despite the thematic boldness, the daring brutality, and the dauntless references to female sexuality, *Aurora Leigh* is a strongly conservative poem.

Having chastised Barrett Browning for her unfeminine coarseness in figuring rape and references to prostitution, contemporary reviewers also attacked her for creating an implausible figure in Marian Erle, arguing that no working-class girl could possess such language and dignity. Undeniably, Marian is an idealised figure, as Cora Kaplan observes in attributing such idealisation to Barrett

114

Browning's 'aversion to realistic portrayals of working-class women' (Introduction to *'Aurora Leigh' with other Poems*, p. 25). What Kaplan neglects to add is that the characters are not only idealised in *Aurora Leigh*, they are hardly characters at all; they possess no finely nuanced and registered shades of consciousness, and apart from Aurora Leigh herself who addresses the reader in a language necessarily poetic rather than prosaic, they are emblematic sketches: Romney is a misguided socialist, Lord Howe an aristocratic liberal, Aurora's aunt a gentry spinster. As Virginia Woolf observed, when she assessed *Aurora Leigh*'s formal challenge to the supremacy of the novels of the mid-Victorian period in representing social problems, the characters are 'summed up with something of the exaggeration of a caricaturist', a failing that is unavoidable, Woolf sensibly suggests, as blank verse does not permit that subtle development of character that comes from the effect of one character upon another, nor does it allow for plausible conversation between characters. Crisply summing up the problem, Woolf concludes, 'Blank verse has proved itself the most remorseless enemy of living speech' (*Virginia Woolf: Women and Writing*, p. 142).

Vigorously employing blank verse and multiple images of degradation and exploitation, Barrett Browning vividly places Marian's rape before the reader, if not in its details then in its absence. Social and literary decorum dictates that Marian's story remain unsaid, yet its marginal status intensifies its volatile content:

> We wretches cannot tell out all our wrong
> Without offence to decent happy folk.
> I know that we must scrupulously hint
> With half-words, delicate reserves, the thing
> Which no one scrupled we should feel in full.
>
> (vi. 1220–4)

Marian is the victim of man's violence, not merely his seduction, and besides helping to transform her from fallen woman to the 'Marian' figure that she becomes,[1] this emphasis underlines the violence that is a central theme of the poem. Aurora becomes a mother to Marian, making those 'half-words' whole, repairing as much as she is able the injury she has suffered, and in the way of all mothers described by Aurora in evoking her own Italian childhood, 'kisses full sense' into what Marian cannot say. In giving voice and protection to Marian, Aurora rejects a social evil consistently attacked by Barrett Browning: the sexual hypocrisy of respectable women. If there is one place where *Aurora Leigh* takes a radical stand, it is when it daringly deploys erotic imagery and when it refuses to be silent about sexuality.

In an intriguing pattern for a woman who led such a severely sequestered life yet identified with a male poetic tradition, Barrett Browning favours active, phallocentric images for poetic creation. The maker and the subject of the poem are imagined as male and female in *Aurora Leigh*, as we see in the lines that shocked contemporary critics: 'Never flinch, / But still unscrupulously epic, catch / Upon the burning lava of a song / The full-veined, heaving, double-breasted Age' (v. 214–17). As I suggested earlier, *Aurora Leigh* attempts to mould the thematic content of the Victorian 'female' novel to the form of Classical 'male' epic. Here, Aurora exhorts herself and other poets to 'represent the Age', to employ epic form despite its current literary unfashionability and to catch in the volcanic image of 'burning lava' the voluptuous female time, heaving with nurturing life in its 'full-veined' breasts. Moreover, the image suggests some of the paradoxical mythologisation of women in the Victorian period: the poet must actively create a swiftly moving song out of an age which, even if it is the present one, is also immutably stable in its association to mother earth. Making poetry is straightforward, unflinching, male work, but the female subject of the poem is more complicated: woman is both symbol of the 'heaving' present and of an almost primordial past. Furthermore, Aurora Leigh's self-description as working poet employs an image of poetic action suggestive of thrusting, male sexuality:

> . . . I stood up straight and worked
> My veritable work. And as the soul
> Which grows within a child makes the child grow, –
> Or as the fiery sap, the touch from God,
> Careering through a tree, dilates the bark
> And roughs with scale and knob, before it strikes
> The summer foliage out in a green flame –
> So life, in deepening with me, deepened all
> The course I took, the work I did.
>
> (III. 327–35)

The simile links poetic and organic growth with images of vital, thrusting movement. The poetic / arboreal sap is 'fiery', it careers, dilates, manifests itself in obtrusions of 'scale and knob', until it blazes, 'strikes out' into green flame.

In 1861 Thackeray rejected one of Barrett Browning's poems, 'Lord Walter's Wife' for the *Cornhill* on the grounds that 'there are things my squeamish public will not hear', hastening to assure her that the wife of Browning and the mother of Pen was sacred to English readers. Barrett Browning's response was to the point: 'It is exactly because pure and prosperous women choose to *ignore* vice, that miserable women suffer wrong by it everywhere' (*L*.EBB, 2:244–5). The poem in question is a spirited attack on male hypocrisy. An engaged man declares to his friend's wife that he finds her 'too fair', and deliberately encouraging his attentions, the woman, Lord Walter's wife, instructs him in the unhappy social truth that men treat all women as sexual commodities to be used and discarded. Had she succumbed to his advances he would no longer find her so desirable: 'Too fair? – not unless you misuse us! and surely if, once in a while, / You attain to it, straight way you call / Us no longer too fair, but too vile' (6: lines 31–4). The poem is vitalised by a woman's anger, felt not only for herself but on behalf of all women who are either deified or degraded by men. Twenty years earlier, in writing to Mary Russell Mitford, Barrett Browning berated respectable women, 'Fair wives of honourable husbands', who will 'shrink from breathing the same air with a betrayed woman', yet will gracefully sit down to dinner with male adulterers (*L*.EBB/M, 1:295).

During the Crimean War, Barrett Browning wrote to an old friend that 'there are worse plagues, deeper griefs, dreader wounds than the physical. What of the forty thousand wretched women in this city? The silent writhing of them is to me more appalling than the roar of the cannons' (*L*.EBB, 2:213). In *Aurora Leigh* the wounds are both physical and symbolic: Marian is violently wounded by rape and in a hellish scene of diseased bodies swelling the aisles of the church where Romney and Marian are to be married, all is an oozing 'peccant social wound'. The image of the wound is crucial not only to the poem, but also to Barrett Browning's work as woman intellectual/poet. In refusing to ignore the wounds inflicted upon prostitutes, in compelling society to look at the 'offal' it makes of 'fallen' women and also of the poor, and in symbolising social evil as social wound, she creates herself as a ministering healer to an infected world. If society has been cleft in two by a symbolic knife, if women are cleft by rapacious men, then Barrett Browning will, through her poetry, heal the wounds – but not as auxiliary helper in the way that Martineau designed her work to serve male theory. Barrett Browning is a principal actor in the work of healing. She rejects the retrograde function of ancillary usefulness, refuses the role of 'female nurse' to a diseased world – behaves, in fact, in accordance with her actual view of the profession of nursing. As much as she admired Florence Nightingale as an individual, she was sharply critical of the way that nurses enact the 'safe' roles inscribed for them by a male-dominated society: 'Every man is on his knees before ladies carrying lint . . . if they stir an inch as thinkers or artists from the beaten line (involving more good to general humanity than is involved in lint) the very same men would curse the imprudence of the very same women and stop there . . . I do not consider the best use to which we can put a gifted and accomplished woman is to *make her a hospital nurse*' (*L*.EBB, 2:189). In *Aurora Leigh*, Barrett Browning stirs more than an inch as 'thinker' and 'artist' from the beaten line.

If one considers that the image which unifies *Aurora Leigh* is that of maternal nurturance, that Aurora is symbolically suckled by the hills of her Italian childhood, that Romney feeds the great carnivorous mouth of the poor through his Christian socialism, it may seem contradictory to suggest, as I do, that an imagery of wounding is also central to the poem. However, this is obviously less a pattern of contradiction than it is one of dialectical relationship: injury and nurturance are governing concepts which inform each other, and which, in their dialectical turn, direct the entire poem. Contrary to what one might expect, however, the mammocentric imagery does not work in quite the same way as that of wounding because symbolic and literal nurturance possesses its own contradictory implication not always ascribable to the constitutive relationship between wounding and healing. Even Marian's nurturance of her bonny baby is invested with an almost malevolent quality: as she suckles him, she seems to consume him greedily in an image of appropriation, 'drinking him as wine'. Moreover, Lady Waldemar's breasts both attract and repel. They are an unspoiled source of life and an image of demonic eroticism: the paradox suggests that contradiction between the deification and degradation of women which Barrett Browning attacks in her poem, 'Lord Walter's Wife'. Lady Waldemar offers a dazzling display of ripe female sexuality:

. . . How they told,
Those alabaster shoulders and bare breasts,
On which the pearls, drowned out of sight in milk,
Were lost, excepting for the ruby clasp!
They split the amaranth velvet-bodice down
To the waist or nearly, with the audacious press
Of full-breathed beauty. If the heart within
Were half as white! – but, if it were, perhaps
The breast were closer covered and the sight
Less aspectable by half, too.

(v. 618–27)

Proceeding through a sequence of false appearances and concealed truth, the description shows that 'aspectable' things are not what they seem. Nature herself (in the seductive shape of milky breasts) seems to drown out female ornamentation (the pearl necklace), yet the visible ruby clasp indicates Lady Waldemar's embellished sexuality. A single grey hair in her luxuriant bronze tresses contrasts ironically with the symbolism of her amaranth-velvet bodice (the purple colour of a mythical flower which never fades). The display of vibrant sexuality implies its own degeneration, and, significantly in terms of what Lady Waldemar does to Marian, the radiant whiteness of her breasts conceals the dark heart within. Lady Waldemar is what her name implies – the 'weal' which 'mars' all she touches.[2]

The depiction of women in *Aurora Leigh* is framed by Barrett Browning's employment of three interwoven colour images: green, red, and white. The first symbolises the serenity Aurora enjoys in the time she is freed from her aunt's instruction in English womanhood; the other two tend to express, even when employed by Aurora herself, the prevailing nineteenth-century fragmentation of woman into a creature fractured by seemingly irreconcilable, and therefore dangerous, attributes. Sometimes speaking this imagery of fragmentation, Aurora moves from the green, calm (but stultifying) time of her young womanhood to her mature, vibrant, fiery part in building the New Jerusalem:

I had a little chamber in the house,
As green as any privet-hedge a bird
Might choose to build in, though the nest itself
Could show but dead-brown sticks and straws; the walls

> Were green, the carpet was pure green, the straight
> Small bed was curtained greenly, and the folds
> Hung green about the window which let in
> The out-door world with all its greenery.
>
> (I. 567–74)

No *Jane Eyre* red room this, no symbolic chamber of female anger or prison of female desire, but rather the calm, cool space of the English countryside where, employing the bird imagery that is everywhere in the poem, Aurora describes herself nesting in her green chamber/ privet hedge. Some reviewers accused Barrett Browning of melodramatic borrowings from Brontë's novel, of making Romney both St John Rivers and Rochester, the stern seeker of missionary helper rather than sexual partner and the misguided lover blinded by fire. Romney, however, is neither as chillingly austere as St John Rivers nor as passionately vital as Rochester for the obvious reason that he is not, as I have suggested earlier, a character whom we suspect of having much feeling at all. He is a deluded spokesman for Christian socialism who learns that a 'famishing carnivorous mouth, – / A huge, deserted, callow, blind bird Thing' (his image for the poor) needs more than worms in the form of utopian politics to fill it.[3]

The first significant employment of the red/white imagery occurs in Aurora's description of her mother's portrait executed after her death. The face, throat and hands possess a 'swan-like supernatural white life', yet the body wears a red brocade dress, and to the child Aurora the face is 'by turns' 'Ghost, fiend, and angel, fairy, witch, and sprite'. This is the paradoxical female face of so much Victorian art – the angelic sprite who winds her hair around the neck of a knight in Waterhouse's 'La Belle Dame Sans Merci', the fiendish, contorted figure of Hunt's 'The Lady of Shalott', Rossetti's 'Lady Lilith' whose massive neck and powerful jaw forebode an awful female mystery.[4] Confronted as a child by a contradictory representation of her mother, as a woman Aurora must integrate these iconised fragments of Victorian womanhood.

When she hears of Marian's flight from London, Aurora employs the commonplace imagery of purity and whiteness to assure Romney that his lost bride will stay as pure as 'snow that's drifted from the garden-bank / To the open road'. In Marian's own powerful evocation of her despair, however, the imagery becomes more complicated. She describes herself, pregnant and destitute, wandering the roads in France:

> And there I sat, one evening, by the road,
> I, Marian Erle, myself, alone, undone,
> Facing a sunset low upon the flats
> As if it were the finish of all time,
> The great red stone upon my sepulchre,
> Which angels were too weak to roll away.
>                                   (VI. 1269–74)

The raped woman, spoiled yet innocent, soon to give birth to a joyful child from brutal rape, reddened by the blood of defloration literally and symbolically 'engraved' upon her white body, likens the setting sun to a red stone upon her sepulchre. There is a foreshadowing of the end of Hardy's Tess here, a character also figured in the red and white imagery of purity and defloration: Tess sleeps on an oblong slab at Stonehenge, is a sacrificial victim to sexual hypocrisy, and is awakened by a strong ray of the rising sun as the police arrive to arrest her for the bloody stabbing of Alex d'Urberville. In Marian's language, the red imagery links the dying day, the exhausted woman, and the weakened angels; all seems to be in a paradoxically fiery decline and suggests a significant contrast to Aurora on her twentieth birthday. A radiant, vital and virginal Aurora, fresh from her vernal nest in the morning, foreshadows a depleted, violated Marian at sunset. On Aurora's morning, she is dressed in white, hopefully self-wreathed in ivy as symbol of the poetic power to come: 'The June was in me, with its multitudes / Of nightingales all singing in the dark, / And rosebuds reddening where the calyx split' (II. 10–12). The green calyx splits to reveal the ripening rose and suggests the departure of a maturing Aurora from the green enclosure of her room.

If Marian suffers a symbolic fiery ordeal as she feels the weight of 'a great red stone' upon her grave, then Romney suffers a literal one when he is blinded in the fire set by local peasants, incensed by the 'drabs and thieves' he has housed in his Phalanstery. He describes himself as 'A mere bare blind stone in the blaze of day', an image which connects with Marian's evocation of gravestone and sunset (and also an image whose alliterative, jarring assonance recalls the closing of the seventh section of *In Memoriam*, 'On the bald street breaks the blank day'). Fusing the traditional myths of poet as witness to a transcendent order and of woman as sympathetic consoler, Aurora repairs the injuries suffered by Marian and Romney.

The informing structure of wounding and healing in *Aurora Leigh* is emphatically etched by imagery of knifing. 'There, ended childhood' declares Aurora on the death of her father. Her life becomes 'Smooth endless days, notched here and there with knives, / A weary, wormy darkness, spurred i' the flank / With flame, that it should eat and end itself / Like some tormented scorpion' (II. 219–22). Barrett Browning sustains the imagery of knifing as Aurora describes her aunt's discipline as a 'sharp sword set against my life', her aunt's gaze as 'two grey-steel naked-bladed eyes' searching through her face, and a young man at a dinner party as possessing 'A sharp face, like a knife in a cleft stick' (I. 691, 328; V. 629). Moreover, Aurora's sense of injured self is sometimes surprisingly gruesome, even sado-masochistic: 'So I lived' she says, 'A Roman died so; smeared with honey, teased / By insects, stared to torture by the moon' (II. 890–1); in London she likens the city sun to the 'fiery brass' of cages used in Druidic sacrifice 'from which the blood of wretches pent inside / Seems oozing forth to incarnadine the air' (III. 172–5); and in justifying her refusal of Romney, she suspects that 'He might cut / My body into coins to give away / Among his other paupers' (II. 790–1).

Knifing and bleeding are prominent symbols in the severe condemnation of female sentimentality which Romney imprudently issues to Aurora:

> . . . Your quick-breathed hearts,
> So sympathetic to the personal pang,
> Close on each separate knife-stroke, yielding up
> A whole life at each wound, incapable
> Of deepening, widening a large lap of life
> To hold the world-full woe. The human race
> To you means, such a child, or such a man,
> You saw one morning waiting in the cold,
> Beside that gate, perhaps. You gather up
> A few such cases, and when strong sometimes
> Will write of factories and of slaves, as if
> Your father were a negro, and your son
> A spinner in the mills. All's yours and you,

All, coloured with your blood, or otherwise
Just nothing to you.

(II. 184–98)

From Romney's perspective of patriarchal socialism, women lack
the male faculty of abstraction from personal experience to a general
theory of society: wounded women give up their entire beings at
one emotional 'knife-stroke', leaving no room in their maternal laps
for the woes of the world. Through Romney's sexist sermon, Barrett
Browning seems slyly to respond to those critics who derided the
poems *she* wrote about factories and slaves, and also to a powerful
Victorian myth about intellectual women – if women can only write
about what is 'coloured' with their blood, can only think in terms of
'yours and you', then their minds must be symbolically stained by
the somatic signs of their womanhood. In the success of Aurora
Leigh and in her own career, Barrett Browning defies the ugly
implication that the intellectual lives of women must be marred by
biological destiny.

In proposing to Marian, the cutting edge, as it were, of Romney's
imagery is deflected from disdain for women's sentimentality to a
passionate plea for the class unity that will be realised through their
marriage:

. . . though the tyrannous sword,
Which pierced Christ's heart, has cleft the world in twain
'Twixt class and class, opposing rich to poor,
Shall *we* keep parted? Not so. Let us lean
And strain together rather, each to each,
Compress the red lips of this gaping wound
As far as two souls can . . .

(IV. 122–8)

Assimilating Christian and socialist doctrine, Romney aligns the
origin of class antagonism with the fall from unity which originated
in the piercing of Christ's body. Despite the eventual insufficiency
of Romney's materialistic remedy for social evil, Barrett Browning,
in deploying this imagery, expresses that yearning for re-integration
of the mythical bond between man and his world which she, in
common with many of her Victorian contemporaries, believed had
been stretched to its most 'gaping' extent in the nineteenth century.
Romney acknowledges that fallen, class-conscious man can do little

more than 'compress' the wound, and from the manner in which
Barrett Browning imagines the Church scene where rich and poor
come to witness this 'compressing' marriage, it would seem there
*can* be no successful healing. The social body is deeply infected.
Employing a language of violence and pestilence which reminds us
of the suffering scorpion burnt by flame, the Roman eaten by
insects, and the Druidic human sacrifices, Barrett Browning paints a
grotesque picture.

The vision is infernal. How could a woman who had been
secluded from society until the age of 39, and after that who had
resided in Italy under the adoring protection of her husband, a
woman who was a mother, who had written heart-rending poems
about the untimely death of children and of female self-sacrifice
such as 'Isobel's Child' and 'Bertha in the Lane' – how could this
revered example of female virtue and delicacy describe that half of
the wedding party which comes from 'Saint Giles' in the following
language?

> . . . Faces? . . . phew,
> We'll call them vices, festering to despairs,
> Or sorrows, petrifying to vices: not
> A finger-touch of God left whole on them,
> All ruined, lost – the countenance worn out
> As the garment, the will dissolute as the act,
> The passions loose and draggling in the dirt
> To trip a foot up at the first free step!
> Those, faces? 'twas as if you had stirred up hell
> To heave its lowest dreg-fiends uppermost
> In fiery swirls of slime, . . .
>
> (IV. 579–89)

As far as one can judge from reading her letters, the closest Barrett
Browning ever got to such hellish faces was on a rare cab trip to
Shoreditch in search of Flush, dog-napped from Wimpole Street.
However, she was very close to such scenes of pestilential misery
through her daily reading of newspapers, periodicals and novels of
social realism (particularly of Sue, Hugo, and Balzac). Moreover, all
readers of *The London Times* in the 1840s would have read
uncensored reports of testimony before the various Parliamentary
committees investigating conditions in the factories, mines and
slum areas of the poor. The reports reveal a hellish world of stench,

squalor, and disease, of open privies, of prostitutes and beggars living in dens which resembled animal lairs rather than human dwellings.

In February 1843 Barrett Browning read the entire Report of the Royal Commission on the Employment of Children and Young Persons in Mines and Manufactories (one of its Assistant Commissioners was her close correspondent, R. H. Horne): as a consequence of that reading, she was compelled to write her first poem of social protest, 'The Cry of the Children', which appeared in *Blackwood's Magazine* in August of that year. As an avid reader of virtually every kind of Victorian text, she was no stranger to representation of working-class suffering, and this, of course, is really the point – those faces 'festering to despairs' come from her extensive reading. In itself, the informing relationship between reading and writing in a poet's life is hardly remarkable, but by virtue of the limitations of Barrett Browning's experience, her work was generated more by text than it was by direct observation, and it seems as if these sections of *Aurora Leigh* are the hellish distillation of her readings in the Victorian discourse of the poor.

Let me emphasise that Barrett Browning's vision of the pestilential poor does not necessarily bespeak fear and loathing of the working class (in fact, her vision is governed as much by sympathy as it is by revulsion); the important point here is that her representation of that class is derived from the discourse of the poor with which she was most acquainted. The Parliamentary Papers, in particular, consistently employ a language of the inferno: bodies tumble together in crowded hovels, dunghills dominate the landscape, and all is festering and pestilential. Witnesses to this misery were by no means unsympathetic to what they saw (quite the contrary), but the language of their testimony frequently seems derived from the Christian imagery of hell – a stinking, festering hole. In a complex process of representation whereby the poor are implicitly punished by their own vice, they are imaginatively placed in the topos of the damned.[5]

'Only a person with the wildest imagination' would have used the image of hell to describe the poor, observes Gardiner Taplin in his disparagement of *Aurora Leigh* (*The Life of Elizabeth Barrett Browning*, p. 324). This is undeniable, and Barrett Browning was not the only Victorian writer to possess such an imagination. In Chapter 22 of Dickens's *Bleak House* (included in the seventh monthly number which appeared in September 1852) Messrs Snagsby and Bucket go in search of Jo, descending deeper in the depths of Tom-all-Alone's; they pass 'along the middle of a villainous street, undrained, unventilated, deep in black mud and corrupt water – though the roads are dry elsewhere – and reeking with such smells and sights that he, who has lived in London all his life, can scarce believe his senses. Branching from this street and its heaps of ruins, are other streets and courts so infamous that Mr Snagsby sickens in body and mind, and feels as if he were going, every moment deeper down, into the infernal gulf.' Barrett Browning, who was working on her 'infernal' sections of *Aurora Leigh* in the early 1850s, was by no means singular in figuring the slums and their inhabitants as hellish, even if she was denied that direct observation of London alleys which Dickens experienced on his night-time excursions with the Metropolitan Police.

In some ways, however, Dickens's surrealistic vision of swelling London streets and grotesque humanity also owes less to direct observation than to a fantastic imagination – or, rather, less to the actual urban scene than to representation of it. Hogarth's 'Gin Lane' could well be a source for Field Lane in *Oliver Twist* and for the scene in *Aurora Leigh* at St Giles's Church when the stinking poor arrive to witness the marriage of social classes. As Oliver is dragged along by the Artful Dodger, the air is 'impregnated with filthy odours' and he sees 'heaps of children, who, even at that time of night, were crawling in and out at the doors, or screaming from the inside . . . little knots of houses, where drunken men and women were positively wallowing in filth' (Chapter 8). On the way to St Giles's Church, chosen by Romney as the place for his transgressive convention of rich and poor, Hogarthian bodies invade the streets of Belgravia:

> Lame, blind, and worse – sick, sorrowful, and worse –
> The humours of the peccant social wound
> All pressed out, poured down upon Pimlico,
> Exasperating the unaccustomed air
> With a hideous interfusion. You'd suppose
> A finished generation, dead of plague,
> Swept outward from their graves into the sun,
> The moil of death upon them.
>
> (IV. 542–50)

The metaphor of the 'social cleft' is both repeated and literalised as the symbolic wound in the social body literally stinks, presses out its suppurating matter. The people clog the streets, ooze into the church 'in a dark, slow stream, like blood', and Barrett Browning pushes her infernal imagery to a hideous conclusion as the movement of the crowd is likened to that of bruised snakes crawling and hissing out of a hole 'with shuddering involution'. As the stinking poor makes its serpentine procession, the upper classes sit with handkerchiefs to their noses and Barrett Browning aligns her pestilential, carnivalesque imagery with her poetics of healing by having one of the aristocrats observe that the present spectacle, 'this dismembering of society', resembles the tearing apart of Damien's body by horses. The social wound, the ruptured body, the bloody procession, all seem to congeal in a brutal image of the dismembered body/social state. In order to understand how Barrett Browning saw her vocation as poet intellectual in terms of cure for the wounded social body, it is necessary to examine her political etiology, so to speak, and her prescribed remedies. Defilement is the disease and artistic service is the medicine.

# 7

# Defiled Text and Political Poetry

A poem that begins with the admonition from Ecclesiastes, 'Of writing many books there is no end', *Aurora Leigh* is pervaded by metaphors of writing, the most notable being that employed by Aurora in likening man's soul to a multiply inscribed text. Refuting enlightenment beliefs in the soul as 'clear white paper', she imagines it as:

> A palimpsest, a prophet's holograph,
> Defiled, erased and covered by a monk's –
> The apocalypse, by a Longus! poring on
> Which obscene text, we may discern perhaps
> Some fair, fine trace of what was written once,
> Some upstroke of an alpha and omega
> Expressing the old scripture.
>
> (I. 826–32)

Richly invested with Barrett Browning's philosophical and political values, the lines signalise her recurrent preoccupation with the traditional Christian myth of lost unity. Man's soul is likened to a scripture which once possessed its own perfect form and its own internal coherence: as Christ declares in Revelation 1:8, 'I am Alpha and Omega, the beginning and the ending', so man, in an ideal correspondence to this unity, once possessed a unified soul/text. But the soul/text which once resembled the holograph inscribed by a prophet, who was, in his turn, inspired by the original inscriber of all things, has been defiled by later writers: man's original soul/text has been debased from its primary meaning and transformed from oracular revelation to pastoral romance (the apocalypse inscribed by a Longus). Associating herself with the Biblical prophetic tradition, proclaiming herself as God's new interpreter and inscriber of the ideal world which will replace that sundered by the social cleft, Barrett Browning instructs man in discovering traces of the original text in the degenerate palimpsest. If soul, text, and form have been debased through inscribed interpretation, erasure, and deformation, so, too, the alpha and omega of Victorian life has become obscured by the inscriptions of materialism, commercial individualism, and socialist politics. In a much less ambiguous prophetic stance than that adopted by Harriet Martineau at Niagara Falls, Aurora Leigh performs the ideal mission of the poet as Barrett Browning described it in her Preface to 'A Vision of Poets' – she reclaims the oracular function of poetry and destroys the 'evil' of a 'social incrustation over a great idea'. Empowered by vocation to reveal the connections between God, man, culture, and society which have been obscured in a secular world, the ideal poet is made a woman poet in *Aurora Leigh*. Moreover, she is a political poet whose ideas echo the conservative thought of Barrett Browning, an intellectual we may associate with the traditional function as Gramsci describes it.

Barrett Browning's political thought frequently resembles that aspect of Carlyle's which excoriates mercantilism and mechanisation. In her *Contributions towards an Essay on Carlyle*, taken from letters to R. H. Horne written during 1843, Carlyle is, as one might expect, the antithesis of Martineau's intellectual inspiration, Jeremy Bentham; he speaks a 'soul-language', is the figurative opener of a long closed, bricked-up, 'encrusted' window in the 'blind wall of his century' (6:312–21). To peer through the window opened by the force of Carlyle's swirling, vital prose is to see, if one is Elizabeth Barrett Browning, not very far back in the century. It is to have a vision of the Romantic revolutionary spirit embodied and mythologized in the figures of Byron and Shelley, to glimpse the heroic energy of Napoleon, and to diminish the material achievements of the English middle class. 'When we drive out, from the cloud of steam, majestical white horses, / Are we greater than the first men who led black ones by the mane?' asks the lowly poet in 'Lady Geraldine's Courtship' (2: lines 207–8). According to Barrett Browning's politics, clearly not: her poet observes that if man touches the ocean floor, strikes the star, or wraps 'the globe intensely with one hot electric breath', he is only displaying technological power which is within his tether and of his making. 'Materialist / The age's name is', declares Romney to Aurora as they debate the proper ways to remedy the evils of that age. To understand the full significance of these evils in *Aurora Leigh* and the conservative weight of their remedies, it is necessary to examine the antagonism to English middle class values expressed in Barrett Browning's other political poetry.

Much of this poetry is more overtly concerned with Italy than it is with England. An impassioned partisan of Italian nationalism, Barrett Browning mourns and celebrates Italian history in 'Casa Guidi Windows', published in 1857, and in a collection, *Poems Before Congress*, published in 1860 and greeted by *Blackwood's Magazine* with the following affronted declaration: 'We are strongly of opinion that, for the peace and welfare of society, it is a good and wholesome rule that women should not interfere with politics' (*Blackwood's Magazine*, 87:490). However, the two part 'Casa Guidi Windows', an impressionistic meditation on Italian culture and politics viewed from the fenestrated seclusion of Barrett Browning's intense readings, contains strong criticism of the British commercialism celebrated at the Crystal Palace in 1851 and of England's failure to support Italian aspirations. To all sympathisers with the Italian cause, unity had seemed likely in 1848; but conflict between different revolutionary factions had debilitated the struggle and the restoration of Austrian military rule served to darken all hopes of Italian nationhood by the end of 1849. Europe after the events of 1848 is painted by Barrett Browning as a 'Fair-going world', bent upon exhibiting glories of trade and trophies of imperialism, and deaf to the cries of people suffering under domestic and foreign tyranny. England displays the signs of imperial might – the corals, diamonds, porcelains, intricate glassware, and models of the steamships that make her the queen of 'liberal' trading nations – but where is the 'light of teaching' for the poor, asks Barrett Browning, where is the 'help for women sobbing out of sight / Because men made the laws?' And England is not singular in her indifference:

> No remedy, my England, for such woes?
> No outlet, Austria, for the scourged and bound,
> No entrance for the exiled? no repose,
> Russia, for knouted Poles worked underground,
> And gentle ladies bleached among the snows?
> No mercy for the slave America?
>                    (3: Part 2, lines 641–6)

In a manner suggestive of Gramsci's definitions of traditional intellectual activity, she scathingly attributes England's 'woes' to contemporary spineless liberal politics and to rampant mid-nineteenth-century mercantilism. According to Gramsci, the traditional intellectual believes (or wants to believe) in the existence of an 'historical continuity uninterrupted even by the most complicated and radical changes in political and social forms'. This structure of feeling impels such intellectuals to 'put themselves forward as autonomous and independent of the dominant social group' ('The Intellectuals', pp. 5–7). Barrett Browning's politics are defined by a self-sustained myth of transcendent poetic practice and by strong antagonism to the dominant middle class. In the Preface to *Poems Before Congress*, she sarcastically imagines an English politican who would say, 'This is good for your trade; this is necessary for your domination . . . [but] it will profit nothing to the general humanity; therefore away with it! – it is not for you or for me' (3:315). In general, her politics express a yearning for a utopian society in which economic development and better ways of existence for 'humanity' have little to do with each other: the relationship, for example, between Victorian commercial expansion and improved living conditions escapes her idealistic polarisation of trade and the social good. That the industrial revolution produced intense and far-reaching misery is beyond question, but the threat and visibility of that misery generated a surveillance and consolidation of the working classes which produced certain improvements, however minimal, in the working and living conditions of those who suffered.

To be sure, Barrett Browning's attacks upon English politics are voiced from her adopted Italian perspective, but she had consistently practised a poetry of social criticism from the time she was the secluded English 'poetess' of 1838.[1] 'The Soul's Travelling', her first flight into such poetry, bears a suitably uplifting motto from Synesius, the late fourth-century Christian Neoplatonist: 'Now, to spread one's intellectual wings'. The poem is characterised by that irregularity of form and carefully constructed appearance of inspired and spontaneous verse which reveals its origins in Barrett Browning's most intensely 'Spasmodic' period: dwelling in the city, a cacophonous place from which he imaginatively travels to the quiet of the country, the speaker/poet catalogues the noises of a teeming town – a town noticeably Hogarthian in its anticipation of the carnivalesque church scene in *Aurora Leigh*:[2]

> The champ of the steeds on the silver bit,
> As they whirl the rich man's chariot by;

> The beggar's whine as he looks at it, –
> But it goes too fast for charity; . . .
> The gin-door's oath, that hollowly chinks
> Guilt upon grief, and wrong upon hate;
> The cabman's cry to get out of the way;
> The dustman's call down the area-grate;
> The young maid's jest, and the old wife's scold;
>
> (2: lines 15–33)

In an ironic turn at the end of the stanza, all the dissonant noises of champing steeds, whining beggars, of drunken oaths which 'chink' as glasses and coins chink together, of dustmen's calls down area-grates which 'grate' upon the reader, are drowned out by the ringing bells and blaring trumpets greeting the Queen's coronation. In desperation the poet imaginatively flies from the Blakeian town to find 'a grassy niche / Hollowed in a seaside hill', where the only sound is 'Distance-softened noise made more old / Than Nereid's singing, the tide spent / Joining soft issues with the shore / In harmony of discontent'. Paradoxically, this unpeopled spot offers 'a harmony of discontent' because the poet still feels that which makes the 'city's moan', and the poem concludes with the recognition that all travelling of the poetic imagination from city streets to unspoiled nature is necessarily futile. All men and all poets must fly to God's throne where 'the archangel, raising / Unto Thy face his full ecstatic gazing, / Forgets the rush and rapture of his wings!' Expressly critical of degraded city life full of shriek and moan, the poem argues that the poet possesses a special gift of escape from dissonance through his imagination, and finally suggests that both city dissonance and country harmony can only be, must be, transcended in a flight to God. The glory of this flight lies in a falling away of self-consciousness from the archangel and from the poet: as the angel forgets 'the rush and rapture of his wings', so the poet loses awareness of his power which has lifted him to God's glory.

In this early poem, Barrett Browning foreshadows the dedication of Aurora's poetic power to the building of a New Jerusalem. But before her union with Romney and before her understanding that 'Art's a service', Aurora lives in a London as disturbing as that evoked in 'The Soul's Travelling'. Enshrouded literally and symbolically by a fog which is more strangely comforting than it is threatening, and feeling 'serene and unafraid of solitude', she writes inferior poetry.

There, in a proverbial garret whose windows reveal the chimney pots of a tangled city rather than the stately turrets of Romney's country house that Aurora viewed from her green chamber, she sees:

> Fog only, the great tawny weltering fog,
> Involve the passive city, strangle it
> Alive, and draw it off into the void,
> Spires, bridges, streets, and squares, as if a sponge
> Had wiped out London, – or as noon and night
> Had clapped together and utterly struck out
> The intermediate time, undoing themselves
> In the act. Your city poets see such things
> Not despicable.
>
> (III. 179–87)

Here she is surprised by 'a sudden sense of vision and of tune' and writes poetry that implicitly fills the absence created by the shrouding fog, a creeping, deadly force which seems to kill the city, to 'strangle' it and 'draw it off into the void'. Somewhat schematically in terms of Aurora Leigh's aesthetic values (and those of Barrett Browning) this poetry is, of course, commercially successful but inspired by no belief in the mission of the poet. According to Aurora, 'I did some excellent things indifferently, / Some bad things excellently. Both were praised, / The latter loudest' (III. 205–7). In the lengthy aesthetic meditations of Book v which, among other things, question the rigid imposition of form upon content, Aurora distills her views in these terms: 'Inward evermore / To outward, – so in life, and so in art / Which still is life' (v. 227–9). The London poetry produced by the 'city poet' has originated in an 'outward' world, which though sometimes shrouded by fog, is the materialistic world feeding and applauding a skill ungoverned by transcendent vision; at the end of the 'novel-poem' figuring an epic quest and thereby defying governing rules of appropriate form, Aurora Leigh's poetry is properly directed by an 'inward' vision which will build a new city, and, one might add, a new poetics itself which reconciles the early Spasmodic inspiration of 'A Soul's Travelling' with politics and society.

Whether writing poetry about Italian history, English politics, or poetry itself, Barrett Browning tends to form her arguments in terms of confinement and liberation. Until she left England as Mrs Robert

Browning, Elizabeth Barrett was literally confined to a domestic space she described as a prison, guarded by closed doors against which she wanted to dash herself 'with a passionate impatience of the needless captivity'. She writes of talking exclusively by post and gloomily likens herself to someone incarcerated in a dungeon driven to scrawling mottoes on a wall. The image of the closed door is elaborated in her letters after her marriage: she speaks of the time before she left England as one in which all the doors of her life were closed to her, shutting her in 'as in a prison'. Before one marvellous door stood Browning, who, after much dedicated persuasion, released her from the obsessive grip of a father who had forbidden *any* of his children to marry. A month after her marriage, she observed that had she asked her father's permission, it would have been like 'placing a knife in his hand' (*L*.EBB, 1:275, 293). It is hardly surprising that a father whose pathological will was unyielding, who refused permission for Barrett Browning to travel to Italy in the autumn of 1845 (a journey urged upon her by her doctors and her friends) causes his daughter to cast him in the role of knife-wielding patriarch. Yet that father who brandishes the symbolic knife (which in *Aurora Leigh* also cleaves the social body) was consistently, if ambiguously, defended by his daughter. She declared to Browning that 'the evil is in the system' which sanctions paternal enforcement of filial submission by that 'most dishonouring of necessities, the necessity of living'. In terms of her career as a political intellectual, the most significant connection she makes between the patriarchal 'system' and society is to be found in her association of domestic and socialistic tyranny.

Conceding in 1848 that the cooperation of individuals and families designed to organise more economically 'the means of life' may be beneficial, she is vehemently opposed to such spontaneous small scale cooperation becoming a 'government scheme': 'All such patriarchal planning in a government issues naturally into absolutism, and is adapted to states of society more or less barbaric' (*L*.EBB, 1:359). Socialism was thoroughly repugnant to her, a political system that stifled individualism and called forth in her writings a language suffused with fervent emotionalism. 'I love liberty so intensely that I hate Socialism. I hold it to be the most desecrating and dishonouring to humanity of all creeds. I would rather (for me) live under the absolutism of Nicholas of Russia than in a Fourier machine, with my individuality sucked out of me by a social air-pump' (*L.*EBB, 1:452). Preferring the absolutism of tyranny to the dehumanisation of socialism and speaking from an essentialist perspective, she mythologises, even literalises, individuality as an essence that can be forcibly extracted from the human body, while at the same time she implicitly likens this explicitly political individualism to the familial individualism of rebellious children held under the knife of patriarchy. Her intense loathing of socialism is further revealed in her reactions to the death of Margaret Fuller Ossoli. She flatly declared that 'it was better for her to go' as 'only God and a few friends can be expected to distinguish between the pure personality of a woman and her professed opinions', opinions Barrett Browning felt were 'deeply coloured by those blood colours of Socialistic views' (*L.*EBB, 1:460). Deeply sympathetic to Margaret Fuller as a wife and mother, finding in her life many parallels to her own exile from a mother country, she found Fuller's politics that much more repulsive.

In a telling image from *Aurora Leigh*, Barrett Browning indicts socialism in Lord Howe's misguided support of Romney's social programmes. According to Aurora, Lord Howe is:

> A born aristocrat, bred radical,
> And educated Socialist, who still
> Goes floating, on traditions of his kind,
> Across the theoretic flood from France,
> Though, like a drenched Noah on a rotten deck,
> Scarce safer for his place there.
>
> (IV. 710–15)

He floats on French socialist theory, but unlike Romney, his detachment keeps him from getting wet. Vincent Carrington, Romney's painter friend, describes Lord Howe as standing 'high upon the brink of theories, / Observes the swimmers and cries "Very fine," / But keeps dry linen equally, – unlike / That gallant breaster, Romney!' (III. 115–18). Heroic swimmer as he is, however, Romney is finally defeated by the sea of engulfing theory (even if he is blinded by fire), by that wave of socialist doctrine formed by Louis Blanc and Fourier and which crossed the channel in the 1830s. Romney's literal blinding seems to be a punishment for his political blindness. Unable to see the folly of his utopian socialism, he loses his sight in a fire at the Phalanstery he establishes at his country estate. If Brontë punishes Rochester for his vaunting masculinity, as some critics believe, then Barrett Browning certainly punishes Romney for his politics.

As a political conservative favouring the values of the land-owning classes in England, as a conservative poet lamenting the 'defilement' of a once heroic culture, Barrett Browning speaks as a Gramscian traditional intellectual and abhors the liberalism and mercantilism of the swelling middle classes. In her two powerful poems attacking the exploitation of children she holds mercantile greed accountable for their suffering. 'The Cry of the Children', the poem written after reading the full report investigating employment of children in mines and factories, emphasises the sounds of the factory machinery that drown out the sobs of child-workers. She employs droning, monotonous rhyme and metre to make the reader experience the dreadful and dizzying effects of the factory. The seventh stanza is evocative of the concrete imagery deployed in *Aurora Leigh*:

> For all day the wheels are droning, turning;
> Their wind comes in our faces,
> Till our hearts turn, our heads with pulses burning,
> And the walls turn in their places:
> Turns the sky in the high window, blank and reeling,
> Turns the long light that drops adown the wall,
> Turn the black flies that crawl along the ceiling:
> All are turning, all the day, and we with all.
> And all day the iron wheels are droning,
> And sometimes we could pray,
> 'O ye wheels' (breaking out in a mad moaning),
> 'Stop! be silent for to-day!'
>
> (3: lines 78–88)

The unrelenting assonance, the repetition of 'turning' whereby the turning of the machinery makes the children's hearts turn, the walls turn, the sky turn, the flies turn, the sense of all movement generated by that droning movement of 'iron wheels' so that industrial manufacture determines and perverts natural movements of the human body, of the sky, and of insects – all this strongly anticipates Dickens's image of the mad, melancholy elephants in *Hard Times*. There, in Bounderby's factory, the piston of the steam-engine works 'monotonously up and down like the head of an elephant in a state of melancholy madness'. Dickens makes the movement of machinery become the movement of perverted nature. Barrett Browning, however, converts nature into a movement that resembles the machine and thereby more directly (if less imaginatively) indicts the factory system and those who profit from it. The poem concludes with an accusing lament from the children: how long, they cry, 'Oh cruel nation, / Will you stand, to move the world on a child's heart' (lines 152–3). With the pun upon stand, the poem interrogates British mercantilism: how long will it stand, endure, a commercial power that stands, rests upon, depends upon, exploitation, and how long will it figuratively stand with its crushing weight upon the heart of a child? The cry in this poem seems to issue from the centre of Blakes's 'London', where the speaker hears 'mind-forg'd manacles' in every cry of every man and every infant.

In the second of her poems of social protest dealing with children, 'A Song for the Ragged Schools of London', written in 1854 for a charity bazaar organised by her sister, Barrett Browning relies upon the familiar association of the Roman and British empires in order to make the song a monitory one. Listening in Rome to hymns of praise for Britain's imperial power, her rich natural resources, her morally correct middle class, the speaker advises, 'Lordly English, think it o'er, / Caesar's doing is undone!' England should remember that she already has 'ruins worse than Rome's' in her 'pauper men and women':

> Women leering through the gas
> (Just such bosoms used to nurse you),
> Men, turned wolves by famine – pass!
> Those can speak themselves, and curse you
> But these others – children small,
> Split like blots about the city,
> Quay, and street, and palace-wall –
> Take them up into your pity!
>
> (3: lines 40–7)

Characteristically defying the patriarchal injunction that women writers avoid discussion of sexuality, she insists that the English see their mothers' breasts in those of the prostitutes, and in an ironic allusion to the myth of the founders of Rome (Romulus and Remus who were suckled by wolves), the British poor, the detritus of

Empire, have become wolves. 'Pass', instructs the speaker, for these women and men will curse you, but the children cannot, and they are imagined by Barrett Browning as blots upon the gilded façade of British imperial power and as literal disfigurations of the urban scene. These children again seem to inhabit a Blakeian city, but where Blake's brilliant imagination could make the speaker of 'London' *hear* how 'the hapless Soldier's sigh / Runs in blood down Palace walls', Barrett Browning more literally sees the children as visual blots on those walls enclosing the centres of empire.

In these two poems of social criticism informed by Barrett Browning's political opposition to the English mercantile middle class and by her strong belief that this class 'defiles' a potentially shining and heroic world, the speaker undertakes to voice the suffering of those unable to articulate their own misery. When the children do speak in 'The Cry of the Children', it is in the context of an interrogation of English power, in a poetic frame which deploys the rhetoric of accusation: 'Do ye hear the children weeping, O my brothers' begins the first stanza; 'Do you question the young children' begins the second; and the closing stanza of the poem contains the children's question as to 'how long' they must suffer. The second poem is a barely mediated request from the famous poet-mother to her sisters on behalf of the poor children of London: 'Our own babes cry in them all.' Both poems plead for liberation from miserable confinement: that the poet must speak for the oppressed intensifies the actual conditions of oppression which make the suffering voiceless. But at the same time that voice of civilised outrage tends to temper the misery being described simply by virtue of the fact that the suffering must be mediated by a voice of privilege. The most stirring of Barrett Browning's poems of social protest is the one in which the speaker is empowered by her hatred of her oppressor to articulate her own rage. Speaking in the language of brutal literalness that frequently characterises *Aurora Leigh*, she is the pursued figure of 'The Runaway Slave at Pilgrim's Point'.

In September 1833 Barrett Browning professed herself profoundly 'glad' that the recent Parliamentary Bill freeing the West Indian slaves had passed, despite the exacerbation of financial difficulties for her father caused by the legislation.[3] Her anti-slavery poem was written for a Boston bazaar held in 1848 and is a savagely ironic interrogation of the freedom proclaimed by white pilgrims arriving in New England. So fiercely hateful is the tone of the poem, so proudly adamant is its anger, that in a first reading it comes as a shock to realise in the ninth stanza that the speaker is female: a slave who narrates the story of having strangled the child she has borne from rape by her white masters (the poem implies she has been raped by more than one man). She mocks the disjunction between the American myth of freedom and the reality of her experience by literally and figuratively taking a stand:

> I stand on the mark beside the shore
> Of the first white pilgrim's bended knee,
> Where exile turned to ancestor,
> And God was thanked for liberty.
>
> (3: lines 1–4)

She then bends her knee on the spot that marks, 'stands' for liberty in the way that she 'stands' for oppression, and addresses the poem to the 'pilgrim-souls' whose presence she feels in this place. She kneels to curse the land blessed in the name of freedom, to curse the patriarchal line of oppressors, for she is triply oppressed as slave, as black, and as woman. The slave she loved has been dragged from her ('I crawled to touch / His blood marks in the dust') and the hated child she carried on her breast is 'an amulet that hung too slack'. The child's whiteness is unbearable, and the genuine horror of the poem lies in the mother's hatred of her infant. She sees her master's hated look in the child's innocent eyes, the white man's struggles for political liberty in the moans of her baby as he struggles to free himself from the shawl with which she has bound him. In a violently ironic reversal of the master/slave relationship, the black female slave becomes the oppressor of a white male infant, and the irony is intensified by the reader's awareness of the only power such a figure *can* exercise to brutally pervert the nurturing relationship between mother and baby. Finally obliterating his mocking difference from her and thus reconciling herself to him, she strangles the infant and buries him in the forest: 'Earth, 'twixt me and my baby, strewed, – / All, changed to black earth, – nothing white, – / A dark child in the dark!' (lines 184–6).

Raped, flogged, a cursing, bleeding figure who finally jumps from the rock in a dreadful parody of the liberation achieved by white pilgrims as they stepped on to this same rock, she is Barrett Browning's wounded woman taken to the extremes of figuration. Leaping, she cries 'I am floated along, as if I should die / Of liberty's exquisite pain.' Lacking the racial status and class meaning that makes Marian Erle appealing to Romney Leigh, and lacking an Aurora Leigh to nurture and enfold her into a matriarchal household, she possesses the one thing that Barrett Browning could not, or would not, give Marian – a cursing, authentic voice empowered by rage.[4] If her later poem 'A Curse for a Nation' (1859) is any guide, Barrett Browning was reluctant to voice directly a woman's curse, to repeat in her own poetic persona the indictments of slavery so chillingly articulated in the earlier stanzas. Half-knowingly, it seems, she anticipates the dictum that was *Blackwood's Magazine*'s response to the poem: 'To bless and not to curse is woman's function' (87:494).

The poet-speaker resists instructions from an angel to write a 'Nation's curse' for America, claiming that she is bound in gratitude and love to that country and deeply grieved for her own:

> . . . 'Evermore
> My heart is sore
> For my own land's sins: for little feet
> Of children bleeding along the street:
>
> 'For parked-up honours that gainsay
> The right of way:
> For almsgiving through a door that is
> Not open enough for two friends to kiss:'
> (3: lines 17–24)

The prologue concludes with the poet's acquiescence in the angel's judgment that 'A curse from the depths of womanhood / Is very salt, and bitter, and good,' and in having the poet speaker agree to write this curse, Barrett Browning places her in an ambiguous position, a figure burdened with contending imperatives suggestive of those imposed upon women poets in a male-dominated culture. The angel issues a stern instruction, 'Write! Write a Nation's curse for me / And send it over the Western Sea.' The poet falters, three times refusing to write the poem, until overmastered by the logic of the angel. When she declares 'To curse, choose men. / For I, a woman, have only known / How the heart melts and tears run down', he responds that her curse will be that much more effective coming from her womanhood: 'So thus I wrote, and mourned indeed, / What all may read, / And thus, as was enjoined on me, / I send it over the Western sea' (lines 49–52).

The elaborate apology *for* the poem serves both to intensify the criticism articulated *in* the poem and to reveal an important ambiguity in Barrett Browning's career as woman poet engaged by politics: that is to say, the force of the curse and the immensity of the evil cursed are emphasised by a woman's inadequacy to the cursing task, and the American nation must be in a pretty bad way if a woman's curse is needed. The woman is not powerful enough to deliver the appropriate curse and yet *too* powerful to be doing such a thing. It seems to me that important questions relating to the definition of a woman's poetic voice in the Victorian period, to Barrett Browning's affiliation with a male poetic tradition, and to her chosen ratification of conservative political thought, are raised by this poem. Possessing no sustaining female poetic tradition, from where does the Victorian woman poet derive her authority to speak? What are the suitable subjects for poetry written by women? Does the Victorian woman poet possess the intellectual strength to perform strong political criticism? Enacting a scene of male authority and female obedience which recalls Harriet Martineau's subaltern status, Barrett Browning's female poet can perform a male function when 'enjoined' to do so by a male voice.

Somewhat ironically, then, a recurrent emphasis of the political poetry written by a woman poet 'authorized' by a male voice and affiliated with male poetic practice is a plea for liberation. Slaves must be freed from oppression, children from exploitation, nations from foreign domination, and society from the injurious, materialistic, middle-class ideologies that have created the 'social cleft' and 'defiled' a once heroic culture. What then of women, whether they be poets 'authorized' by male angels or transformed by Barrett Browning into metaphors of imprisonment? If, in a certain sense, English society is symbolically raped, if the Italian motherland is brutally penetrated and exploited by Austrian imperial forces, if raped working-class women symbolise careless exploitation of the poor, how do we characterise Barrett Browning's sexual politics? How does she view woman's actual experience when she is not employing it as metaphor? It would seem that conservative politics not only led her to excoriate the middle class for its materialism; she also believed that most women are intellectually inferior to most men and that woman's art must be made the attendant of patriarchy. As I shall now argue, Elizabeth Barrett Browning's comments about women and her rhapsodic closing of *Aurora Leigh* must dislodge much of the feminist meaning recently read into her career.

# 8

# Woman's Art as Servant of Patriarchy: the Vision of *Aurora Leigh*

One of the most vexed questions raised by feminist literary criticism is the degree to which women writers may be said to possess a voice of their own. Reduced to its fundamentals, the question is twofold: is there such a thing as a women's language, and if there is, what is the relationship between that language and the one employed by those who, in one way or another, have possessed the social and cultural power to create the language against which, and within which, women may be said to define their own? If women writers have worked within the context of male-dominated systems of discourse, then how is women's discourse to be defined? Is it, for example, to be discovered in symbolic forms which betray, even in the texts most consciously propitiative of male authority, an unconscious and angry subversion of dominant linguistic modes? These are large, and at this developed point in feminist literary criticism, rather obvious questions, yet they are clearly related to my examination of the ways in which women intellectuals in the Victorian period create and understand their own literary and intellectual performances.

Despite the conflicts I have identified in Harriet Martineau's career, women's language itself is never an explicit issue for her: she never consciously employed imagery related to female experience, and although she wrote extensively about women's lives, she rarely paid attention to herself *writing* as a woman. It is otherwise with Elizabeth Barrett Browning. As I have argued, she models her poetic and intellectual career upon traditionally male lines, yet the work most fully expressing her aesthetic and political beliefs is the poetic narrative of a woman writer whose experience is rendered through bold imagery associated with female experience. For that reason, it has become a provocative text for feminist critics engaged in the debate about women's language: it is also a text whose eventual

143

dedication of the woman poet to a life of social and political service seems to present a contradiction between liberal feminism and patriarchal attitudes. In my view, however, the sexual politics of *Aurora Leigh* are coherent with *all* of Barrett Browning's conservative politics in general.

Cora Kaplan's reading of the poem, informed by supple discussion of Barrett Browning's place in the tradition of nineteenth-century women writers, interprets *Aurora Leigh* as a revolutionary text: 'In spite of its conventional happy ending, it is possible to see it as contributing to a feminist theory of art which argues that women's language, precisely because it has been suppressed by patriarchal societies, re-enters discourse with a shattering revolutionary force, speaking all that is repressed and forbidden in human experience' (Introduction to *'Aurora Leigh' with Other Poems*, p. 11). My reservations about this aspect of Kaplan's reading rest on an interrogation of the ahistorical assumption that there *is* such a thing as 'women's language', a system of communication inherently available to women and not to men and unmolested by the social and cultural forces that create language itself – forces, indeed, which actually create (and discipline) women as a separate sex. In arguing that the language of a subjugated class (women) have been 'suppressed by patriarchal societies', Kaplan tends to bypass obvious, dialectical points about language, culture, and society.

At the risk of rehearsing the unnecessary, it seems to me essential to point out that if language is in some sense 'made' by culture and society, and if culture and society have been controlled by patriarchy, then any language 'suppressed' by these patriarchal formations must, to whatever degree and in whatever form one wants to argue, also be controlled by the hegemonic structures of patriarchy. This is not to question the challenging vitality of Barrett Browning's language and imagery in *Aurora Leigh*. But whether such language and imagery originate in a conscious, liberal feminism or in repressed revolutionary impulses which find expression in mediated symbolism, is less relevant to my overall examination of women's intellectual activity in a male-dominated culture, than a consideration of whether this language and imagery are implicitly 'authorized' by the formations they may be said to subvert. Women's language may indeed be subversive, may indeed speak 'all that is repressed and forbidden' by a dominant culture, as Kaplan suggests. But in its subversion, in its speaking of the 'repressed and forbidden', it also speaks the hegemony of the cultural and social formations which repress and forbid. The feasibility of political action through linguistic subversion is not the nub of my disagreement with Kaplan and others, and neither do I consider feminist criticism futile because it is necessarily complicit in the patriarchal formations enabling its existence. Rather, I want to deny the essentialist integrity of something labelled 'women's language', and also to submit that, if anything, this language would be cultivated by patriarchy, rather than supressed by it. A language which 'speaks' the confinement of women to domestic space, to their own world of female mysteries, to speaking a language of the body, of feelings and of community, is surely a language of little threat to male social and cultural power.[1]

Cora Kaplan also believes that Barrett Browning is chronically opposed to the realistic portrayal of working-class characters, that she emphasises 'radical distinctions' between social classes, and that her 'vicious picture of the rural and urban poor' bespeaks 'painful contradictions in a liberal feminist position on art or politics' (ibid., p. 11). Putting aside for the moment the question of whether Barrett Browning is, indeed, liberal or feminist, it seems to me that Kaplan's judgement is itself a discriminatory contradiction: one cannot praise Barrett Browning's employment of women's language and condemn her unsympathetic reification of the working classes into types. The postulation of women's language is, itself, a form of reification. In a synthesising assessment of Barrett Browning's sexual politics, Kaplan finally claims that because she centres 'the woman as speaker-poet' who replaces 'all male prophets' and because this figure 'dominates the symbolic language of the poem', *Aurora Leigh* dynamically confronts patriarchal attitudes (p. 35). *Aurora Leigh* is certainly confrontational: its enemy, however, is not patriarchy but the middle-class materialism which found a convenient ally in patriarchal formations.[2] Barrett Browning's political thought is essentialist and conservative: women, the working classes, the intellectual, the poet – all possess intrinsic qualities that must be liberated from their confinement by the bonds of mercantilism and competitive individualism.

As an essentialist in sexual politics, Barrett Browning unequivocally ratified the concepts of 'masculine' and 'feminine' thought: after the death of Margaret Fuller, she evaluated the bulk of her writings as 'quite inferior to what might have been expected from so masculine an intellect' (*L.EBB/DO*, p. 32). To speak of a masculine intellect evidently presupposes a feminine one, and as far as one can judge from Barrett Browning's letters and poetry, the feminine is inferior. Harriet Martineau is consistently praised by Barrett Browning for the 'male' qualities of her mind, and the following remarks about her fellow-invalid, addressed to an old friend in 1844, reveal Barrett Browning's sanction of the patriarchal allocation of men and women into categories of strong and weak thinkers: 'No case of a weak-minded woman and a nervous affection; but of the most manlike woman in the three kingdoms – in the best sense of man – a woman gifted with admirable fortitude, as well as exercised in high logic, a woman of sensibility and of imagination certainly, but apt to carry her reason unbent wherever she sets her foot; given to utilitarian philosophy and the habit of logical analysis' (*L*.EBB, 1:196–7). The model for intellectual superiority is the conventionally male one: Martineau is not nervous, possesses fortitude, and exercises the power of logical reasoning. When Barrett Browning wrote to H. S. Boyd that Martineau is 'the most logical intellect of the age, for a woman', she believed – with her contemporaries – that it was unusual for a woman to be logical (*L*.EBB, 1:225). In the Victorian discourse of sex and gender, logic is a male property, just as nurturance is a female one. Barrett Browning's employment of imagery long associated with women's experience must be located within the context of her entire sexual politics; that is to say, within that entangling matrix of sex, gender, and intelligence which determined Barrett Browning's firm identification with male-dominated modes of political thought and literary production.

She believed woman the intellectual inferior of man, emphatically announcing herself not a 'very strong partizan on the Rights-of-Woman-side of the argument . . . I believe that, considering men and women in the mass, there IS an *inequality* of intellect, and that it is proved by the very state of things of which gifted women complain; and more than proved by the manner in which their complaint is received by their own sisterhood' (*L*.EBB/M, 3:81). In this tautological denigration of female intellectual power, women are proved inferior by their record, which implies that if they *were* intellectually powerful, then feminists would have nothing to complain of. The manner in which feminists complain confirms woman's intellectual inferiority. The actual constraints placed upon the lives of Victorian women, the necessity of fitting female desire for intellectual autonomy to the shapes of male cultural authority, tend to be evaded or ignored in Barrett Browning's sexual politics.

For example, that need for women to be educated in which Martineau so strongly believed (if only so women might assent rationally to their subjugation) is of little interest to her: she confided to Robert Browning that women have 'minds of quicker movement, but less power and depth' than men; 'there is a natural inferiority of mind in women – of the intellect . . . the history of art and of genius testifies to this fact openly'. She made no secret of her dislike of everything to do with 'women and their mission' (her terms) and, as she confessed to Browning, early in her career she relinquished whatever interest she may have had in 'the Martineau-doctrines of equality' (*L*.RB/EBB, 1:116, 357, 373).[3]

Before her marriage to Robert Browning, Elizabeth Barrett made it clear that she shared his highly ambiguous assessment of women's intellectual and artistic capabilities. In a complex strategy of praise and criticism, Browning deems women too good to be in Parliament, implicitly too delicate for participation in the privileged rough and tumble of Westminster, and in late June of 1846, wrote to Elizabeth Barrett that it would be 'exquisitely absurd . . . essentially retrograde a measure' for Harriet Martineau's call for female members of Parliament to become reality: 'Parliament seems no place for originating, creative minds – but for the second-rate minds influenced by and bent on working out the results of these – and the most efficient qualities for such a purpose are confessedly found oftener with men than with women' (*L*.RB/EB, 2:280). This is one form of the insidious praise of women constituting Victorian deification and degradation of the 'softer sex.' Parliamentary practice calls for 'second-rate minds', practical rather than 'originating, creative' ones: men are more likely to possess these practical second-rate minds than women, which seems to score one for the female side, but such praise also implies that women are inadequate to sustained, administrative work. As Barrett Browning's response to the enjoining angel in 'A Curse for a Nation' suggests, women are both too good and not good enough to do a man's work of confrontational political criticism. Woman is an iconised figure of contradiction, the excessively inscribed portrait of Aurora's mother which she interprets as 'Abhorrent, admirable, beautiful / Pathetical, or ghastly, or grotesque', depending on what she has been reading. Elizabeth Barrett replied to Browning's views of women and Parliament by declaring that not only do women lack the physical strength for such work (which Browning had also suggested), but they 'have not instruction, capacity, wholeness of intellect enough' to be in Parliament. Admittedly, this is a woman writing to the man she would marry in less than three months, and her letters in this period of their correspondence are more concerned with the joys and difficulties of their romance than with sexual politics. However, the statement that women lack the 'instruction, capacity, wholeness of intellect' to participate in the political life of their country is not the statement of a woman on her way to confronting patriarchy, nor is it pregnant with the promise of 'speaking all that is repressed and forbidden in human experience', which is how Kaplan reads *Aurora Leigh*. Rather, it seems to me, this statement reveals how Barrett Browning complicitly elaborated the patriarchal deprecation of women's minds.

Rarely disclosing female resentment of male cultural, social, and political authority, Barrett Browning's sexual politics, then, are essentialist and conservative. It is surprising, therefore, to discover, how fervently she admired George Sand.[4] In 1844, she addressed two sonnets to Sand, 'A Desire' and 'A Recognition', but despite the virtual adoration of a woman notoriously defiant of convention, what Barrett Browning desired for Sand and what she recognised in her, affirm the essentialist views characterising her sexual politics.

The desire is that Sand, an androgynous figure ('Thou large-brained woman and large-hearted man'), should transcend the 'applauded circus' of her literary performance. Sand's 'tumultuous senses' are likened to lions, a simile which associates her roaring vitality with male aggressiveness: the leonine, uproarious senses almost overwhelm the defiant 'moans' of Sand's soul, which, by virtue of Barrett Browning's dualistic division of Sand into gyno-brained and andro-hearted figure, may be associated with a female mind/spirit. Barrett Browning's desire for Sand emerges as a plea for her to amaze her enthralled audience with a flight to sublime womanhood, vanquishing in this symbolic battle of male senses and female soul, that part of Sand which has been dominant – and dominant only through a physical power:

> . . . that thou to woman's claim
> And man's mightst join beside the angel's grace
> Of a pure genius sanctified from blame,
> Till child and maiden pressed to thine embrace
> To kiss upon thy lips a stainless fame
> (2: lines 10–14)

The 'recognition' of the second sonnet is that of Sand as 'True genius, but true woman!' Sand has attempted to mask her womanhood, to deny her woman's nature with 'manly scorn'. Yet a cry which evokes the female 'moan' of the first sonnet betrays Sand's womanhood: 'that revolted cry / Is sobbed in by a woman's voice forlorn', and again Sand must ascend to a higher stage where her essential womanhood, having been self-acknowledged, will be dissolved 'on the heavenly shore / Where unincarnate spirits purely aspire!' In the first sonnet, Sand will sprout two pinions 'white as wings of swan', generated by that part of her separate from the leonine senses, which will carry her upwards to a sanctified throne of womanly fame. In the second sonnet the beat of her 'woman-heart' will generate her ascension:

> . . . and while before
> The world thou burnest in a poet-fire,
> We see they woman-heart beat evermore
> Through the large flame. Beat purer, heat, and higher,
> Till God unsex thee on the heavenly shore
> Where incarnate spirits purely aspire!
>
> (2: lines 9–14)

The first sonnet moves from denial to recognition of womanhood: the second from denial to recognition, and then to God's eventual 'unsexing', which would suggest that the eventual transcendence of all worldly taxonomies cannot be achieved without self-acknowledgement of one's essential being. Transcendence of the social, material self is the privilege of those who recognise a paradox – the social, material self originates in a power which is *not* social or material.

The sonnets also evoke Barrett Browning's recurrent preoccupation with the imagery of ascension, particularly apparent in 'The Soul's Travelling', where the poet manifests his greatest power in a paradoxical loss of self-awareness that assists his ascension to God's throne. Although inspired by Barrett Browning's enduring admiration of a woman who brilliantly flouted dominant nineteenth-century ideologies of sex and gender, the Sand sonnets are essentialist in doctrine: they postulate a 'pure' womanhood, unstained and innate, and they express conservative and traditional ideologies of woman's power and her potential for artistic self-expression.

If it is difficult to discover in these sonnets a feminist politics, it *is* fair to say that Aurora Leigh's tart indictment of the education foisted on her by her aunt expresses female scorn. In a satiric interrogation of the subjects thought suitable for women's minds, Barrett Browning shows Aurora acquiring a jumble of useless information and social skills designed to make her a desirable commodity in the marriage market. She learns the 'collects and the catechism', a 'complement of classic French', a 'little algebra', the 'internal laws of the Burmese empire'. And she is educated in the conventional male views of female intellectual ability: 'I read a score of books on womanhood / To prove, if women do not think at all, / They may teach thinking' (I: 428–30). In terms of Barrett Browning's sexual politics, however, it is significant that in the angry arguments between Aurora and Romney about woman's contribution to remedying social evil and her potential for producing great art, Aurora is more contemptuous of a male inability to feel than she is of male cultural authority. The angry woman utters the familiar attack on male insensitivity. It is not Romney's politics that Aurora really objects to when she refuses his proposal, not his desire to fit women into the convenient social slots of wife, nurse, and helper, but rather that he is emotionally barren, as figuratively blind to Aurora's feelings as he is literally blind to her face at the end of the poem. To a sexually vibrant Aurora on her twentieth-birthday morning, Romney is a cold fish. Aurora wants poetic fame, but she also wants sexual fulfilment.

In London ten years later, professionally successful, even 'applauded' by that literary circus entertained by George Sand, Aurora muses on her solitary state. Praised by all the periodicals but bereft of physical love, she sits unhappily alone praying to God the Father / God the Artist, who understands her dilemma as woman poet. Despite a certain daring intimation of ungratified female sexual desire in these lines, they are deeply conventional in the heartfelt praise of a patriarchal deity. This may be 'women's language' that Aurora speaks, but it speaks woman's service to male authority:

> O my God, my God,
> O supreme Artist, who as sole return
> For all the cosmic wonder of Thy Work,
> Demandest of us just a word . . . a name,
> 'My father!' thou hast knowledge, only thou,

How dreary 'tis for women to sit still,
On winter nights by solitary fires,
And hear the nations praising them far off,
Too far! ay, praising our quick sense of love,
Our very heart of passionate womanhood,
Which could not beat so in the verse without
Being present also in the unkissed lips
And eyes undried because there's none to ask
The reason they grew moist.

(v. 435–48)

With a play upon the passionate beat of a woman's heart and the metre of her verse, Aurora implies that artistic creation is unfulfilling to the woman poet unless she is sexually loved, kissed upon the lips. This is not to argue that Barrett Browning should have made *Aurora Leigh* a feminist polemic for the rewards of a celibate intellectual life, or that she should have disdained the Christian beliefs central in her life and in her culture. What I am trying to get at here is her ratification of a deep-rooted foundation of Victorian patriarchy – women serve men, and men and women together serve God. The making of poetry and the making of love are associated to show that woman's poetry is created from her own sexuality, indeed that poetry and sexuality are part of the 'cosmic wonder' that is God's 'work'. Having heard Marian's story, Aurora assumes that Romney has married Lady Waldemar. She regrets her own refusal of him, for in so doing she has refused God's 'cosmic wonder' of making poetry through love, and love through poetry: 'Now, if I had been a woman, such / As God made women, to save men by love, – / By just my love I might have saved this man, / And made a nobler poem for the world / Than all I have failed in' (VII. 184–88). Questioning her womanhood, her failure to 'save' Romney through sexual love, she denigrates her literary achievement by believing that to have 'written' Romney in marriage she would have made a 'noble' text far superior to any she has produced. She then concludes that he is lost, 'And, by my own fault, his empty house / Sucks in, at this same hour, a wind from hell / To keep his heart cold, make his casements creak / For ever to the tune of plague and sin' (VII. 190–3). Unmade into a 'noble' poem by Aurora, that is to say not sexually loved by her, Romney's body is like an empty house, sucking in an evil wind. She has figured herself as passionately warm, her heart and verse beating with desire:

Romney, also alone, is made cold by the dissonant 'tune' of Lady Waldemar's evil; hers is a cold sexuality manifested in those marble breasts designed for display, not warm nurturance. Romney's body/house 'creaks' where Aurora's body and verse beat with the pulse of female desire.

Having evoked her own emotional life in vibrant, symbolically sanguine terms as she spills her life's blood into her poetry, and having made Romney a frozen theorist by deploying cold, white imagery, Aurora suggests that women possess a quality which permits them transcendence of the symbolised dualism: they can undo their iconised fragmentation through a legendary female ability to relinquish identity to the more powerful sex. While explicitly praising woman's ability to transcend ugly, aggressive self, Aurora actually perpetuates the unfortunate myth that women lack a strong sense of individual identity: we women, says Aurora, 'yearn to lose ourselves / And melt like white pearls in another's wine'; man 'seeks to double himself by what he loves, / And makes his drink more costly by our pearls' (v. 1078–81). At the end of the poem Aurora dissolves the contradictions of red and white imagery by melting the purity of her art and sexuality into Romney's vision, and Romney, in his turn, ceases to appropriate women's feelings to his male politics. The rosy, Florentine dawn that concludes the poem anticipates the forthcoming expression of Aurora's sexuality in marriage with Romney and a dissolution of his emotional anaesthesia through that union.

The closing lines of *Aurora Leigh* constitute a densely allusive hymn to work, sexual love, and the vision of a new city built from the consummation of man and woman, intellect and feeling, blindness and vision. It may very well be that Barrett Browning's eroticised imagery in the poem and the daring references to female sexuality *do* signify an unrecognised defiance of male cultural authority that can only be expressed through symbolic language; but the appropriation of Aurora's art and sexuality by male power is executed with such certainty that whatever defiance of androcentric authority we may discern in the poem is overwhelmed by the orgasmic reconciliations of male and female, politics and art, material and spiritual. Romney praises 'the love of wedded souls', which is the earthly counterpart of God's love:

> Sweet shadow rose, upon the water of life,
> Of such a mystic substance, Sharon gave

A name to! human, vital, fructuous rose,
Whose calyx holds the multitude of leaves,
Loves filial, loves fraternal, neighbour-loves
And civic – all fair petals, all good scents,
All reddened, sweetened from one central Heart.

(IX. 884–90)

All political and social action will originate in and be sweetened from their marriage, from the rose of sexual love consummated and celebrated in the Song of Solomon: Judaic wedding song, Christian doctrine, social action, all centre in the rose image which evokes the vibrant twenty-year-old Aurora who feels the June within her, 'rosebuds reddening where the calyx split', and the present, mature Aurora, a ripe and blooming flower. And Aurora is also the radiant light of the morning star, destined for tutelage by the darkened, weary, blind Romney in her contribution to their joint work. In terms which express Barrett Browning's vision of woman's art as servant of patriarchy, and in a hortative structure reminiscent of the male angel and the woman poet in 'A Curse for a Nation', Aurora is instructed by Romney to become the privileged, witnessing poet of Barrett Browning's aesthetic discourse:

. . . Art's a service, – mark:
A silver key is given to thy clasp,
And thou shalt stand, unwearied, night and day,
And fix it in the hard, slow-turning wards,
To open, so, that intermediate door
Betwixt the different planes of sensuous form
And form insensuous, that inferior men
May learn to feel on still through these to those,
And bless thy ministration. The world waits
For help.

(IX. 915–24)

The artist labours to unlock doors of perception, to mediate between material and spiritual 'planes', and the term 'wards' indicates not only the mechanisms of a lock, but also implies places of confinement of the individual to the stifling materialistic ideologies which Barrett Browning despised. The poet's hard function is to trace the first writings of that 'old scripture' which inscribe a more spiritual existence.

Aurora is exhorted by Romney 'to press the clarion on thy

woman's lips . . . And blow all class-walls level at Jericho's'. Sandra
Gilbert and Susan Gubar read these closing lines as a revolutionary
fantasy too dangerous to be articulated by Aurora, and they suggest
Romney's sanctification of revolution through marriage is a severe
compromise of Barrett Browning's own politics: the 'millenarian
program Romney outlines is not, of course, his own; it is the
revolutionary fantasy of his author – and of her heroine, his
wife-to-be, discreetly transferred from female to male lips'. That the
programme is revolutionary is undeniable, and Gilbert and Gubar
are clearly correct in noting that all must be made new, even though
'a divine patriarch, aided by a human patriarch and his helpmeet' is
doing the renovation (*The Madwoman in the Attic*, pp. 579–80). Yet
what is to be made new, and the means of making it new, are figured
in highly traditional, even reactionary terms which, if placed in the
context of Barrett Browning's sexual politics, make the ending of
*Aurora Leigh* less a compromise than a fulfilment of her
'revolutionary fantasy'. It is important to examine the lines which
follow Romney's call for Aurora to level class barriers: she must do
so in order that all men and all women may be flattened to an
equality of subjugation to God's will so they might ascend, like
George Sand, to an 'unsexing' of their incarnate state. To be sure,
this is revolutionary, but not, it seems to me, in any way that
suggests a compromise of Barrett Browning's beliefs. Men's souls
'here assembled on earth's flats' must 'get them to some purer
eminence':

> . . . The world's old,
> But the old world waits the time to be renewed,
> Toward which, new hearts in individual growth
> Must quicken and increase to multitude
> In new dynasties of the race of men;
> Developed whence, shall grow spontaneously
> New churches, new oeconomies, new laws,
> Admitting freedom, new societies
> Excluding falsehood; he shall make all new.
>                                        (IX. 941–9)

New churches precede new economic systems and new laws in this
taxonomy of Christian revolution: after all Romney has already
decreed that there must be 'fewer programmes . . . fewer systems':
'Less mapping out of masses to be saved, / By nations or by sexes!

Fourier's void, / And Comte absurd, – and Cabet puerile' (IX. 867-9). This is Romney's *and* Aurora's *and* Barrett Browning's vision – coherent with all her politics, and, to whatever degree it might be seen as revolutionary or feminist, a vision inspired first and always by a patriarchal God who demands hard work from his woman poets. Work is a 'key' word at the end of *Aurora Leigh* – the literal key enabling the poet to unlock the symbolic wards that restrain man from seeing connections between 'sensuous' and 'insensuous' world. The woman poet labours in service to God, mankind, and man.

'I have *worked* at poetry – it has not been with me revery, but art. As the physician and lawyer work at their several professions, so have I, and so do I, apply to mine' (*L.*EBB/RHH, p. 263). Writing to Horne in 1844, Barrett Browning insists upon her professional status as working poet. In one of the 1844 Poems, 'A Fourfold Aspect', the speaker traces a child's fearful understanding of its mortality, gleaned from reading of the death of heroes. So awful are these stories that the child wakes shrieking in the night and spends its days mournfully preoccupied with the dead. The poem turns upon a lesson the child must learn: death leads to Heaven and in the mortal meantime man must pray, think, learn, and work: 'Work: make clear the forest-tangles / Of the wildest stranger-land' (3: lines 119-20). This imperative originates in the Victorian preoccupation with clearing the wilderness, that renovation of the wasteland imagined, for example, in 'The Coming of Arthur', the first of Tennyson's *Idylls of the King*, and figured in these lines: 'And so there grew great tracts of wilderness, / Wherein the beast was ever more and more, / But man was less and less, till Arthur came.'[5] And when Arthur does come, he drives out the 'heathen', slays the beasts, fells the forest 'letting in the sun'. Tennyson's Camelot is one version of the Victorians' New Jerusalem, the city built from barbarism, darkness, and despair. Earlier in the poem when she indigantly refuses Romney's offer of marriage and partnership in practice of his despised social theory, Aurora declares 'I too have my vocation, – work to do . . . Most serious work, most necessary work / As any of the economists' (II. 455-60). As Arthur clears the wilderness, so Aurora dedicates her poetry to the establishment of a renewed social order. And in an appropriation of Romney's language of social action, she says the artist must 'keep up open roads / Betwixt the seen and unseen' (II: 468-9). The actual social and political action of improving sanitation, extending the railway, clearing the slums, creating the empire, becomes a metaphor for poetic action.

'Blessed is he who has found his work; let him ask no other blessedness', thunders Carlyle in *Past and Present*: he who works, makes 'instead of pestilential swamp, a green fruitful meadow with its clear flowing stream' (p. 197). Women must become 'worthy wives and mothers of a mighty nation of workers' announces Charles Kingsley to his female audience at Queen's College in 1848. Barrett Browning's enduring insistence on the cultural function of the poet intellectual *in* the world originates in this imperative to work: the poet clears a symbolic path, unlocks a symbolic door, dissolves the encrustations of debasing materialism covering man's soul. Carlyle's Gospel of Work is the good news elaborated by Aurora and Romney at the end of the poem. Men, women, creatures all, must work: 'Let us be content, in work', is repeated with slight variation in a hymn of praise sung throughout the night as Aurora and Romney await the new day. Aurora describes Romney crying out the litany which has united them:

> And then calm, equal, smooth with weights of joy,
> His voice rose, as some chief musician's song
> Amid the old Jewish temple's Selah-pause,
> And bade me mark how we two met at last
> Upon this moon-bathed promontory of earth,
> To give up much on each side, then take all.
> 'Beloved!' it sang, 'we must be here to work;
> And men who work can only work for men,
> And, not to work in vain, must comprehend
> Humanity and so work humanly,
> And raise men's bodies, still by raising souls,
> As God did first.'
>
> (IX. 843–54)

The poem ends in reconciliation of male and female, material and spiritual, vocation and desire, in much the same way as the ending of Tennyson's 'The Princess', where a new beginning marks a new Eden, and where men and women are 'distinct as individualities' yet so harmoniously in tune with a new order that 'Then comes the statelier Eden back to men'. The Prince instructs Ida to 'Look up, and let thy nature strike on mine, / Like yonder morning on the blind half-world . . . O we will walk this world, / Yoked in all exercise of noble end, / And so thro' those dark gates across the wild / That no man knows' (*Poems of Tennyson*, part 7, lines 330–42). In both poems the dawn signals a new beginning and chastened lovers dedicate themselves to clearing the wilderness and to liberating man (and woman) from confinement to materialistic ideology. As Aurora is married to Romney and female art wedded to male socialist politics, the novel-poem *Aurora Leigh* becomes a form-giving epithalamium for the essentialist sexual politics formed primarily through Barrett Browning's very early apprenticeship to male modes of intellectual training and aesthetic practice. In this poem we hear a woman's voice speaking patriarchal discourse – boldly, passionately, and without rancour.

In the twenty-fourth of Barrett Browning's *Sonnets from the Portuguese*, which were composed during the years 1847 to 1850 and published with some reluctance on her part in the latter year, she rejoices in the radiant enclosure of her marriage:

> Let the world's sharpness, like a clasping knife,
> Shut in upon itself and do no harm
> In this close hand of Love, now soft and warm;
> And let us hear no sound of human strife,
> After the click of the shutting. Like to life –
> I lean upon thee, Dear, without alarm,
> And feel as safe as guarded by a charm,
> Against the stab of worldlings, who, if rife,
> Are weak to injure.
>
> (3: lines 1–9)

The love she and Browning feel for each other closes up the wounding knife of the world: the sword which has pierced Christ's body and the knife which has symbolically severed the social flesh, are drawn back, clicked shut, quite simply, by love. But the sword and the knife are also defeated, clicked shut, by poetry itself: as these sonnets give form to her passionate feelings for Robert Browning, so all her poetry gives form to her intellectual life and to her politics. Enjoying no sustaining sense of attachment to a female literary tradition, self-educated in conventionally male disciplines, literally barred by illness from a female intellectual community, she aligns herself with a poetic tradition celebrating a privileged relationship of the poet to God and figuring the poet as enjoined by that relationship to be active in the world. As a Gramscian traditional intellectual, she integrates poetry and politics in conservative criticism of values she associated with the English middle class: materialism, mercantilism, and aggressive individualism. Dear to the popular Victorian imagination as delicate 'poetess', she actively contributed to the Victorian intellectual discourse seeking an understanding of a changing world and the place of poetry in that world. Less politically prominent in society than Harriet Martineau and less renowned as a woman intellectual than George Eliot, in actuality she was a good deal more political and a good deal more intellectual than literary history has imagined.

# Part Three

# George Eliot: the Authority of a Woman Intellectual

'What name do you think I have been baptized withal? Rather a learned pun, Deutera, which *means* second and *sounds* a little like daughter.'

(Mary Ann Evans to
Mrs Charles Bray, 8 November 1843)

# 9

# Iconic Sage

In *The Mill on the Floss*, when Maggie Tulliver first enters the study of Tom's tutor, the Revd Walter Stelling, she cries, 'O, what books! . . . How I should like to have as many books as that!' In a sharp governance of such desire, the less than stellar Mr Stelling has this to say about intelligent little girls: 'They've a great deal of superficial cleverness; but they couldn't go far into anything. They're quick and shallow.' It is instructive to place Mr Stelling's comment alongside a not untypical entry from George Eliot's Journal, recorded for 13 June 1855:

> Began Part IV of Spinoza's 'Ethics'. Began to read Cumming, for article in the *Westminster*. We are reading in the evenings now Sydney Smith's letters, Boswell, Whewell's 'History of Inductive Science', 'The Odyssey', and occasionally Heine's 'Reisebilder'. I began the second book of the 'Iliad', in Greek, this morning.[1]

A day in the life of Marian Evans, woman intellectual, clearly puts Mr Stelling in his sexist place: she not only got to 'have' more books than he could have read, let alone understood, she also got to write them, garnering in the process a harvest of critical tributes to her mind. Of the many contemporary laudations of Eliot's fertile intellect, that of Henry James is, perhaps, the most finely appreciative of a woman who was enabled to direct her sharp intelligence into gratifying work. In reviewing *Middlemarch*, James points to the 'constant presence of thought, of generalizing instinct, of *brain*, in a word' behind the novel, and in his essay on Cross's *Life*, he pays passionate tribute to 'the magnificent mind, vigorous, luminous, and eminently sane', to Eliot's 'intellectual vigor, her immense facility, her exemption from cerebral lassitude'.[2] Despite certain disappointments which Eliot dealt to her critics (for some she lamentably failed to repeat the delightful rural realism of *Adam Bede* and for others she rather too scrupulously showed nineteenth-century men and women subject to determinative webs of heredity and environment), she enjoyed within her lifetime an iconic status as intellectual novelist. For us, the pseudonym 'George Eliot' is virtually identical with the vigour and accomplishment of woman's mind in the nineteenth century.

At this point in literary criticism, 'George Eliot' is a well-established institution unto itself. Whether viewed from the perspectives of intellectual history, theories of fiction, or feminist criticism, Eliot looms as a monolithic figure; as sibylline sage, extensively celebrated and finely dissected in all her eminent Victorianism and incipient Modernism, she powerfully signalises achieved female intellectual ambition in the Victorian period. Yet as many of her critics have noted, her writings about intelligent women often betray the conflict between female intelligence and male authority we see traced in the desire of Maggie Tulliver and the judgement of Mr Stelling. In my view, this conflict is present almost everywhere in Eliot's work. From the brutal literalism of one of her first pieces of fiction (*Janet's Repentance*) where Robert Dempster physically disciplines a wife whose 'superior education' and refined mind led her to choose marriage to an ambitious lawyer rather than employment as a governess, through the essays that analyse the contributions of women's writing to European culture, to the final collision between Gwendolen Harleth's scintillating intelligence and the male worlds of social and moral governance represented by Henleigh Grandcourt and Daniel Deronda, Eliot describes, sometimes explicitly and sometimes not, compelling conflicts between the desires of intelligent women for autonomy and a male authority seeking to govern such desires. I shall argue that Eliot's delineations of this conflict, together with her varied dissolutions of it, are essential in understanding her intellectual career. As Eliot observes at the end of *Middlemarch*, Dorothea Brooke has struggled 'amidst the conditions of an imperfect social state': the curbing of female intellect by male authority is surely one of the most debilitating social imperfections Eliot either seeks to eradicate or to evade in her writings. That she so regularly returns to this conflict reveals a great deal about the career of a woman who achieved a remarkable degree of independence and recognition in the cultural formations of her time. Eliot's career tantalisingly reminds us of Maggie Tulliver's unhappy life in the sense that both novelist and female character possess sharp minds and desires for intellectual recognition, but where the novelist transforms herself from provincial young woman to metropolitan intellectual, she relegates her character to the rushing waters of the Floss.

Let me make it clear immediately that my approach to Eliot is not one that traces intellectual influences. The relationship to Eliot's thought of the philosophical and social theories of figures such as David Friedrich Strauss, Ludwig Feuerbach, Auguste Comte, and Herbert Spencer, to say nothing of the work of George Henry Lewes, has been so commandingly established that rather than re-presenting and re-citing these well-documented intellectual affiliations (except where they seem appropriate to my analysis), I shall be more concerned with Eliot's performance as a woman intellectual, the significance of her views about women's minds as expressed in her essays and letters, and the way in which she ambiguously represents intellectually ambitious women in her fiction.[3] Analysing Eliot's deployment of what Fredric Jameson terms 'strategies of containment', I shall trace her containment of a conflict both richly consistent with, and peculiarly at odds with, her own situation: the tension between woman's mind and male culture. Jameson suggests that when ideologies collide, when seemingly irreconcilable conflicts threaten formal coherence, a writer may manage such tension by relegating to another place what is incoherent, contradictory, even intolerable. As William Dowling usefully describes the process, a strategy of containment provides 'a way of achieving coherence by shutting out the truth about History' (*Jameson, Althusser, Marx*, p. 77).[4] In Eliot's writings about woman's mind and male culture, the topos where coherence is achieved does, indeed, exist outside history, outside time: there, woman possesses universal, atemporal, and inherent characteristics making her immune from the stifling, subjugating restraints of male-dominated culture and society.

Of the three important women thinkers examined in this study, Eliot is the one who most consciously 'made' herself *as* an intellectual. Her career is a narrative of self-creation, the story of a powerfully intelligent woman graced with an impressive ability to discipline and expand her intellect through sustained scholarly study. To the end of her writing life, Eliot directed her comprehensive mind across a wide scope of cultural, social, scientific, and political thought. Her reputation in literary history deservedly rests upon her work as a novelist, yet the range of her intellectual interests, the extent of her learning, and the fame she achieved as a brilliant woman in her own time, identify her pre-eminently *as* an intellectual whose reputation as novelist, essayist, reviewer, translator, and scholar is subsumed under this designation. Her profession is intellectual itself.

Her ambition, achievements, and fame do not, however, free Eliot from the conflicts inherent in the career of any intellectual woman in the Victorian period. If anything, because of her unparalleled success, Eliot's career displays a peculiarly high degree of conflict and contradiction. Her success, it seems to me, also leads us to expect more from her than we do from other Victorian women intellectuals; that is to say, her sexual politics disappoint in ways that the conservative androcentric views of Eliot's less talented female contemporaries do not. Unfairly and irrationally, we expect Eliot's learning, intelligence, and success to make her extra-resistant to her male-dominated culture. My discussion of Eliot's sexual politics, which follows analysis of her presence in Victorian culture as iconic sage, aims to avoid this unfair expectation and to balance an assessment of her androcentric thought with recognition of her necessary complicity with the culture enabling her success. In the sections of this chapter that deal with *Romola*, *Felix Holt, the Radical* and *The Mill on the Floss*, I suggest that the conflicts in Eliot's texts are sometimes so disjunctive that they lead to a confrontation of equally autonomous ideologies whose only dissolution seems to be an implicit cancellation of ideology itself. This dissolution leaves its fragmented trace in the form of subjugated female intelligence and Eliot exacts certain painful prices from her female characters in return for the cancellation of the structures of power and authority which restrain them.

The critical institution of 'George Eliot' was founded in Eliot's own lifetime, the cornerstone laid by Eliot herself, inventing herself as a woman intellectual, training herself to the life of the mind, and assimilating different structures of thought. Although she was similar to Martineau in her subjection to influential English middle-class beliefs and practices (even in her interrogation of them) and similar to Barrett Browning in her self-mythologisation as the intellectual who is witness to a morally deficient society, she did not view herself as performing work of 'auxiliary usefulness', nor as fulfilling an ancillary role in a culture dominated, for the most part, by men. Willing herself to believe in historical continuity uninterrupted by political change, persistently returning to the past in her fiction either to deny or to repair disjunctive rupture, Eliot transforms herself from industriously intelligent provincial girl to majestically sibylline moral voice. Refusing the ancillary role of organic intellectual who legitimates ideologies of a dominant social class, Eliot constructs an imperious, if sympathetic, persona in her novels and essays that interrogates English middle-class values. Through this interrogation, she generates herself as an intellectual belonging to Gramsci's category of traditional practice. And this is the canonised myth of George Eliot, both in her own time and in ours: the sagacious, cool presence peculiarly untainted by the vulgar business of the world, the 'magnificent' mind betraying and transcending sex and gender.

Paradoxically and predictably, however, from the moment of 'George Eliot's appearance in print, the issue of sex and gender intrudes itself upon almost all critical discussion of Eliot's work. Having adopted a male pseudonym to avoid the customary association of women writers with particular themes and to protect herself from potential criticism for her liberal writings in the *Westminster Review* and her co-habitation with a married man, Eliot found her work constantly evaluated in terms of its fidelity (or not) to 'female' or 'feminine' qualities. She is praised and blamed for writing like a woman – and for writing like a man. No wonder Mary Ann Evans decided to call herself 'George Eliot'.[5]

After the female authorship of *Adam Bede* became known the *Saturday Review* admitted that the novel had been 'generally accepted as the work of a man . . . it was thought to be too good for a woman's story'; the reviewer goes on to declare that it was 'with the usual pretty affectation of her sex' that the 'authoress' wanted 'to look on paper as much like a man as possible'. Here, Eliot seems to score one for both sexual sides by realising her understandable 'female' ambition to write like a man. In an otherwise complimentary evaluation of *The Mill on the Floss*, the *Westminster*'s anonymous reviewer associates the melodramatic events in Eliot fiction with some sort of primordial female time: they 'crop out of the rich culture of her mind, like the primitive rocks of an earlier world . . . are vestiges of a Titanic time, before the reign of the peaceful gods commenced'. Sex and gender are nowhere specific in this image, yet the 'peaceful gods' are surely Athenian, Apollonian ones, and the Titanic world was ruled as much by raging female forces as by male ones. In assessing the propriety of the Maggie Tulliver/Stephen Guest episode, the *Dublin University Magazine* delivered the first of its two attacks upon Eliot, notable in the almost twenty-five years of laudatory criticism she received in her lifetime: 'The lengthened treatment of a mystery so full of doubt and danger, by an Englishwoman writing for readers of both sexes, speaks as poorly for her good taste as the readiness wherewith a large-hearted girl yields up all her noblest scruples, her tenderest sympathies, to the paltry fear of seeming cruel in the eyes of a weak, unworthy tempter.' Author and character are brought dangerously close to being 'fallen' women in this invidious equation. 'The man never lived, I do believe, who could have done such a thing as this,' declares an outraged Swinburne, who believed Maggie was 'debased' by Stephen and the female novelist strangely infatuated with a character to whom any 'real' man would take a horsewhip.

Somewhat more dispassionately but in the same vein, Henry James, in an unsigned review in the *Nation*, compares Eliot to Maria Edgeworth and Jane Austen, finding Eliot 'stronger in degree than either of these writers. . . . She brings to her task a richer mind, but she uses it very much in the same way. With a certain masculine comprehensiveness which they lack, she is eventually a feminine – a delightfully feminine writer . . . George Eliot has the exquisitely good taste on a small scale, the absence of taste on a large (the vulgar plot of *Felix Holt* exemplifies this deficiency), the unbroken current of feeling and, we may add, of expression, which distinguish the feminine mind.' In praising her for improving upon the purely 'feminine' Edgeworth and Austen, James also faults her for not having enough of that 'masculine comprehensiveness'. As a last representative example of the Victorian critic's concern with Eliot's sex, the remarks of Richard Simpson, perhaps the most judicious of her critics, are particularly pertinent. Suggesting that 'she may be too far separated from the ordinary life of her sex to be a good judge of its relations', that the 'direct power and the celebrity of authorship may obscure and replace the indirect influence and calm happiness of domestic feminine life'. Simpson declares she has taken up a 'male position', that 'the male ideal becomes hers, – the ideal of power, – which, interpreted by her feminine heart and intellect, means the supremacy of passion in the affairs of the world'. Improperly for a woman, she desires power; moreover, because she can only imagine power in 'feminine' terms, most of her male characters are subjugated, in one way or another, by female passion. Simpson smartly puts Eliot in her 'feminine' place.[6]

After the publication of Cross's *Life* in 1885, the issues of sex and gender are submerged in the deified greyness of what David Carroll apty terms a 'lifeless silhouette'.[7] 'Female' and 'feminine' are subordinated by the terminology of sagehood and Eliot becomes sibylline – obviously still female, but by virtue of her 'magnificence' ascending to an androgynous zone. The myth of 'George Eliot' which was born in the sequestered precincts of the Priory (the London home of Eliot and Lewes for 17 years) gains vitality after her death as she is accorded an intellectual apotheosis. In his last discussion of Eliot's life and work, Henry James talks of the 'sanctity' of a visit to Eliot's drawing-room, of the 'atmosphere of stillness and concentration, something that suggested a literary temple'.[8] In this temple, Eliot was worshipped as an intellectual goddess, a mythical Athena with a Victorian woman's heart.

The myth of 'George Eliot', which began in her own time and in certain significant ways has continued to the present, dispels unsettling contradiction and buttresses established ways of thinking and feeling threatened by an intellectually powerful woman. Contemporary reviewers of Eliot's novels faced the unsettling conjunction of woman and mind, of second sex and intellectual prominence; preferring dualism to dialectic, they sought to untie the knot of 'feeling' and 'rationality' by labelling Eliot undeniably 'feminine' despite a certain 'masculine' quality of mind. Or, to reverse the dualistic reading, in celebrating Eliot as the masculine intellect dwelling at ease with feminine consciousness, as the powerful male mind in woman's weaker body, a male-dominated culture defends itself from a disruptive anomaly. Eliot, therefore, becomes iconic sage in her own lifetime, a process helped immeasurably through that sovereign narrative voice which retains sympathetic and omniscient understanding of individual moral failing.

My aim is to place her firmly on political and historical ground, to examine the strategies of containment she employed in managing the conflict between woman's mind and male authority in her writings. I want also to focus upon the related conflict between an ideology of free individualism sanctioned by the liberal, humanist circle to which she belonged, and the strong desire expressed in her fiction for a mythical pre-industrial world. It is female characters who often become metaphors for nostalgic conservatism, emblems of Eliot's residual desire (as a traditional intellectual) to affiliate herself with the land-owning classes in England rather than with the liberal, educated middle class which encouraged and eventually adored her. Yet these female characters are subversive in unexpected ways, yearning for the past rather than the future, often revolutionary in their wishes to overthrow cultural, social, and political structures founded on male middle-class values. Through these female characters Eliot expresses some of the conflict she experienced in creating for herself the authority of a woman intellectual. 'I am so tired of being set on a pedestal and expected to vent wisdom – I am only a poor woman,' she said to Georgianna Burne-Jones (Burne-Jones, *Memorials of Edward Burne-Jones*, 2:103–4). She was, however, complicit in her cultural apotheosis, necessarily collaborative with patriarchal discourse as proof of her iconised wisdom.

At the beginning of her career as George Eliot, Mary Ann Evans becomes, in a sense, twice male: the woman novelist adopts a male pseudonym, speaks from a specifically male narrative perspective, and, moreover, begins to sound the first chords of that wise voice resonating throughout her fiction. In *Janet's Repentance* the narrator laughs at his boyhood self in the Milby parish church 'appearing in coat-tails for the first time', observing that 'unimaginative boys find it difficult to recognize apostolical institutions in their developed form', and excusing himself with the aside that 'it is the way with us men in other crises that come a long while after confirmation'. As Eliot becomes more technically proficient, remedying such lapses of narrative coherence as we find in *Janet's Repentance* where the amazing ubiquity of the male narrator remains unjustified (he seems to be everywhere without invitation, including the Dempster household), the voice becomes less explicitly gender identified, while retaining the authority conventionally associated with male cultural power.

In the view of most of her critics, Eliot's narrative voice achieves its most sympathetic resonance in *Middlemarch*; according to Sandra Gilbert and Susan Gubar, the voice in that novel transcends 'gender distinctions' by virtue of its 'meditative, philosophical, humorous, sympathetic, moralistic, scientific' qualities. Such qualities, these critics assert, find their origin 'above and beyond the ordinary classifications of our culture' (*The Madwoman in the Attic*, p. 523). It seems to me, however, that the power to combine all these impressive attributes of mind in one narrative voice, the ability to unite a 'man's mind and woman's heart' (as Gilbert and Gubar describe it), is a power that originates in a cultural authority which in itself requires further analysis. The ability to perform an act of such synthesis, to bring male and female sensibilities together, comes from a confidence to speak about culture that in Victorian society tended to be enjoyed more by male than female intellectuals. And

assuming for a moment that Eliot herself believed she possessed a
'man's mind and woman's heart', which she united in her narrative
performances, then in believing this, she is complicit in an allocation
of intellect and feeling by sex and gender that must keep her very
much within those 'ordinary classifications' of culture to which
Gilbert and Gubar refer. My point is not to distinguish between
whether Eliot authentically feels this power to perform such
synthesising feats or whether she does an excellent job of mimicking
the authority to do so. I wish to emphasise her implicit choice of a
model of commanding narrative voice. She may bring her 'woman's
heart' to her 'male' work of knowing in *Middlemarch*, but the very act
of bringing them together bespeaks a cultural confidence acquired
through her self-fashioning as the male 'George Eliot'.

Feminist readings of Eliot come at the end of a century of criticism,
and the narrative of her reputation during that time frequently
confirms the strength of the myth she helped to create of and
for herself. In the most general terms, the reputation begins
with contemporary approbation only tempered by fears that
the 'femininity' might be overwhelmed by the 'masculine
comprehensiveness'; this praise, occasioned by the pleasing
confluence of brains and woman's body, continues after her death,
is in fact intensified by the sternly moral woman who emerges from
Cross's *Life*. However, late nineteenth-century swipes at Victorian
pieties knocked Eliot from her pedestal and she becomes a ridiculed
figure, a 'Pallas with prejudices and a corset'.[9] Twentieth-century
pre-feminist critical discussion of Eliot tends to treat her work as the
product of a great disembodied, genderless brain. Now in the 1980s,
the reputation is under revision by feminist critics, either unhappy
with Eliot's lack of feminist political action and her punitive
patronage of female characters or finding in her texts evidence of
angry subversion of dominant male modes of fictional discourse.

Leslie Stephen's critical biography, published in 1902 for the
*English Men of Letters* series, is an androcentric mid-point between
Victorian efforts to reconcile female feeling and male brain and
twentieth-century pre-feminist assessments of Eliot as a genderless
intellectual. In paying ambiguous tribute to Eliot's mind, Stephen
implicitly endorses the patriarchal readings which have preceded
his own; he concludes, in relieved fashion, that Eliot's creation of
male characters betrays her femininity: 'In spite of her learning and
her philosophy, George Eliot is always pre-eminently feminine'. As
he sees it, however hard Eliot tries to make Adam Bede definitively

'of the masculine gender', she cannot succeed because jealousy of good-looking women prohibits control of 'a kind of resentment with which the true woman contemplates a man unduly attracted by female beauty' (*George Eliot*, p. 74–5). The key phrases here, of course, are 'in spite of her learning and her philosophy' and 'true woman'. In Stephen's view, essentialist womanhood triumphs, vanquishing the hard-earned 'masculine' scholarship, and his late Victorian patriarchal attitudes allocate woman's qualities to a universal, immutable sphere. Man lives in a more temporally circumscribed realm of acquired learning and philosophy. In further complication of Stephen's praise of Eliot's powers, essentialist womanhood reveals itself in negative terms; Eliot's adroitly sympathetic creation of Hetty Sorrel as victim of her own limited mind is dismissed by Stephen as evidence of authentic 'womanly' resentment of male attraction to pretty girls. Stephen also views the idealisation of Adam Bede as an intelligent daughter's accolade to the father. Certainly, Stephen's intimate acquaintance with intelligent daughters lends weight to this judgement, but the assessment is entirely conventional: the daughter needs to propitiate the stern father, must offer fictive idealisation as the price for patriarchal approval, or, to be more biographically precise in Eliot's case, fraternal acceptance.

However, Stephen does take a refreshingly sceptical look at the deification of Eliot which began in her lifetime. He remarks that she listened 'with too much complacency to adoring and "genial" critics who collected her "wise, witty, and tender sayings", and took her for a great poet and philosopher as well as for a first-rate novelist' (pp. 147–8). Protected by Lewes from negative criticism of her work, lovingly accorded iconic status by such worshippers as Alexander Main and Edith Simcox, she was, perhaps, encouraged to believe in her own mythologised reputation. And if she did, then surely such belief was not unwarranted. If one thinks of the Sunday afternoon salons at the Priory, conducted at the height of Eliot's literary fame in the 1860s and 1870s, the images of revered enthronement become vividly literal as a stream of visitors sits at her feet and seeks words of wisdom from the woman who was the 'Mutter' not only to Lewes and his sons, but also intellectual matriarch to a tribe of admirers.

Predictably, enthroned icons tend to have their waspish detractors and disappointed viewers. For example, Eliza Lynn Linton's recollections of a literary life (1899) are not kind to Eliot. Meeting her shortly after her arrival in London, she found her 'under bred and provincial, . . . not yet the Great Genius of her age, nor a philosopher bracketed with Plato and Kant, nor was her personality held to be superior to the law of the land' (*My Literary Life*, pp. 94–5). At the height of Eliot's success, Linton deemed her 'artificial, *posée*, pretentious, unreal . . . interpenetrated head and heel, inside and out, with the sense of her importance as the great novelist and profound thinker of her generation' (p. 99). Interestingly, corroborative evidence of Linton's views comes from a more feminist and less professionally competitive source. Mary Ponsonby, member of the original committee to found Girton College and Maid of Honour to Queen Victoria from 1853 to 1861, confesses that she had put Eliot 'on such a towering pinnacle' that inevitably a meeting must disappoint. But, says, Ponsonby, she was '*manièrée* and stilted . . . there seemed to be a weight of responsibility on her as if each word must be considered in its effects and result' (*A Memoir, some Letters and a Journal*, p. 91).

Edmund Gosse, participating in the dismantling of Victorian idols that took place in the 1890s, has this to say about Eliot's reputation: 'No writer was ever more anxious to improve herself and conquer an absolute mastery over her material. But she did not observe, as she entertained the laborious process, that she was losing those natural accomplishments which infinitely outshone the philosophy and science which she so painfully acquired. She was born to please, but unhappily she persuaded herself, or was persuaded, that her mission was to teach the world, to lift its moral tone, and, in consequence, an agreeable rustic writer, with charming humour and very fine sympathetic nature, found herself gradually uplifted until, about 1875, she sat enthroned on an educational tripod, an almost ludicrous pythoness.' Rebellious as he may have thought himself, Gosse still betrays those patriarchal attitudes he so movingly repudiates in *Father and Son*: Eliot has 'natural accomplishments' which outshine painfully acquired learning; foolish woman that she is, she fails to understand that she was 'born to please' and mistakenly undertakes a mission to be a man of letters. Gosse's almost embarrassing image of her as enthroned 'pythoness' suggests a barely suppressed fear of woman's intellect. Learned women are monstrous creatures.[10]

Gosse's splenetic reaction confirms the idealisation of Eliot by her contemporaries. Revered for the womanly qualities of her mind, she seems to have been a 'man's' woman intellectual: sincerely admired for her assiduous scholarship, she remains 'feminine' despite her brain. Strangely enough, or perhaps not so strangely, Eliot continues to be a 'man's' woman intellectual for some of her twentieth-century readers. Where she was praised, with some relief, by Victorian critics for her femininity, in twentieth-century assessments of her learning, she seems to enter a world where sex and gender are inconsequential. Where her Victorian male critics search for 'feminine' qualities which both elevate and denigrate Eliot's achievements, her later critics de-sex her. She becomes pure 'brain', located in a freakish, sexless, and genderless topos of intellect – which implies, of course, that she has overcome all impediments of second sex and second gender and ascended to a realm of unsullied mind. Such attitudes point to a radical ambiguity in the critical praise of Eliot's career, indeed to an ambiguity that reveals deep-seated male attitudes to female intellectual achievement in general. It would seem that an outstandingly learned woman must be diminished, consciously or unconsciously, by her culture: either revered as a woman despite her learning or treated as if she is not a woman at all. Androcentric cultures thus deploy strategies of containment to manage the intolerable contradiction embodied in Eliot's achievements. By making her either irredeemably, charmingly 'feminine' or transcendently without sex or gender, she is relegated to an unproblematical place.

What Q. D. Leavis identifies as 'the legend of the masculine blue stocking' tends to dominate pre-feminist twentieth-century critical writing about Eliot.[11] By making minimal reference to Eliot's status as a *woman* intellectual and novelist, her critics implicitly praise her for not thinking like a woman. Such dubious salutes to her mind suggest the ambiguous praise sometimes accorded social groups who do not enjoy full social and cultural opportunities; these groups are frequently congratulated for possession of qualities not conventionally associated with them. For example, in promoting George Elliot to the pantheon of Victorian sages, John Holloway never once refers to the disabilities or advantage she might have suffered or enjoyed by virtue of her status as female 'sage'. By implication, she is deemed fit for 'sagehood' because she does not bear traces of her womanhood.[12] Holloway examines the fertile relationship between philosophical thought and rhetoric: the sage 'gives expression to his outlook imaginatively'. Paying particular attention to Eliot's moral concern with the 'high responsibilities of literature' in undertaking to represent life, Holloway considers it a fine thing that her 'didactic intention' is perfectly clear from her novels, and imposing a unified, organic structure upon her work, he perceives her fiction and non-fictional writings as philosophically coherent (*The Victorian Sage*, p. 111). He defines Eliot's philosophy in terms of the by now closely analysed moral teaching which infuses her fiction: the imperatives of individual responsiblity to society, of renunciation of destructive ego in favour of sympathetic understanding, of recognition of the social laws which benevolently govern man's existence. But however commandingly and astutely Holloway defines Eliot's social and moral thought, he tends to inflate moral teaching into philosophical system, almost as if, writing in the early 1950s, he participates in the exaltation of Eliot as philosopher/teacher begun almost a century before. And obviously with no such intention, he also characterises her intellectual production as she herself implicitly mythologised it and as I define it in terms of the cultural theory which frames my overall analysis of Victorian women intellectuals; Holloway perceives Eliot as a traditional intellectual who speaks to the community from a long-established rather than newly-constituted position.

Moreover, the features Holloway identifies in Eliot's work as expressing her thought, if not her philosophy, such features as 'characteristic setting in the recent past . . . linking a particular story to known historical conditions . . . meticulous charting of social and economic patterns' (pp. 123–4) are not always so coherently present, so easily identifiable, or so free of conflict as Holloway would have us believe. In dispatching Eliot to sexless and genderless Victorian sagehood, in relegating her to a world of moral sagacity unmolested by sexual politics, Holloway tends to create a figure who experienced no conflict between intellectual ambition and cultural authority in her career, no contention between conservative ideology and progressive views in her politics; that is to say, she reigns whole and complete in his study, sprung, as it were, Athena-like from the head of male Victorian culture.

To be sure, Holloway is writing some twenty years before feminist literary critics began to revise canonised readings of Eliot's life and work. But my point is not to rehearse the obvious (that before feminist literary criticism Eliot was not usually discussed as a *woman* writer) but rather to draw attention to some of the actual ways in which she *was* discussed: that is to say, she is seen by some pre-feminist critics as a kind of novel-writing creature entirely *without* sex or gender, which is something significantly different from critical blindness to the sexual difference of women's writing.

Moreover, *not* to discuss the sex and gender of a writer is to evade one of the multiple determinants of literary production. What I am identifying here is a tactic of critical defence, a strategy of containment in fact, which suggests that pre-feminist or indeed non-feminist critics might have been all too aware of the problematical conjunction of female sex, extraordinary intellect, and at least four major novels which take as their governing theme the unsatisfactory life of women. For example, the readings of Eliot made by one of her most impeccable critics, Barbara Hardy, rarely, if ever, address such an issue: to be sure, Hardy's primary concern is with matters of form, language, and imagination, with 'the novelist's investigation of life, made through the particularities of a literary genre' (as she puts it in the introduction to her collected essays and lectures on Eliot). But those essays and lectures on *Middlemarch* and *The Mill on the Floss* strangely evade the constraints placed upon Dorothea Brooke, Rosamund Vincy, and Maggie Tulliver by virtue of their sex, and the conflict between woman's mind and male authority to be found everywhere in Eliot's writings.[13]

In his 1966 essay examining the powerful effect of the past upon character and event in Eliot's fiction, Thomas Pinney constructs an impressive argument for resemblances between Eliot and Wordsworth, noting they 'both faced the world alone, without the support of the traditional religious explanations of man and the world . . . Both of them are seeking in their work to discover a principle of coherence and order that will give isolated man a sense of home in the world'. Yet in his sensitive exploration of the determinative effects of past affection upon present action, Pinney not once refers to Eliot's sex – to say nothing of her gender. Despite Pinney's strong historical emphasis upon Eliot and Wordsworth as literary and social figures seeking a pre-industrial order thought to have been swept away by the Victorian dust and doubt deforming the social and moral landscape, he dislocates Eliot from her actual presence in history.[14]

Obviously Pinney is not alone in this implicit dislocation and I focus upon his essay as usefully representative of pre-feminist criticism of Eliot. In fact, not one of the other ten essays collected in *George Eliot: Twentieth-Century Views* (ed. George Creeger, 1970) discusses Eliot as a woman novelist; not one acknowledges, for example, that the struggles of Maggie Tulliver are determined in part by the simple fact that she is a girl, and a too clever one by half as her father recognises. Even the critic whose name is synonymous with analysis of relationships between culture, society, and the individual, fails to take account of Eliot's sex and gender. Raymond Williams, writing in 1973 and deeply sensitive to Eliot's provincial origins and desire for intellectual eminence, nowhere mentions her struggles as an ambitious young *woman* in the provinces. In grouping her with Thomas Hardy and D. H. Lawrence in his analysis of the entrenched snobbery of the British intellectual establishment, he fails to distinguish her from her ambitious fellow provincials in terms of sex and gender. In all these readings, Eliot becomes a de-sexed, de-gendered presence, performing much like Karl Mannheim's ideal intellectual, untainted by political polemic as she floats free of crucial social and cultural determinants of her career, mythologised into Henry James's 'magnificent mind' image that seems to defy historical and political meaning.[15]

It seems to be entirely possible that the idealisation of Eliot in her own time and the evasion of her sex and gender in pre-feminist criticism signify an implicit refusal to recognise the many other women who were active and important in cultures controlled, for the most part, by men. Victorian society can point to that sign, that enthroned emblem of intellectual womanhood which is 'George Eliot', and delude itself (and those subjugated by its prescriptions for woman's role and function) that intelligent women share an equal role with men in the creation of culture. The fulsome recognition of *one* woman intellectual may be read as a sign of absence: the thousands of women who were editing periodicals, writing essays and novels, translating difficult works of Continental literature and philosophy, are not recognised by the idealisation and elevation to iconic status of George Eliot. The lives of those women are the subject of another study, but it seems to me that Eliot as 'feminine sage', as intellectual priestess, as the woman invited for an Oxford weekend at the home of Benjamin Jowett, as the privileged guest at a University which denied women access to its precincts – this is a 'George Eliot' pointing the way to those lives. So, too, the 'George Eliot' who seems to escape the contingencies of history and politics, who is de-sexed and de-gendered by her pre-feminist critics, points the way to many female lives of unrecognised intellectual merit. Pretending that this eminent 'sage' is not a woman is one way of pretending that intellectual women enjoy equal opportunities with men to create culture.

Either through being emphasised or omitted, a conjunction of male sex and intellectual authority has governed responses to Eliot's work and continued to define her reputation in literary history until recent feminist criticism of her work. In its turn, however, that feminist criticism must address itself to Eliot's own strategies of containment when she confronts the conflict between woman's mind and male authority. Boldly locating herself in the privileged realm occupied by Victorian men of letters, speaking in a voice that blends the conventional Victorian attributes of male intellect and female feeling, she participates in a discourse of essentialist sexual politics and thereby gains for herself the admiration of Victorian patriarchy.

# 10
## Instructed Women and the Case of *Romola*

Eliot's reputation as a timid feminist, at best, is well documented by her cautious endorsement of social measures designed to rectify the institutionalised discrimination practised against women in her time. The least equivocal approval of political action to be found in her letters comes in her sanction of a petition drawn up in 1856 by Barbara Leigh Smith calling for amendment of the laws relating to married women. The terms of her approval, however, are somewhat ambiguous. Congratulating Sara Hennel for having 'taken up the cause' in signing the petition, Eliot revealingly adds that she thinks the proposed laws 'would help to raise the position and character of women', a hoped for elevation which tends to diminish the present character of women as Eliot perceived it.[1] That Eliot retained her dim view of women's characters is confirmed by Emily Davies, founder of Girton, who discovered in 1876 that the mandate for girls' education set forth by arguably the most prominent Victorian woman intellectual was peculiarly gauzy, almost comically abstract.

Davies describes her increasing frustration when confronted by Eliot's evasion of political action through a kind of meandering discourse, punctuated by 'active' affirmations of her views interjected by Lewes. In Davies's account of the interview, Eliot was fearful that educated girls will be led away from 'individual efforts to be good'. Davies briskly assured her that this was somewhat improbable as girls in Victorian society were rarely directed to be anything other than 'good'. Eliot then complained that girls want 'to do some great thing' and, unable to do that, do nothing; she concluded by insisting that the most important thing for girls to learn is that 'the state of insensibility in which we are not alive to high and generous emotions is stupidity'. Realising Eliot had become strangely oblivious to the thrust of her own female ambitions 'to do some great thing', Davies decided she had stayed long enough; she recalls that 'at this stupidity stage' she abandoned her attempts to shift the interview from abstract discussion of moral insensibility to concrete suggestions for improving women's higher education (*L.*, 6:286–7). Had Davies read Eliot's remarks about Girton written to Mrs Nassau John Senior in October 1869, she might have been less baffled: in this letter Eliot announces she has had 'no practical connexion with the proposed college, beyond subscribing to it, and occasionally answering questions which Miss Davies has put to me about the curriculum which would be desirable. I feel too deeply the difficult complications that beset every measure likely to affect the position of women and also I feel too imperfect a sympathy with many women who have put themselves forward in connexion with such measures, to give any practical adhesion to them. There is no subject on which I am more inclined to hold my peace and learn, than on the "Women Question" ' (*L.*, 5:58). Actually, Eliot did give 'practical adhesion' to the establishment of Girton, not, however, with notable generosity; considering that she received £7000 for the publication in fourteen monthly parts of her novel about an educated woman in Renaissance Italy, her subscription of fifty pounds 'from the author of *Romola*' to Girton seems unusually cautious.[2] Whether expressed at the Priory, in her letters, essays, and novels, or in her financial contributions, Eliot's hope for woman's intellectual development is not always sanguine.

Eliot's hostility to feminist action and her disparagement of women less accomplished than herself, has been explained by some feminist critics as evidence of the price of her eminence in a male world. Sandra Gilbert and Susan Gubar, for example, argue that Eliot 'demonstrates her internalization of patriarchal culture's definition of the woman as "other" ' through her 'continued guilt over societal disapproval, her avowed preference for male friends, her feminine anti-feminism, her self-deprecatory assumption that all other forms of injustice are more important subjects for her art than female subjugation, her extreme dependence on Lewes for encouragement and approbation, her inability to face the world as a writer and read even the most benevolent reviews of her work' (*The Madwoman in the Attic*, pp. 466–7). Such 'internalization' leads, as one might expect, to contradiction, resolved, according to Gilbert and Gubar, through what they term 'acts of vengeance' committed by Eliot against her own characters (p. 479). Although these critics expansively identify and dissect the source of contradiction in Eliot's work, they tend to resist political and historical analysis in favour of an undefined patriarchy within which the woman writer is either rebellious or conformist. For me, patriarchy is a complex ensemble of beliefs and practices, of which women intellectuals are simultaneously resistant and complicit parts. Eliot's attitudes towards her women characters and woman's 'character' disclose her active, necessary compliance with the patriarchal culture that gave her intellectual birth, and nourished and applauded her. That she was also subversively resistant to this culture (as I shall demonstrate in discussion of Romola, Arabella Transome, and Maggie Tulliver) only corroborates her patriarchal genesis and affiliation. Eliot's androcentric attitudes are best understood when we perceive their integral meaning in her self-directed performance as traditional intellectual. Her sexual politics must be analysed in the context of all her politics.

As I have already noted, Gramsci argues that the traditional intellectual feels himself to be part of an 'historical continuity uninterrupted even by the most complicated and radical changes in political and social forms'. This attitude causes such intellectuals to 'put themselves forward as autonomous and independent of the dominant social group' ('The Intellectuals', pp. 5–7). Eliot's writings about women and her creation of female characters in her fiction express a will to believe that women possess intrinsic characteristics impervious to social and political change, which will, in effect, make them autonomous and eventually triumphant over the male, materialistic, middle-class values dominating Eliot's society. In other words, the subversive desires of a number of Eliot's female characters may be said to represent her political conservatism (which is not to deny such desires also express Eliot's serious concern about women's unhappy lives). Paradoxically, these female characters seek escape from the confinements of their present culture in order to retrieve a more organically coherent time (whether it be located in fifteenth-century Florence or the English Midlands of the 1830s), and their desires express the wishes of the traditional intellectual for an autonomy unmolested by the power of emerging social classes who are in the process of producing their very own organic intellectuals. In Eliot's thought, therefore, women tend to represent negative criticism of those ideologies of competitive individualism and mercantilism abhorred by Elizabeth Barrett Browning, a self-mythologised traditional intellectual, and sanctioned by Harriet Martineau, an almost perfect representative of organic intellectual practice. In what follows, I shall first examine

Eliot's problematical attitudes towards women's higher education and women's writing; I shall then focus upon *Romola*, the narrative of an intellectually ambitious woman impeded by male cultural authority and invested with all the immutable, ahistorical autonomy desired by the traditional intellectual.

Eliot certainly believed that women should be educated and accorded equal treatment under the law, yet she desired this equality not so much because a widened vista might enable women to transform their own lives (as she had transformed hers), but because she wanted unhampered expression of woman's mythically inherent characteristics. Woman must make her essential, and essentialist, contribution to cultural development as Eliot understood it.

'We must have freedom and culture for woman, because subjection and ignorance have debased her, and with her, Man,' Eliot announced in 1855. In May 1867 (as we know) she was sympathetic to John Stuart Mill's agitation for women's rights in Parliament and emphasised that women should be 'educated equally with men'; in 1867, she was a cautious supporter of the plans for Girton, saying that even though she was 'much occupied . . . the better Education of Women is one of the objects about which I have *no doubt*'; in 1868, still supporting the plans for Girton, but phrasing that support in strangely ambiguous terms, she announces that women's higher education should prepare them for 'the great amount of social unproductive labour which needs to be done by women'. The 'true gospel', she says, should be recognition by women and men of the 'disgrace' involved in trying to do work for which they are 'unfit' (*L.*, 4:366, 399, 425). Eliot's enigmatic advocacy of higher education for women tends to shift the terms of the argument from specific, ideologically determined situations to abstract, moral issues. Talk of education for women becomes talk of man's general moral failings, and while Eliot may well be correct in her unflagging attribution of man's unjust treatment of women to his generally imperfect state, the evasion of particular issues markedly contrasts with Martineau's forthright attacks on specific instances of injustice and with Barrett Browning's unembarrassed assertions that woman is intellectually inferior to man.

Evasion of the particular through discussion of the ideal also informs Eliot's writings about women and literature. Eliot chose to write only two essays about women's literary production (the review of the writings of Margaret Fuller and Mary Wollstonecraft which appeared in the *Leader* in October 1855 is too brief to be considered in this context);[3] she also chose to focus her discussion on the writing of seventeenth-century French aristocrats in one essay and on the silly novel-writing of nineteenth-century English 'ladies' in the other. Through such evasive limitation, she shuts out the ideological contention resident in the phrase 'Victorian woman intellectual' and removes herself from Victorian culture and society. In 'Woman in France: Madame de Sablé' (1854) and 'Silly Novels by Lady Novelists' (1856), the readers of the *Westminster Review* are instructed by an anonymous voice in the qualities, good and bad, of women's writing. Behind that voice, beginning the ascendency of her rise to cultural fame, discovering her cultural confidence, establishing herself as a woman intellectual, is Marian Evans, deploying certain strategies to deal with a potentially disabling conflict between gender and authority.

In these two essays about women writers and woman's potential for intellectual excellence (to say nothing of recognition by her society), Eliot employs a strategy of containment which creates a topos of essential and essentialist female characteristics: in that place, fenced by dominant attitudes towards sex and gender, woman is dislocated from her conflictive place, allocated her timeless contributions to the advancement of culture. In these essays woman is freed from contradiction. She is unmolested by history and untroubled by the social and cultural ideologies that directed a woman better read than most of her male contemporaries and capable of sustained scholarly study, to call herself 'George Eliot'. Moreover, Eliot's strategy of containment also relegates the intolerable 'lot' (one of her favoured terms) of intelligent nineteenth-century women to an undiscussed, unacknowledged place.

'Woman in France' maintains that in science the 'mere knowing and reasoning faculties' have no sex, a view which mythically dissociates the cognitive and rational mind from all the historical, cultural and social forces that construct the idea of 'sex' itself. Eliot argues that in art and literature 'which imply the action of the entire being, in which every fibre of the nature is engaged, in which every peculiar modification of the individual makes itself felt, woman has something specific to contribute'. This something specific is a special class of sensations and emotions, the maternal ones 'unknown to man' and never to be 'cancelled', and introducing 'a distinctly feminine condition into the wondrous chemistry of the affections and sentiments, which inevitably gives rise to distinctive forms and combinations' (*E.*, p. 53).[4] So far, this biology-as-destiny argument unsurprisingly asserts that woman's physical difference from man inevitably leads to difference in aesthetic production, which does not necessarily suggest a difference in equality of achievement. But biology-as-destiny in Eliot's argument *does* mean inequality of achievement; as she develops her discourse of physical, psychological, and aesthetic difference, she develops an imagery that values male over female, and she plots a strategy containing woman in her essentialist, ahistorical, unproblematical place. Unaccosted by historical change, woman becomes an emblem of the autonomous immutability desired by the traditional intellectual.

Locating its sagacious voice in its own time, the essay declares that even when 'a complete development of woman's intellectual and moral nature' is attained, the psychological difference between the sexes will still be 'a permanent source of variety and beauty, as long as the tender light and dewy freshness of morning affect us differently from the strength and brilliancy of the mid-day sun' (*E.*, p. 53). However fulsomely Eliot praises the writing of seventeenth-century French women for its refinement, grace, and wit, it is writing which by virtue of the contrast between tender light, dewy freshness, and the strength and brilliance of high noon, is writing produced by immature minds. Moreover, Madame de Sablé's 'forte' was 'to show that sympathy and appreciation which are as genial and encouraging as the morning sunbeams' (*E.*, p. 74).

The writing of French women is not the only thing Eliot surreptitiously diminishes through imagery of early morning and high noon. In reviewing George Meredith's 'Arabian Entertainment', *The Shaving of Shagpat*, in January 1856, she remarks that 'In an historical as well as in a physical sense, the East is the land of the morning' (*Leader*, 7:15–17). Needless to say, an unembarrassed elevation of Western over Eastern culture is hardly peculiar to George Eliot, but her imperialist judgements are relevant in considering her assessments of difference between male and female writing and in seeing connections between cautious sexual politics and the conservative aspects of her political thought in general. Meredith's oriental story-telling elicits the judgement that 'priority of sunshine' gives the East its precedence, but *not* a pre-eminence. The East is thereby implicitly aligned with women's prose as she describes it in her essay on French women writers, prose radiant with morning grace but deficient in substantial brilliance. And Eliot was not the first to make such an alignment. In Mary Shelley's novel, Frankenstein effects a similar conjunction when he recalls the reading of Persian, Arabic, and Sanskrit with his friend, Clerval; when one reads the works of the Orientalists, Frankenstein declares, 'life appears to consist in a warm sun and a garden of roses . . . How different from the manly and heroical poetry of Greece and Rome!' (*Frankenstein*, p. 330). In the Meredith review Eliot confidently elaborates Western disparagement of Eastern civilisation, an attitude she expressed with unusual fervour on her return from Spain in 1867. Having inspected the paintings in the Prado and the cathedral in Seville, she wrote to Barbara Bodichon that she considered these Spanish cultural monuments sufficient 'to justify Western civilization, with all its faults, and transcend any amount of diaper patterns even if they were coloured as the Moors coloured . . . Europe has been filled with ideas over and above what they ever possessed' (*L.*, 4:351). Fusing her judgement of woman's intellectual achievements with her patronising view of alien civilisations, Eliot allots a primary *and* subordinate place to the aesthetic achievements of exotic cultures and the writing of French seventeenth-century female aristocrats: first in time but not in substance.

Eliot admits that the writing of Madame de Sablé and her friends (primarily letters, memoirs, romances written to amuse each other) must be ranked below that of Madame de Sévigné, Madame de Staël or George Sand: these three soar 'like tall pines' from 'a thicket of hawthorns, eglantines, and honeysuckle'. This must be a truly fertile thicket, for there the sweetly reticent writing of Madame de Sablé and her friends is shaken from them, in Eliot's horticultural image, 'like the petals which the wind shakes from the rose in its bloom'. What is important for Eliot about these rosaceous writers is that they wrote *as* women: 'They were not trying to make a career for themselves'; they wrote 'without any intention to prove that women could write as well as men, without affecting manly views or suppressing womanly ones' (*E.*, pp. 54–5). They 'seconded a man's wit with understanding – one of the best offices which womanly intellect has rendered to the advancement of culture'. Shifting the essay into a trans-historical mode, Eliot asserts that these women, possessing 'womanly characteristics', knowing their essentialist limits, felt what is known to all women at all historical periods, that intuitive 'dread of what over-taxes their intellectual energies, either by difficulty or monotony, which gives them an instinctive fondness for lightness of treatment and airiness of expression, thus making them cut short all prolixity and reject all heaviness' (*E.*, p. 58). Women intuitively know they must not overtax their minds in the way they know they must not overtax their bodies.

But if these are trans-historical 'womanly characteristics', what of Eliot and her fellow women intellectuals? Did Harriet Martineau, Frances Power Cobbe, Barbara Bodichon, Caroline Norton and Emily Davies (to name a few) take things easy? We know that they did not, and we also know how different all this is from Eliot's own career, from her disciplined self-taxing, her relish of intellectual 'difficulty', her tolerance of the 'monotony' entailed, for example, in the study of more languages than Mr Stelling ever managed to master. And how very different, too, is the style Eliot praises here from the prolixity and heaviness which often lend weight to her own mature writing. Very definitely seeking to make a career from her writing life, and if not aiming to write like a man, then certainly assuming the authoritative style characteristic of the *Westminster*'s reviewers (for the most part the collective male 'we') and certainly assuming 'manly' views in her impersonation of male narrators (in *Janet's Repentance*, for example), Eliot dons an intellectual persona associated with a male way of writing. It is not a light and airy one.[5]

Why were French women of the seventeenth century superior to those stagnating in England and Germany? Because they were 'admitted to a common fund of ideas, to common objects of interest with men; and this must ever be the essential condition at once of true womanly culture and of true social well-being' (*E.*, p. 80). Splendid as this is, we need to remember that the judgement is based upon analysis of the letter writing and memoir making of a handful of privileged French aristocrats. What 'common fund of ideas'? What 'common objects of interest with men' are we talking about here? If Eliot wanted to talk about the intellectual achievements of French women, why did she not talk about George Sand, a woman about whom she said 'one might live a century with nothing but one's own dull faculties and not know as much as those six page [from Sand's *Jacques*] will suggest' (*L.*, 1:278)? Why does Eliot not scrutinise an intellectual world in which women like herself chose to work rather than opting to protect themselves from anything which might 'overtax' their intellectual energies? It is significant that Eliot's plea for equal participation for women in culture and society ('this must ever be the essential condition at once of true womanly culture and of true social well-being') does not mention the impediments to that participation felt by women in seventeenth-century France *and* in Victorian England; and neither does she base her plea upon specific historical analysis of those 'ideas' and 'common objects of interest', those discourses in which women might participate. Moreover, the appeal for equal time for women in intellectual discourse is articulated in the language of ahistorical inherency: 'true womanly culture' implies a realm of immanent female characteristics.

In sum, to choose analysis of the salons of intelligent seventeenth-century French women is not to choose analysis of the situations of intelligent nineteenth-century English women. My aim is not to indict Eliot for disappointing sexual politics or for the failure to write a feminist tract; rather, I have tried to show how the conflicts in the 'Woman in France' essay reveal her strong ideological bond to patriarchal culture and to certain conservative modes of thought. The absences of this essay disclose the presence in Eliot's career of what must have been a very real and painful dilemma: how to reconcile her own consciousness as woman intellectual with the values of the androcentric culture which permitted her to have that consciousness in the first place. In 'Woman in France', Eliot's strategy of containment, that defensive manoeuvre relegating a conflict between woman's desire for intellectual autonomy and male cultural authority to another place, is to dislocate herself from Victorian life altogether.

When Eliot did address herself to the situation of intelligent English women she was far less charitable than when saluting the women of France. In a letter written in 1848 to John Sibree, she characterises Hannah More in terms that anticipate Edmund Gosse's venomous characterisation of herself as freakish 'pythoness': Hannah More is 'that most disagreeable of all monsters – a blue-stocking – a monster that can only exist in a miserable false state of society; in which a woman with but a smattering of learning or philosophy is classed along with singing mice and card-playing pigs'.[6] In some ways, this might be read as a strong feminist statement, yet it is a strangely double-edged one. By implication, an authentic, decent society would be one in which a well-read and learned woman would not be anomalous; but Eliot embeds an élitist view of intellectual women in her avowed distaste for blue-stockings. She is disdainful of women who have only a 'smattering of learning or philosophy', a scorn expressed in her early fiction when the male narrator of *Janet's Repentance* engages in stock male ridicule of intellectually pretentious women. He derides the provincial ambition of Miss Pratt by ironically referring to her possession of 'no less than five hundred volumes', her competence 'to conduct a conversation on any topic whatever', and her occasional 'dabbling a little in authorship, though it was understood that she had never put forth the full powers of her mind in print' (*S.C.L.*, pp. 268–9).

Miss Pratt announces that she 'has ever considered fiction a suitable form for conveying moral and religious instruction'. This misguided view, of course, is the direct object of Eliot's witty attack in 'Silly Novels by Lady Novelists' where she defines the silliest novels of all to be those of the oracular species – 'novels intended to expound the writer's religious, philosophical or moral theories'. This essay, as Thomas Pinney aptly puts it, is 'slashing': it performs a spectacular demolition of novels where, in Eliot's droll terms, every lover has a manly breast, minds are redolent of various things, hearts are hollow, friends are consigned to the tomb, infancy is an engaging period, the sun is a luminary that goes to his western couch or gathers the rain-drops into his refulgent bosom. When not entertaining the *Westminster* reader in this fashion, Eliot employs a veritable cookbook of culinary metaphors serving to relocate these lady novelists from the library to the kitchen, undeniably where Eliot thinks they belong. The 'recipe' for production of novels of the 'oracular species' is as follows: 'Take a woman's head, stuff it with a smattering of philosophy and literature chopped small, and with false notions of society baked hard, let it hang over a desk a few hours every day, and serve up hot in feeble English, when not required' (*E.*, p. 310). Employing a culinary proverb to warn women from rushing into print unprepared for the consequences, she recites, 'Be not a baker if your head be made of butter,' and she refutes the 'standing apology' for bad women's writing (that women are hampered from doing anything else) by saying that society is held culpable for everything from 'bad pickles to bad poetry'. Even a well-kneaded metaphor, so to speak, takes on a particularly appropriate meaning when Eliot, sounding rather like someone speaking from a club-chair at the Carlton, declares, 'We had imagined that destitute women turned novelists, as they turned governesses, because they had no other "lady-like" means of getting their bread' (*E.*, p. 303).

Attacking the acquisition of superficial learning as an impetus for women's writing, Eliot scorns paraded knowledge as vulgar vaunting of intellectual ambition. The sly severity of Eliot's essay originates, I think, in certain élitist values that have as much to do with her sense of herself as an intellectual as with her views of 'lady novelists'. These élitist values also buttress the strategy of containment that relegates to another, unacknowledged place the conflict between female desire for cultural autonomy and male intellectual authority. She declares that authentically cultured people of either sex do not put themselves forward: 'A really cultured woman, like a really cultured man, is all the simpler and less obtrusive for her knowledge. . . . She does not give you information, which is the raw material of culture – she gives you sympathy which is its subtlest essence' (*E.*, p. 317). Woman's knowledge is associated with 'sympathy', a quality conventionally ascribed to female role and function in the nineteenth century, and woman, so to speak, has advanced to the cooked state of culture, leaving behind that 'raw' material which is information. She is implicitly dissociated from the modes of behaviour displayed and sanctioned by the male English middle class in the nineteenth century – no competitive, aggressive individual she, no Maggie Tulliver demanding acknowledgment of her mind. Confident in her inherited, not acquired simplicity, she remains serenely unobtrusive, symbolising the historical continuity desired by the traditional intellectual and the timeless, immutable essence of womanly qualities. She is immune to history, culture, and society.[7]

One function of these essays about women's literary production is to make a strategy of containment out of the form of the Victorian essay-review or review-essay itself.[8] By basing a sensible plea for an equal role for women in shaping culture and society upon a review of three books about aristocratic women who wrote long ago, very little, and very airily at that, Eliot removes the conflict between desire and authority from the nineteenth century. She defuses it of its urgency. By attacking the easiest of targets (silly novels) Eliot also manages the conflict through entertainment and wit, through a voice which speaks from privileged bastions of male authority – in this case the *Westminster Review*. Intelligently refined seventeenth-century French women and pretentious Victorian lady novelists possess intrinsic characteristics (good in the French and bad in the Victorian) which make them immune to historical restraint (again a good thing and a bad thing): such mythical autonomy removes them from the contingent urgency of actual history which governs, curbs, and restrains.

Mindful of Eliot's support of higher education for women (however cautious) and of the dilemma she must have felt in regard to her problematic genesis in androcentric culture, I still want to emphasise that in the only two extensive essays she wrote about women's writing she is less concerned with the actual ways Victorian intellectual women might transform their lives, than she is with avoiding discussion of the powers which constrain them. When Marian Evans became 'George Eliot', the essayist was taken over by the novelist, and conflicts and dilemmas explored in more complex ways by virtue of the formal possibilities of fiction. However, Eliot's strategy of containment remains the same: it is to remove intellectual woman from history and to relocate her in a realm of inherency. In Eliot's one novel that deals specifically with the ambitions of an 'instructed woman', Romola de' Bardi Melema finds the enquiring nature of her intelligence directed to emphatic recognition of her essential womanhood. She begins as scholarly assistant to her father and she ends as tutor to her husband's illegitimate son.

'We cannot but think,' declares the anonymous reviewer of *Romola* in the *Westminster Review*, 'that this long and elaborate disquisition on the relations between the sexes as a moral question is set forth by George Eliot too much in the colours of the nineteenth century' (*C.H.*, p. 216). What the *Westminster* reviewer undoubtedly identified in *Romola* was a pattern already traced in *The Mill on the Floss*: the desire of a female character for self-governance obstructed by male figures of restraint. Maggie Tulliver's desire for recognition of her intelligence is, as we know, squashed by Mr Stelling (among others) and her desire to make her own moral choices so constrained by the relentless admonitions of her brother that even her rejection of Stephen Guest is directed as much by fear of Tom's anger as by regard for her cousin Lucy. Romola's desires are governed by her father, her husband, and, in a significant difference from *The Mill on the Floss*, by a far more powerful figure of male authority than Tom Tulliver – Savonarola. *Romola* names female intellectual ambition as egregious 'suffering Self' and sternly redirects it to Christian charity.

The minutely observed scenes of Florentine life and character manifest the meticulous research Eliot undertook for the writing of her historical novel and at times *Romola* seems a vivified Renaissance canvas.[9] Articulated in a kind of verbal painting, burnished with golden colour, and crammed with movement, Florence is animated by the sights and noises of 'old clothes stalls, the challenges of the dicers, the vaunting of new linens and woollens, of excellent wooden-ware, kettles, and frying pans'; it is peopled by gesticulating barbers, haggling goldsmiths, comic peasants and plotting politicians. Crowding the bridges, swelling the narrow streets, peasants and politicians alike seem to spill over the edges of Eliot's novelistic canvas as the Medicis are expelled from power, Savonarola enjoys a brief period of protection from Charles VIII of France, and Romola discovers the treachery of her handsome Greek husband. As Peter Conrad observes, Eliot visualises fifteenth-century Florence with 'the luminosity, the almost hallucinatory vividness, with which every flower or leaf is picked out in a Pre-Raphaelite painting'; Eliot's 'determination to be exact about Florentine table equipage, tunics and shops' is borne out in every scene (*The Victorian Treasure-House*, p. 119). Romola herself, with her statuesque form, her face 'without any tinge of the rose', her abundance of reddish gold, wavy hair, is a Pre-Raphaelite icon; a secularised madonna, she seems to fill the canvas of every scene in which she appears just as Rossetti's broad-shouldered, thick-necked, voluptuous women dominate his paintings, as Nina Auerbach demonstrates in her study of the iconography of Victorian womanhood.[10]

When we first see Romola, she is reading to her blind father, an anti-clerical, impoverished scholar and possessor of a distinguished library. An embittered, selfish man, he laments the loss of his son to the Dominican order and resents his replacement as research assistant in the female form of Romola. Ironically, Romola is reading the story of the blinding of Tiresias from Politian's *Miscellanea*. But Bardo is no seer, no blind man gifted with prophecy: instead, he seems a fugitive from a Browning dramatic monologue – if not relishing the worth of the marble that will make his tombstone or the value of his bronzes, then avidly calculating the material value of his library. From his patriarchal perspective, Romola is not a 'fitting coadjutor' for the male work of knowing and he rewards her intellectual industry with the ungrateful (and long-winded) announcement that 'the sustained zeal and unconquerable patience demanded from those who would tread the unbeaten paths of knowledge are still less reconcilable with the wandering, vagrant propensity of the feminine mind than with the feeble powers of the feminine body'. He meets Romola's propitiating reminder that she exactly follows his instructions with the querulous assertion that she fainted 'in the mere search for the references I needed to explain a single passage of Callemachus' (*R.*, p. 97). Smiling 'with a bitter sort of pity' and speaking in the stilted language Eliot believed would render the idiom of an educated, late fifteenth-century Florentine, he announces, 'I cannot boast that thou are entirely lifted out of that lower category to which Nature assigned thee, nor even that in erudition thou art on a par with the more learned women of this age' (p. 101). 'Sweet daughter' Romola may be to him, but she is a daughter kept firmly in her subjugated place by peevish reminders of her intellectual inferiority.

'The more learned women of this age' invoked by Bardo included in their humanistic sisterhood Cassandra Fedele (1465–1558), who is twice referred to in connection with Romola's intellectual ambitions. As Margaret King observes, women 'constituted a small minority among humanists; yet their participation was significant' ('Book-Lined Cells', p. 67). The women humanists typically came from prominent families located in court cities and, of course, were educated by men (often their fathers) in the languages, literature, history, poetry, and moral philosophy of Greece and Rome. These learned women tackled the difficult material of humanist studies and composed works in the conventional humanist forms of orations, dialogues, treatises, and poems. Fedele's fame rested upon her oration on the liberal arts, recited at the University of Padua in 1487; according to King, even though the oration was not original, it was remarkable 'because a woman had acquired the skills necessary to compose it without error and to deliver it with poise to an audience of some of Europe's most learned men' (p. 69). The fame of Fedele's oration has made her an ideal for Romola and an intimation for the reader of how Romola might have lived were it not for the selfishness of her father, the insidious sexual attraction of her treacherous husband, and the spiritual chastisement of Savonarola. Evidently, Eliot was already thinking about Cassandra Fedele in 1854. While she does not specifically refer to Fedele in the 'Woman in France' essay, it seems reasonably certain Eliot has her in mind when she justifies a 'turn to France for the highest examples of womanly achievement in almost every department' by declaring, 'We confess ourselves unacquainted with the productions of those awful women of Italy, who held professional chairs, and were great in civil and canon law' (*E.*, p. 54).[11]

On the first occasion that this scholarly woman is mentioned, Romola vows to her father she will study diligently: 'I will become as learned as Cassandra Fedele. I will try and be as useful to you as if I had been a boy, and then perhaps some great scholar will want to marry me, and will not mind about a dowry; and he will like to come and live with you, and he will be to you in place of my brother . . . and you will not be sorry that I was a daughter' (*R.*, p. 100). Articulating the abject lament of so many daughters in Victorian fiction, Romola makes a pitiful offering of Fedele to propitiate the father; but when Romola discovers that her adored Greek husband can outdo Florentine politicians in perfidious plotting and that her father's library is to be sold by Tito to the invading French, she thinks of Fedele in more useful terms. She decides to leave Florence and Tito: 'She had invented a lot for herself – to go to the most learned woman in the world, Cassandra Fedele, at Venice, and ask her how an instructed woman could support herself in a lonely life there' (p. 393). Residual propitiation of the father is still present, however; Romola's ambition is described as a desire to become 'wise enough to write something which would rescue her father's name from oblivion'. Writing for the father directs her to Venice, but she gets no farther than a hillside outside Florence. There, she is recognised and accosted by Savonarola, her 'invented lot' demolished by his stern intervention, her dream of an 'instructed' life for women (even if it is a life of intellectual duty to the father) thwarted by his lecture on the moral poverty of such a desire. He redirects her back to Florence and the topos of her inherent womanhood.

The chapter in which the significant meeting between Romola and Savonarola occurs is entitled 'An Arresting Voice'. This is the voice that impedes through proclamation of a destiny different from the one imagined or desired: it is the voice of the Annunciation, a subject of enduring fascination for Eliot. In an unfinished and undated fragment, 'Notes on the Spanish Gypsy and Tragedy in General' (included by Cross in his *Life*), Eliot writes of how the subject of 'The Spanish Gypsy' was suggested to her by a painting of the Annunciation, probably by Titian, in the Scuola di San Rocco at Venice: 'Of course I had seen numerous pictures of this subject before; and the subject had always attracted me . . . It occurred to me that here was a great dramatic motive as those used by the Greek dramatists.' The 'motive' for tragedy, as Eliot goes on to describe it here in relation to 'The Spanish Gypsy', is the collision between an individual's joyful expectation of a predictable life (anticipated by Fedalma in her forthcoming marriage to Silva, Spanish count and Christian foe of the pagan gypsies) and the 'annunciation' of a great destiny (performance of her inherited and inherent duty as daughter of the gypsy king, Zarca). Where in 'The Spanish Gypsy' the 'arresting voice' emanates from a father proclaiming his daughter's immutable destiny, in *Romola* it comes from Savonarola, a spiritual 'father' to Romola and able to articulate much more powerfully than her real father the patriarchal injunctions impeding her journey to Cassandra Fedele. In 'The Spanish Gypsy', Fedalma vows, 'I will take this yearning self of mine and strangle it' (Book I); in *Romola*, Romola vows to Savonarola, 'Father, I will be guided. Teach me! I will go back' (p. 436).

The Annunciation, then, as a subject always 'attractive' to Eliot, becomes the effective means of destroying Romola's belief in the possibility of 'inventing' her own 'lot'. Her desire to live independently as an 'instructed woman' (even if it is a desire born of disillusionment with her husband and need to rehabilitate the name of her father) comes into conflict with the moral authority of her surrogate father, Savonarola. In *Romola*, Eliot replaces female desire for autonomy with a coercive discourse of fidelity to community. Deploying his own skilful strategy of containment to manage a rebellious daughter and wife, Savonarola presents a sophisticated argument that relocates female intellectual ambition in another place: he quite literally commands Romola, 'My daughter, you must return to your place.' That place is Florence, stricken by civil discord and disease, and Savonarola 'instructs' the venturesome 'instructed woman' to reinstate herself in her community, to channel her intelligence into social good. 'You are turning your back on the lot that has been appointed for you – you are going to choose another. But can man or woman choose duties?' he asks. Emphasising the irreversible appointment of male and female 'lots', ridiculing futile attempts to choose the direction of one's life, Savonarola becomes more chillingly castigatory as he accuses Romola of wanting 'no rule' but her 'own will'. Patriarchally linking the traditional Christian teaching of obedience to God's will with Romola's own disobedience, he implies that her intellectual ambition is betrayal of a divinely endowed female destiny. What has her 'dead wisdom' done for her? It has left her without a 'heart' for her neighbours, 'without care for the great work by which Florence is to be regenerated and the world made holy'. If she is unable to live for her husband, then she must live for Florence. She has been her father's Antigone, her husband's Ariadne: now she becomes Savonarola's Martha, directed to 'that path of labour for the suffering and the hungry to which you are called as a daughter of Florence in these times of hard need' (p. 438).

When Romola is arrested by Savonarola's commanding voice on the Florentine hillside, she hears herself named as daughter and as wife: 'You are Romola de' Bardi, the wife of Tito Melema.' Nominated as ancillary, she is also painted as such, transformed into a mythological figure rather than accepted as the Romola who wishes to become independent of male discipline. Depicted by Piero di Cosimo as Antigone to her father's Oedipus, her likeness is then commissioned by Tito for a miniature triptych showing the marriage of Bacchus and Ariadne.[12] Literally and psychologically reduced by this last representation, she relinquishes to Tito the crucifix given to her by her dying brother so that he may lock it in the middle panel of the triptych. It seems as if Romola becomes increasingly diminished by her experiences, becomes reduced 'likenesses' of herself, and is finally so chastened by Savonarola's sternly imperative discourse, that she falls to her knees before him in a state of 'yearning passivity' ready 'to thread her life by a fresh clue' (p. 440). Lost in a labyrinth of guilt for the desires named as un-Christian by Savonarola's 'arresting voice', she returns to Florence to tend the sick and feed the hungry. It is not until some two years later when Savonarola refuses to intervene to save her godfather Bernardo del Nero (who has been condemned to death for plotting to restore the Medici), that she makes her way out of the labyrinth, indeed out of the city: 'Again she had fled from Florence, and this time no arresting voice had called her back. Again she wore the grey religious dress; and this time, in her heart-sickness, she did not care that it was a disguise. A new rebellion had risen within her, a new despair. Why should she care about wearing one badge more than another, or about being called by her own name?' (p. 586).

Seeking freedom from all naming, from the imposition of all badges, she longs for a liberation that will paradoxically intensify her passivity: 'To be freed from the burden of choice when all motive was bruised, to commit herself, sleeping, to destiny which would either bring death or else new necessities that might arouse a new life in her' (p. 589). To choose independence, to desire autonomy, is to be constrained at every turn – better to abandon all desire by lying down in a small boat and setting sail for a nirvana of no names, no duties, and no desires. As Daniel Deronda floats to his destiny as Mordecai Lapidoth's 'executive self', so Romola floats to hers as the Madonna of Restoration for a village decimated by plague. Floating without bonds, without motive, without desire, reading no message in the 'far-off symbolic writing of the heavens', she imaginatively sleeps through the cataclysmic events narrated in the succeeding numbers as they appeared in the *Cornhill Magazine*: the aborted trial by fire of Savonarola, the burning of S. Marco, and the murder of Tito Melema by his foster-father Baldessare, whom he has refused to recognise or help when at his most powerful in Florentine politics. Freed from all inscribed duties and identities, Romola sleeps, and sleep becomes the place where Eliot contains contending desires, where she ends the battle between woman's mind and male power. When the woman awakens, she is not only relocated literally away from Florence, she is relocated symbolically in a realm of inherent sexual characteristics.

Romola is called by the early morning sun to a rebirth and baptism in duty; the first sound she hears is the cry of a child bereft of its parents, and she sets to work organising the survivors of plague in the village where she has miraculously landed.[13] Some eight months later she returns to Florence, now 'the blessed Lady' of the valley, the 'sweet and sainted Lady' of the village; taking Tessa, Tito's *contadina* mistress and mother of his two children, into her household, she establishes a kind of beatific matriarchy that is reminiscent of Aurora Leigh's benevolent patronage of Marian Erle and her illegitimate son.

If, as I have argued, Eliot may be said to deploy strategies of containment to evade or to deny an intolerable conflict between woman's mind and male authority, then her Epilogue to *Romola* banishes all rebellious desire and disciplinary 'annunciation' from a place serenely immune to the contingent restraints of culture and society. It is the evening of 22 May 1509. Tessa and her daughter are wreathing garlands for an altar over which hangs a small full-length portrait of Savonarola. Near the doorway opening on to the loggia (in a place thus a little closer to the outside world) sit Romola (in her face 'a placidity . . . which had never belonged to it in youth') and Tito's son. The educated woman, 'instructed' by her father, tutors her husband's illegitimate son in Petrarch. Romola has become a deified matriarch, enthroned in parallel relationship to the deified Savonarola. The antinomies of woman's mind and male authority are banished from this place by virtue of their shared equality of transformed power. She is an animated icon, the female figure of intellectual ambition, disciplined by her experience to tutor her husband's son – an occupation, to be sure, of significant status and merit in the Renaissance, but why is she not also tutoring his daughter, 'a delicate blue-eyed girl of thirteen'? Savonarola is a painted icon, the male figure of authority, looking down upon a household of women. The shared identity of Romola and Savonarola as symbols of transformed, relocated power (her pliable intellect channelled into benevolent teaching, his harsh authoritarianism muted into benevolent image) enacts a cancellation of intolerably antagonistic ideologies.

When Romola sought to free herself from all claims, Eliot observes that she had only heard 'the ring of egoism' in Savonarola's plans for ecclesiastic renovation. In a pattern consistent with Eliot's enduring desire to be as fair as possible to both sides (to put things in their simplest terms), she goes on to observe that this 'ring of egoism' is the 'meaner' part of 'all energetic belief': 'And if such energetic belief, pursuing a grand and remote end, is often in danger of becoming a demon-worship, in which the votary lets his son and daughter pass through the fire with a readiness that hardly looks like sacrifice; tender fellow-feeling for the nearest has its danger too, and is apt to be timid and sceptical towards the larger aims without which life cannot rise into religion' (p. 587). The discourse espousing an ideal reconciliation of the better parts of energetic belief and of tender fellow-feeling – dedication without egoism and tenderness without timidity – finds its visual, reified end in the iconisation of Savonarola and Romola.[14] *Romola* closes with images that make female desire for intellectual power negatively autonomous with male impediment to such power. To be sure, overt patriarchal authority is absent through the death of Romola's father, her husband, and Savonarola, but it is very much present in a scene rich with female worship of an image of that authority. Ironically, the woman who has been made into 'likenesses' of herself throughout the novel now worships the likeness of a man who redirected her wish for 'instructed' independence into acceptance of benevolent subjugation.

To return, now, to the strategies of containment Eliot deploys in assessing women's writing and in giving us the fictive life of one 'instructed' woman, it seems to me that either she evades direct discussion of patriarchal constraints or she shows their documented, historical presence, only, in the long run, to transcend them. Eliot avoids analysis of the situations of nineteenth-century English women intellectuals and she relocates Romola in the realm of female immanence from whose bonds she was breaking free when she heard the 'annunciation' of that 'arresting voice'. At the end of the novel, Romola possesses the immutable, ahistorical autonomy desired, as I suggested earlier, by the traditional intellectual, and she thereby becomes a symbol of Eliot's conservative political views. With the assistance of an actual historical personage, Romola may be said to resist the contingency of history. Finally, Eliot's evasions of Victorian prescriptions for the proper role and function for women and her reliance upon the myth of essentialist womanhood surely serve as self-dislocation from the androcentric culture that both limits woman's possibility and permits Eliot's own intellectual success. In *Felix Holt, the Radical*, published three years after *Romola*, Eliot's awareness of her problematical status as fêted woman intellectual gets expressed in a bitterly subversive sexual politics.

# 11

# Subversive Sexual Politics:
## *Felix Holt, the Radical*

In July 1856 Eliot devoted a long article in the *Westminster Review* to an appreciation of the work of Wilhelm Heinrich von Riehl; in Thomas Pinney's apt assessment, ' "The Natural History of German Life" ' is 'the best statement, through its sympathetic comment on Riehl's position, of the grounds for George Eliot's conservatism' (*E.*, p. 276). I want to suggest that some of the disjunctive complexity of Eliot's most explicitly political and most politically conservative novel, *Felix Holt, the Radical*, has its origin in her praise of the social thought of Riehl. Following Riehl's suggestions for studying 'the People as they are', Eliot ends up subversively rejecting political action through the agency of her own sexual politics. Correlatively with this rejection and coherently with her self-mythologisation as a Gramscian traditional intellectual, Eliot also subverts the dominant ideology of ameliorative change elaborated by organic intellectuals in Victorian England.

Eliot's article is based upon discussion of new editions of two books by Riehl, *Die burgerliche Gesellschaft* (1851) and *Land und Leute* (1853); his work is exemplary, in her view, for a study of the lower classes. At the present, 'a true conception of the popular character' is unavailable. Distorted by those who believe 'the relations of men to their neighbours may be settled by algebraic equations' (a dart at the theories popularised by Harriet Martineau) or by those who practice an 'aristocratic dilettantism which attempts to restore the "good old times" by a sort of idyllic masquerading', the 'people' remain mis-represented (*E.* p. 272). Political economists and upper-class dilettantes alike need to 'check' their intellectual flights and assume a 'concrete' perspective. Noting the failure of European revolutions 'conducted from the point of view of abstract democratic and socialistic theories', Eliot observes that Riehl urges 'a social policy founded on the special study of the people as they are – on the natural history of the various social ranks. He thinks it wise to pause a little from theorizing, and see what is the material actually present

197

for theory to work upon' (*E.*, 289). In *Felix Holt* Eliot makes a fictional application of Riehl's suggestions for a new 'social policy'; she seeks to present the actual material which is the stuff of theory, to give the reader an understanding of the 'natural history of various social ranks' as she understood its meaning in the political scene in 1832 (or in 1866).

Despite her call for an artistic sensitivity to social groups different from those usually encountered in the English novel (a call also sounded in the oft-cited chapter 17 of *Adam Bede* where the narrator urges that art must not banish 'old women scraping carrots with their work worn hands' from fictional representation), her descriptions of the lower classes in *Felix Holt* are static, as muddy as the ale at the Blue Cow (the public house frequented by the navvies). These descriptions are bereft of the power with which Eliot displays the misery of the most fascinating character in the novel: Arabella Transome, a member of the Tory land-owning classes and a woman bearing the terrible secret of long-ago adultery with a socially ambitious lawyer. Strangely withholding the narrative skill that vivifies the suffering of this character from invigorating the political plot, Eliot seems to contradict her own aesthetic imperatives. She invests so much narrative energy in Mrs Transome's unfolding family drama and so little in 'study of the people as they are', that the ideal social novel gets contradicted in her practice. We listen to one or two colourful publicans, eavesdrop in the servant's hall but the lower-class characters end up as wooden, lifeless demonstrations of a 'theory' of representation. Eliot's power to register the painful shades of psychological unhappiness in Mrs Transome distracts her from her purpose, and it is as if Mrs Transome's palpable misery subverts Eliot's abstract ideas about 'true conceptions' of English political life. A bitterly discontented woman gets in the way of a high-minded woman intellectual, or to put this another way, subversive sexual politics interefere with theories of representation.

Eliot's admiration of Riehl's wish 'to pause a little from theorizing' (even though, of course, this means she adopts a 'theory' of representation) may be connected with the two principal concerns of my discussion to this point: Eliot's deployment of strategies of containment to manage the conflict between woman's mind and man's authority and her implicit opposition to the work of organic intellectuals. To 'pause' from 'theorizing' in *Felix Holt* is to enter the mind of Mrs Transome and in doing that Eliot begins to interrogate those systems of political thought directing women's intelligence to private, domestic concerns rather than to public, cultural activity. And to question the theory of those who believe that 'all social questions are merged in economical science' (as Eliot does in the Riehl essay) is to criticise the work of organic intellectuals. As agent of Eliot's anti-theoretical ideology, Mrs Transome performs a spectacular work of sabotage.

Moreover, as many of Eliot's critics observe, the plot of *Felix Holt* is so baroquely involved with changed identities and family secrets that the novel is really less about English politics than the preoccupation with inheritance and discovery of the true father which is the material of so much Victorian fiction. It opens with Mrs Transome awaiting the return of her son Harold from Constantinople where he has resided as a banker for some 15 years. Harold is the son of Matthew Jermyn, the unscrupulous lawyer with whom Mrs Transome has had an affair some thirty years earlier. Jermyn has grown rich, powerful, and respectable in the years since his liason with Mrs Transome. This family drama is, of course, but one thread in the tangled web of plot in *Felix Holt*. Felix Holt himself gets involved in the political disturbances surrounding the elections of 1832, falls in love with Esther Lyon who is not really the daughter of Rufus Lyon, the man she believes is her father, but really the daughter of a Frenchwoman and an Englishman who changed identities with a man now residing in the town where the novel is set . . . and so on. The public theme of politics seems to be under constant siege by the private theme of family drama; or, to cast this problematic in terms of sex and gender, the male plot of corrupt contention for political leadership is so undermined by the female plot of abandoned mothers and illegitimate children that the political meaning of *Felix Holt* may be interpreted as a refutation of male political action.

In *Felix Holt* the strategy of containment deployed by Eliot ironically becomes an ironic containment of women in the private sphere of feeling and sexuality. By relegating woman to a place defined by the absence of a public life, Eliot establishes a deceptively calm stasis. Woman is firmly allocated to the emotional, domestic sphere conventionally associated with her sex: Mrs Transome dwells in bitter self-recrimination for her adultery and in haughty resentment of her diminished social power; Mrs Holt inhabits the weepy territory where mothers querulously seek to control their sons; and Esther Lyon, despite her final renunciation of wealth (and

Byron) and the heartfelt commitment of feminine cleverness to 'teaching', remains a domestic coquette. To be sure, Mrs Holt is harmless, if irritating, and Esther is authentically affectionate and loyal. The case of Mrs Transome, however, is different. From a conventionally powerless position, from the emotional, domestic life to which Eliot confines her, she radically subverts the male world of politics and the male world of patriarchal plotting. Her private, anarchic desires effectively destroy the public ambitions of her former lover and her intractable son. Both men inhabit the active world of male politics and both patronisingly relegate Mrs Transome to an emotional, domestic space. To one she is the faded reminder of an imprudent, passionate past, and to the other an abstraction of quaint Tory politics, rather than a living, breathing, and suffering mother.

   To this point, I have emphasised the intellectual nature of unfulfilled desire in Eliot's female characters. Here I do not mean to suggest Mrs Transome possesses Romola's intellectual ambition, Dorothea Brooke's finely modulated moral intelligence, or the vital mind of Maggie Tulliver. Despite the recognition she received in her young womanhood of being 'wonderfully clever and accomplished' and that she 'had been rather ambitious of intellectual superiority', she is not an unusually gifted woman: solaced only by her faded reputation as a handsome, spirited girl and her love for an illegitimate son, she is obsessed with aging and guilt. But all this is what I want to emphasise about her: the unfulfilled possibilities, the wrong choices, the frustrated desires that are the unhappy history of a rather ordinary upper-class woman living in the country. Eliot's rigid restriction of Mrs Transome to a place conventionally allocated to women (the domestic interior, the feelings) is both an implicit expression of the conflict between woman's mind and male authority *and* a subversion of the forces creating such a conflict. Arabella Transome inhabits a negative sphere of tormented female consciousness. Within that consciousness Eliot confines all the rebellious desire potentially able to undermine male political ambition. In that place we find silence and resentment, vivid reminders of the things Mrs Transome cannot say, bitter memories of the sparkling vitality wasted in marriage to a feeble-minded land-owner and the deflection of her sexuality into rebellious adultery with an eager attorney. Made a saboteur by her sexual history, she can impede the political ambitions of her former lover and her son. That she should possess only one negative form of power reveals Eliot's criticism of the restricted possibilities permitted women when they are regarded primarily as body, rather than as body *and* mind. If men tend to read women primarily as sexual and emotional creatures, then that is how women's power will be expressed – through their sexuality and through their emotions. And in the case of Mrs Transome, this culturally inscribed power is turned against those two men who circumscribe her behaviour. Her female world of destructive sexuality and nagging disappointment demolishes a male world of political action – and implicitly interrogates the usefulness of politics itself.

She also disrupts the male social order. Just as Romola's intellectual desire to live as an 'instructed' woman and, when that desire is chastened by Savonarola, to have no name, no identity, transgresses a male social order nominating woman to her proper function, so Mrs Transome's sexual desire disrupts male continuity in the community of Treby Magna. Her adultery fractures the linear order of inheritance, licenses the aggressive intruder Matthew Jermyn literally to profit from the family he enters through illicit sexuality. As the Virgilian coachman, Mr Sampson, points out in the opening pages, 'Lawyer Jermyn had had *his* picking out of the estate. Not a door in his house but what was the finest polished oak, all got off the Transome estate'. Despite the financial necessity for Harold to leave this estate at the age of nineteen to 'make his way upward in public life', there is an imaginative necessity in his departure: he is born an outsider by virtue of his mother's disruptive sexuality and he becomes one as an adult by virtue of his cultural difference – he returns, an exotic 'Oriental', a suave merchant banker from Smyrna with a taste for 'red pepper' and 'relishing sauces'.[1]

The opening chapter of *Felix Holt* contains a stunning description of an upper-class, intelligent, middle-aged woman reduced by economic circumstance and sexual guilt to small demonstrations of her will and compelled to make do with 'every little sign of power her lot had left her'.[2] Deploying two highly effective images, Eliot creates a sensitive balance of sympathy for a monotonous life and indictment of an irresponsible gentry. She begins with Mrs Transome descending her staircase in a faded, but still elegant black velvet dress: she has the 'imperious air that would have marked her as an object of hatred and reviling by a revolutionary mob'. Yet the only sovereignty she has enjoyed is as a handsome young woman possessing a sparkling but undisciplined mind and finding many

things alleged to be good and true 'dull and meaningless'. Trained
by a 'superior governess' to the superficial assumption of correct
manners and morals, in the hard times of advancing age and
incremental guilt for her transgression, Mrs Transome's knowledge
and accomplishments have 'become as valueless as old-fashioned
stucco ornaments, of which the substance was never worth
anything, while the form is no longer to the taste of any living
mortal' (*F.H.*, p. 28). To this point, Eliot has emphasised the external
signs of dress and manners, but then in a rhetorical turn
characteristic of her instructive narrators, we are directed from the
outer to the inner life – to what remains concealed from the reader
and Mrs Transome's community under that stucco façade. Rather
than absence of worthy substance, we find the presence of appalling
misery. No one has 'divined what was hidden under that outward
life – a woman's keen sensibility and dread, which lay screened
behind all her petty habits and narrow notions, as some quivering
thing with eyes and throbbing heart may lie crouching behind
withered rubbish' (p. 29). The graphic nature of this image shocks
the reader into sympathy and into an astonished, fresh
understanding of an unusually long paragraph of description that
ranges from a young woman laughing at the Lyrical Ballads to a
middle-aged one relishing the curtsies of the parish. The paragraph
begins with an imperious woman descending a staircase in a
draughty country house and concludes with her transformation into
a quivering animal crouching behind rubbish that is as 'withered' as
her heart.[3]

The rich range of imagery and detail employed in this paragraph
contrasts notably with that employed by the disinterested and
disengaged narrator who tells us about political and social change in
Treby Magna. Change in an individual woman is rendered in a
vivid, even passionate, language: change in society and history is
delivered in a dry and weary manner. And so intensely is the change
in the individual described, that Mrs Transome seems to internalise
the language of such description: awaiting her son's return with
dreadful foreboding, she says to herself that it is 'a lucky eel
that escapes skinning'. It is as if she has observed her own
transformation from queenly figure descending the staircase to a
species of trapped animal life. The reader, having been guided
through Mrs Transome's transformation, having been taken with
her down that staircase, then perceives her own internalised
perception of it. Entering the tormented recesses of Mrs Transome's

mind in ways that we never penetrate the consciousness of Felix Holt or Harold Transome, we actually enter that sphere of withdrawn womanhood where Eliot locates the conflict between woman's mind and male authority. Through painful entry into this private space of unhappy womanhood, we become aware of its intense difference from the public space of male power and politics, inhabited with sensuous ease by Harold Transome. In Eliot's descriptions of the public and the private Harold, the former seen as good-natured fellow by his neighbours and the latter as generous but emotionally distant son by his mother, the public and the private worlds determined by sex and gender are ironically disclosed.

Describing Harold as 'a clever, frank, good-natured egoist . . . unspeculative, unsentimental, unsympathetic; fond of sensual pleasures, but disinclined to all vice', the narrator declares that a 'character is apt to look but indifferently, written out in this way': if, however, we were to number Harold among our acquaintances, we would think him 'a good fellow, highly acceptable as a guest, a colleague, or a brother-in-law. Whether all mothers would have liked him as a son, is another question' (*F.H.*, pp. 98–9). Eliot then takes us inside Mrs Transome's mind, giving us the viewpoint of the silenced mother, one of many who are tartly described in these terms: 'It is a fact kept a little too much in the background, that mothers have a self larger than their maternity, and that when their sons have become taller than themselves, and are gone from them to college or into the world, there are wide spaces of their time which are not filled with praying for their boys, reading old letters, and envying yet blessing those who are attending to their shirt buttons' (p. 116). In these 'wide spaces' of female time, Mrs Transome feels a 'bondage' made of the 'finest threads' worse 'than any fetters': it is a bondage of fear that Harold's paternity will be disclosed to him (as indeed it is in a dreadful, silent moment when he sees his resemblance to Jermyn in a mirror).

These descriptions of Mrs Transome's mind reveal not only the ambiguous, even deceptive, qualities of this woman, but also a cultural criticism of the late eighteenth-century values that have produced her. In his political reading of Mrs Transome, Terry Eagleton suggests that the novel 'mourns in her the death of traditional society' and that she is a refutation of 'the novel's official progressivist ideology' (*Criticism and Ideology*, p. 117). In Eagleton's view, the power with which the narrator describes Mrs Transome's uneasy life does not seem to be employed in showing how Treby

Magna is better off because of Felix Holt's elusive radicalism. True
enough, but Eagleton sees Eliot's political thought as more
schematised and coherent than it actually is and he pays insufficient
attention to the narrator's almost hostile assessment of political
change in Treby Magna. Eliot's narrator is far less inclined to
endorse 'progressivist ideology' than Eagleton imagines. For
example, the ending is suffused with a weary irony behind which
the narrator retreats into an indifferent, studied ignorance of events,
abandoning the omniscience that produced the details of social
and individual history constituting the novel: 'not having
correspondence' in those parts, the narrator cannot really say if
there is 'more enlightenment' in Treby Magna than existed before
Felix's involvement with the community. Whatever 'progressivist
ideology' one may discover in *Felix Holt* is considerably modified by
the dyspeptic and heavy-handed refusal to affirm that the farmers
are 'public spirited', the Sproxton men 'sober and judicious', and
the Dissenters 'without narrowness or asperity in religion'.
Eagleton, therefore, is both correct and incorrect about the meaning
of Mrs Transome; undoubtedly, she is an emblem of lost and
ambiguously valued Toryism, but she cannot be said to refute a
progressivism about which the novel is seriously ambivalent.

What is 'mourned' (to use Eagleton's term) in Mrs Transome is not
so much the loss of 'traditional society' as its degeneration. Tory,
traditional society still exists in the novel but in debased, even
dangerous form, its culpability for political disorder manifested, for
example, in the lax management of Sir Maximus Debarry's estate. It
is here that we can perceive Eliot's nostalgia for an organic
community where social classes cooperated in fruitful conservation
of the cultural 'treasure-house' so dear to the Felix Holt who,
appropriated from the novel to become an advocate of social order,
addresses the working men of England in the disruptive year of
1867. And it is in Eliot's nostalgia that we can see her affiliation with
the land-owning classes. As a self-created traditional intellectual,
Eliot wants to believe in an uninterrupted historical continuity. She
sees the positive values of the Tory past, therefore, not as lost, but as
debased through vulgar politics and careless management of the
'treasure-house' of England's history. Eliot implies that had Mrs
Transome and members of her Tory class demanded less pulling of
the forelock and demonstrated more sympathetic understanding of
the lower classes (an understanding that might have been facilitated
by a Riehlian conception of 'the people as they are'), then, perhaps,

Treby Magna would not be left by the narrator at the end of the novel in its unregenerate state of selfishness. Tory values have been debased through parasitic reproduction rather than invigorated through moral revision.

An absence of moral revision in the Tory land-owning classes also reveals the presence of threats to the social order. In *Felix Holt*, English culture and society are endangered by the enfranchisement of an uneducated body of voters in 1832, and Eliot thereby seriously questions the usefulness of political action as she understood it in the months prior to the passing of the Second Reform Bill in 1867. *Felix Holt* seems to put an end to politics through interrogating the liberal views of the class to which Eliot implicitly opposes herself. 'I say, if we working men are ever to get a man's share, we must have universal suffrage, and annual Parliaments, and the vote by ballot, and electoral districts' declaims the trades-union man on nomination day. To this Felix replies 'No! – something else before all that' (p. 248). That something else is a belief in the organic, historical continuity desired by traditional intellectuals opposing themselves to Benthamite theorising and to the political 'engineering' undertaken by Parliament. Parliamentary practice with all its machinery is disruptive, discontinuous; what Felix terms 'the ruling belief in society about what is right and what is wrong, what is honourable and what is shameful' (p. 250) is Eliot's preferred instrument of evolutionary, coherent change.

Eliot's doubt about the usefulness of political reform affirms her self-mythologisation as an intellectual who instructs the community from a privileged narrative sphere above the worldliness of political life. In an oft-quoted letter written towards the end of her career, she characterised her intellectual practice in these terms: 'My function is that of the *aesthetic*, not the doctrinal teacher – the rousing of the nobler emotions, which make mankind desire the social right, not the prescribing of special measures, concerning which the artistic mind, however strongly moved by social sympathy, is often not the best judge' (*L.*, 4:44). Through the antithesis of aesthetics and doctrine, 'the rousing of the nobler emotions' and 'the prescribing of special measures', she places herself in a privileged position. Moreover, if the conflict between woman's mind and male authority originates in cultural and social formations controlled and formed by male political action, then it is not unexpected, even if it seems contradictory, that Eliot would write an explicitly political novel disdaining political action, a novel whose dense family plot smothers vulgar electioneering of Whigs and Tories. *Felix Holt* proposes a radical-conservative ideology, tinged with Eliot's own problematical sexual politics and invested with her achieved authority as farsighted woman intellectual. Radically calling for an end to class antagonism and a concomitant withering away of political action, it conservatively postulates some mythical time and place where there is no need for politics at all. It is in this time and in this place that Felix and Esther are relocated by Eliot at the end of the novel; she relegates all the mucky work of vulgar politics to places outside the unknown town where Felix and Esther live an unremarkable life.

John Blackwood, Eliot's publisher, and Frederic Harrison, her legal adviser in devising the elaborate plot of inheritance, both sensed the slippery nature of Eliot's meaning in *Felix Holt*, even though they did not express it in quite these terms. Blackwood announced that the 'politics are excellent and will attract all parties', which does not promise much for a concise definition of such politics. Harrison delighted in the novel because 'the religious people, the educated, the simple, the radicals, the Tories, the socialists, the intellectual reformers, the domestic circle, the critics, the metaphysicians, the artists, the positivists, the squires, are all quite convinced that it has been conceived from their own point of view' (*L.*, 4:246, 284). What Blackwood and Harrison did not see, of course, was that by diminishing particular ideologies, by appealing to all the interests of all these different groups, Eliot artfully appeals to only one: the group favouring eradication of self-interest, ideology, and politics itself.

What's more, she seems to speak from above and beyond those places where self-interest, ideology, and politics find their origins, and, it must be noted, from above and beyond those places where *she*, as prominent woman thinker, was forced to confront an androcentric culture that both bound woman's possibility *and* encouraged her own intellectual performance. Adopting a disinterested mode that sets the tone for a novel designed to reprimand self-interest, the narrator sets out to tell us how Treby Magna 'gradually passed from being simply a respectable market-town . . . and took on the more complex life brought by mines and manufactures' (*F.H.*, pp. 42–3). Different social, religious, and political groups are viewed from a fair-minded pose of disinterest. Dissenters and Tories are shown to be bigoted in their own particular and harmful ways; however, the religious fanaticism of the Dissenters helps to reconcile them to a 'meagre existence', and the Tories are 'far from being all oppressors, disposed to grind down the working classes into serfdom'. The narrator concludes this even-handed assessment by noting that the 'social changes in Treby parish are comparatively public matters, and this history is chiefly concerned with the private lot of a few men and women; but there is no private life which has not been determined by a wider public life' (p. 45). The sovereign, but sympathetic, nature of this last declaration discloses Eliot's maturing intellectual persona: sagacious, authoritative, graced to connect private and public lives.

Allegedly possessing no hypostatic theory of society that impedes representation of the 'people', wanting only to trace connections between private and public lives, instructing as an 'aesthetic' not as a 'doctrinal' teacher, the voice of *Felix Holt* speaks with the sympathetic sovereignty Eliot perfected four years later in *Middlemarch*. To be sure, the power of this voice owes a great deal to the conventions of authorial omniscience and to the particularly Victorian deployment of narrative which J. Hillis Miller has defined and explored: 'The development of Victorian fiction is a movement from the assumption that society and the self are founded on some superhuman power outside them, to a putting in question of this assumption, to the discovery that society now appears to be self-creating and self-supporting, resting on nothing outside itself.'[4] What needs to be emphasised here, I think, is the manner in which Eliot achieves her sovereignty in this mode of instructive discourse. To teach Victorian society that it rests 'on nothing outside itself' requires great tact and great authority; Eliot displays both. Moreover, in Victorian discourse tact may be associated with the ascription of feeling to women and authority with the ascription of intellect to men. The alignment of narrative tact and authority demands considerable cultural confidence – a confidence enjoyed more by male than by female writers in the Victorian period, yet commandingly possessed by 'George Eliot'.

As I have already suggested, Eliot's sustained display of sagacious sovereignty discloses her willing ability to seize the cultural power required for synthesis of gender-based modes of Victorian discourse. 'Doing in a woman's way a traditionally male task of knowing', as Gilbert and Guber assert, she demonstrates the talent to bring female and male ways together, and in so doing affirms the very existence of those 'ordinary classifications of culture' which these critics believe are transcended in such an action. In her narrative performance in *Felix Holt*, she is complicit in the allocation of intellect to men and feeling to women, just as she is strongly (and simultaneously) resistant to the confinement of woman to the domestic sphere, as her brilliantly subversive creation of Arabella Transome demonstrates.

With Eliot's sagacious (and sometimes subversive) voice in our 'instructed' ears and minds, it is useful to return to the novel in which the problematical desires of her heroine remain just that – desires. In *The Mill on the Floss*, 'male' cultural confidence is so strongly molested by 'female' desire for autonomy, all is so freighted with discordance, that everything goes under in the river. If *Felix Holt* eventually manages to contain disjunctive complexity in such a way that the novel, with its lifeless Felix Holt and disruptively alive Arabella Transome, remains a nagging difficulty rather than a large problem in Eliot's canon, then *The Mill on the Floss*, with its extravagant ending, compels attention as a major critical challenge. No other Eliot novel so painfully evokes the sad containment of female intelligence by male morality. And no other Eliot novel (at least for me) so fully exposes Eliot's own dilemma: how to reconcile her complicity with and resistance to the androcentric culture which, on the one hand, binds her character Maggie Tulliver to self-denial, and, on the other, enables her own dazzling success as woman intellectual.

# 12

# Maggie Tulliver's Desire

Veiled by an anonymity which may have concealed his identity but certainly not his magisterial male confidence, Henry James declared that 'the discursive portions of *Middlemarch* are, as we may say, too clever by half. The author wishes to say too many things, and to say them too well' (*C.H.*, p. 359). The female character in Eliot's fiction who may be charged with a desire 'to say too many things, and to say them too well' is, of course, Maggie Tulliver. But where George Eliot lived on to write *Daniel Deronda* (if only to have it greeted by James as possessing an 'over-cultivated' sense of the 'universal'), Maggie's immodest presentation of her mind is tempered by her experience. As she grows up she restrains her desire to say 'too many things' and understands that saying them 'too well' earns male scorn rather than approbation.

I began my discussion of George Eliot with a scene in *The Mill on the Floss* which the anonymous reviewer for the *Dublin University Magazine* declared to be one where 'the woman's hand is unmistakably shown, and the lack of true perspective becomes most palpable' (*C.H.*, p. 148). Eliot does indeed betray her 'woman's hand' by having Maggie Tulliver desire to possess as many books as the Rev. Walter Stelling, and by deploying strategies of containment to manage the conflict between female mind and male authority in a particularly intense and difficult way. I want now to return to *The Mill on the Floss* and to suggest that in this novel the conflict is at its most intense and the strategy of containment at its most problematical. Because the conflict in *The Mill on the Floss* also stems from Eliot's ambivalent views of past and present as well as from Maggie Tulliver's desire to say a lot of things and say them very well, I shall argue that strategies of containment are deployed by Eliot not only to manage the conflict between woman's mind and male authority: Eliot must confront her own ambiguous attitudes towards past and present. Figuring Maggie Tulliver as a metaphor, these strategies relegate past, present, ideology, and politics to the definitively ahistorical topos of death. In the drowning of Maggie Tulliver we see the destruction of all that constrains her.

Eliot's enigmatic assessment of her own historical time is signalled most clearly by her enduring preoccupation with the past which she sustained until setting her last novel a mere five years or so back in time from its composition. That she situates almost all her fiction in the historical past is interpreted by Steven Marcus as evidence of a desire to control the present. Order imposed on irregular, disjunctive events by narrative is the means to mastery of the present: 'By possessing the past we assert our possession of the present as well; by defining the past in a certain way we control the possibilities of the present' ('Literature and Social Theory', p. 190). Elaborating Marcus's point, one might add that the slim hope of a better present is also implied by narrative closure: the finality of narrative ending we encounter at least up until *Daniel Deronda* shuts off the possibility of positive social or political change occurring in the present, for if the irrecoverable world is the superior one, then the feasibility of useful political action in the present seems uncertain. In Eliot's fiction, concentration upon the past also functions as reassurance for a society troubled at unsettling moments in history. By evoking in 1866 political turbulence and its stable resolution in the Reform Bill of 1832, *Felix Holt*, for example, offers implicit reassurance that history *will* repeat itself, not as tragedy or farce but as dramatic triumph of social order.

At the close of her *Westminster* article on Riehl, Eliot draws attention to certain aspects of his conservative social thought which she finds ideal: 'Riehl's conservatism is not in the least tinged with the partisanship of a class, with a poetic fanaticism for the past, or with the prejudices of a mind incapable of discerning the grander evolution of things to which all social forms are but temporarily subservient' (*E.*, pp. 298–9). If Eliot is affectionately partisan to any social class in her fiction, it is certainly not the one which encouraged and authorised her intellectual production: worthy as they are, the rural lower-middle-class ambitions of Caleb Garth to remain solvent, honest, hard-working, and surrounded by his happy family, are not those which directed Mary Ann Evans's transformation from intelligent, provincial girl to sibylline metropolitan intellectual. The interests of the class to which she is emotionally bound are not the interests which govern her career. Eliot does, however, return with some fanaticism to the past in her fiction, indeed with 'a poetic fanaticism' if one thinks of *Adam Bede* where, as Philip Fisher aptly observes, Mrs Poyser's dairy 'is described with an intensity beyond realism' (*Making up Society*, p.

64). But that 'grander evolution of things to which all social forms are but temporarily subservient' is surely Eliot's secularised, and particularly Comtean, vision of a world unfolding according to a divine plan. *The Mill on the Floss* reveals significant attitudes towards past and present, towards the social class which dominates St Ogg's, and towards the sacrifice of an intellectually ambitious young woman to 'the grander evolution of things to which all social forms are but temporarily subservient'.

The elegaic discourse of *Adam Bede* implies that the world celebrated in that novel can never be recovered: the vital involvement of individuals with their community, the values embodied in Adam's fidelity to his family, in Dinah's power of sympathetic identification, in Mrs Poyser's spotless kitchen – all of this is part of what Peter Laslett terms the world we have lost.[1] Eliot's first narrator, in unfolding the sad story of Amos Barton, scoffs at the 'well-regulated mind' which rejoices in the 'New Police, the Tithe Commutation Act, the penny post, and all guarantees of human advancement'. Eliot fully develops this rejection of modern progress in her evocation of the lost world through the personification of 'Leisure' in *Adam Bede*, the most consciously pastoral of her novels. Because the joys of 'Old Leisure' partially express Eliot's implicit desire for a world unmolested by disruptive historical change, I shall quote the passage at length:

Leisure is gone – gone where the spinning-wheels are gone, and the pack-horses, and the slow waggons, and the pedlars, who brought bargains to the door on sunny afternoons. Ingenious philosophers tell you, perhaps, that the great work of the steam-engine is to create leisure for mankind. Do not believe them: it only creates a vacuum for eager thought to rush in. Even idleness is eager now – eager for amusement: prone to excursion-trains, art-museums, periodical literature, and exciting novels: prone even to scientific theorising, and cursory peeps through microscopes. Old Leisure was quite a different personage: he only read one newspaper, innocent of leaders, and was free from that periodicity of sensations which we call post-time. He was a contemplative, rather stout gentleman, of excellent digestion, – of quiet perceptions, undiseased by hypothesis: happy in his inability to know the causes of things, preferring the things themselves. He lived chiefly in the country, among pleasant country seats and homesteads, and was fond of sauntering by the fruit-tree wall, and scenting the apricots when they were warmed by the morning sunshine, or of sheltering himself under the orchard boughs at noon, when the summer pears were falling.　(*A.B.*, Ch. 52)

In this hymn to pastoral serenity, the slowness of the waggon never caused interminable journeys in bad weather for hard-pressed agricultural labourers, the pedlar was never a surly character who haggled with weary housewives on a stormy day, and modern invention never the source of an improved way of life. The technological advances celebrated by Harriet Martineau are the direct object of Eliot's criticism: the railway, which for Martineau brought previously estranged social classes together and enabled town dwellers to see the seaside and dairy products and vegetables to be brought efficiently to the town, is, for Eliot, the means to gratify idleness. The museums, the technological developments in publishing, which are for Martineau a sign of an increasingly better educated and more rational-minded populace, are for Eliot a sign of cultural degeneration. Leaders similar to those written by Harriet Martineau for the London *Daily News* were, in Eliot's view, happily unavailable to 'Old Leisure'. The narrator disdains modern speed, modern eagerness for new ideas and new amusements, disdains all that Martineau celebrated in her ratifications of the achievements of the English middle class.[2]

To prefer newspapers free of political bias is to reject ideology; to prefer perceptions 'undiseased by hypotheses' is to perceive ideology itself as a symptom of diseased culture and society. The phrase 'undiseased by hypothesis' clearly echoes Carlyle's controlling image in the 'Characteristics' essay: in fact, those objects of the narrator's scorn in *Adam Bede* – periodical literature, exciting novels, concern with first causes – are Carlylean symptoms of a society sick with the disease of self-consciousness, and also the object of Elizabeth Barrett Browning's social criticism.[3] 'Old Leisure' possesses an unusually relaxed cast of mind, tuned not to 'post-time', but to natural time measured by the rhythms of a mythologised country topos. In this ideal place untainted by ideology, a place somewhat reminiscent of Mr Boythorn's rustic paradise in *Bleak House*, time is so fixed that it becomes atemporal: it is always a sunny summer morning and the fruit is always fragrantly ripe. Relegating disruptive historical change to the space outside the mythologised country topos, keeping it, so to speak, on the other side of the 'fruit-tree wall', Eliot virtually literalises her strategy of containment.

In itself, Eliot's employment of pastoral idyll as Victorian social criticism is hardly remarkable; as the towns became dirtier, the urban populace more pressing, the demands for social justice more urgent, the mythological attractions of the country became that much more appealing. Eliot adds her elegaic voice to a nineteenth-century chorus that began with Wordsworth's strong critique in the Preface to the *Lyrical Ballads*, which traces a 'multitude of causes, unknown to former times, [that] are now acting with a combined force to blunt the discriminatory powers of the mind, and, unfitting it for all voluntary exertion'. Wordsworth laments 'the increasing accumulation of men in cities, where the uniformity of their occupations produces a craving for extraordinary incident, which the rapid communication of intelligence hourly gratifies', and he roundly condemns a 'degrading thirst after outrageous stimulation'.[4] What is remarkable is that Eliot's deployment of the pastoral topos as the place where intolerable history is shut out aligns itself with her self-mythologisation as a traditional intellectual resistant to rupturing political change. Here it is only the slow history of *otium* that continues unmolested by alteration.

Where the passage from *Adam Bede* describing 'Old Leisure' argues that negative social and cultural change has taken place, that the self-conscious, self-interested present has destroyed the gentle, ideologically untainted, harmony of a mythical country life, the Proem of *Romola* postulates an unchanging, eternal 'human lot'. The tone, too, is markedly different, not merely by virtue of what is usually characterised as a maturity of novelistic and intellectual imagination, to say nothing of the difference between late eighteenth-century England and late fifteenth-century Florence. Where the narrator of *Adam Bede* is ruefully nostalgic, eventually if reluctantly reconciled to a changed social order, the narrator of *Romola* is majestically judgemental; where the narrator of *Adam Bede* speaks in a wryly resigned tone about social and cultural change, the narrator of *Romola* addresses the reader in the sibylline voice of a maturing 'George Eliot'. Philosophical and sagacious, the narrator speaks about history, culture, and society from above and beyond its determinants.

This narrator evokes a Renaissance 'spirit' of 1492 embodied in a student pondering the eternal mystery of human existence: he has been questioning the stars or the sages, or his own soul, for that hidden knowledge which would break through the barrier of man's brief life, and show its dark path, that seemed to bend no whither, to be an arc in an immeasurable circle of light and glory. The great river-courses which have shaped the lives of men have hardly changed; and those other streams, the life-currents that ebb and flow in human hearts, pulsate to the same great needs, the same great loves and terrors. As our thought follows close in the slow wake of the dawn, we are impressed with the broad sameness of the human lot, which never alters in the main headings of its history – hunger and labour, seed-time and harvest, love and death.   (*R*., p. 43).

This student displays that ambitious curiosity which impels Lydgate's research in *Middlemarch*: like Lydgate, he wants to penetrate the code of human genesis itself, to illuminate the 'dark path' of man's life which *seems* to have no direction, so that it may be seen as a curve in that 'immeasurable circle of light and glory', an image of coherent, radiant enclosure. In contrast to the pervasive insistence in *Adam Bede* upon a social and cultural degeneration, the narrator of *Romola* asserts that the human 'lot' remains unchanged. Eliot's image works to evoke immutable likeness between the 'streams' of natural and human existence; the flow of great rivers is evoked as a shaper of human life, a metaphor for what gives form to man's existence, and the flow of human blood in man's heart (literally and metaphorically) pulsates to unchanging feelings. 'Hunger, and labour, seed-time and harvest, love and death' are eternal 'headings' in the metaphorical text of man's life.

If we attempt to reconcile the 'Leisure' passage from *Adam Bede* and the Proem passage from *Romola* in Eliot's discourse of past and present, it would seem that what changes for the worse is the way in which man *chooses* to do his hungering and his labouring. However, the discourse of past and present becomes more complex when we read on in the Proem to *Romola*. The 'resuscitated spirit' of Florence in 1492 is not only a man hungering, labouring, and so on, but a man whose culture bears a more than passing resemblance to that of Eliot's own Victorian time. Our 'Spirit' turns out to have been

not a pagan philosopher, nor a philosophising pagan poet, but a man of the fifteenth century, inheriting its strange web of belief and unbelief; of Epicurean levity and fetichistic dread; of pedantic impossible ethics uttered by rote, and crude passions acted out with childish impulsiveness; of inclination towards a self-indulgent paganism, and inevitable subjection to that human conscience which, in the unrest of a new growth, was filling the air with strange prophecies and presentiments.   (*R.*, p. 48)

The contending values and manners of fifteenth-century Florence resemble those of nineteenth-century England; they imply the paradigms of conflict Victorians constructed for themselves as a means of giving order to the disturbing effects of rapid social change and unrest upon their lives. Creating such antinomic relationships is one way of understanding what was, perhaps, in actuality not so neatly assignable to such antithetical categories as 'belief and unbelief', 'levity' and 'dread', rigid 'ethics' and 'crude passions', and, in the dualistic assignment most suggestive of Eliot's participation in Comtean discourse, 'inclination' and 'subjection', the former suggesting egoistical choice and the latter acceptance of immutable laws of social progress.

Analysis of these passages from *Adam Bede* and *Romola* suggests that Eliot is saying at least three things: society and culture have changed irrevocably for the worse; despite these changes the human condition remains essentially the same; fifteenth-century culture is not unlike nineteenth-century culture and is probably no worse or better. Moreover, as further complication of Eliot's discourse of past and present, the nostalgic celebrations of the past are also sometimes disrupted by traces of attraction to the ideology very much present, so to speak, in the Victorian period: this is the ideology of self-advancement whose constitutive characteristic of disciplined work was not disdained by Eliot in her struggle to establish herself as a self-supporting woman intellectual in a male-dominated culture. Neither is it disdained by Adam Bede himself. As we move into the nineteenth century in the Epilogue to Eliot's most overtly pastoral novel, we learn that by June 1807 Jonathan Burge's timber-yard has become the property of Adam.[5]

If there is one character in Eliot's fiction who bears the burden of this ideological conflict more than any other, it is Maggie Tulliver. In her, the past is symbolically the place of poetry, imagination, feeling; and in her, too, the present is both the place of an ambition born of aggressive intelligence and, by association, a sterile wasteland of facts and petit-bourgeois stocktaking. The struggle and eventual destruction of Maggie Tulliver may, in part, be read as a political metaphor, her social and cultural status as an intellectually ambitious, passionately imaginative young woman making her a figure who embodies and suffers ideological contradiction. Maggie Tulliver's provocative death cancels the immutable autonomy of the contending political views she metaphorically embodies, and, what's more, liberates her from a form in which she seems to have no home. Eliot's most problematic strategy of containment reveals itself in the relegation of Maggie Tulliver and all she metaphorically represents to the realm of death. Maggie dies in part because she bears the intolerable weight of contending ideas.

Eliot opens Book 4 of *The Mill on the Floss* with the narrator's assumption that the reader has journeyed down the Rhône and noted the dreary villages that stud the banks, the dismal sign of a lost but unlamented world:

> Strange contrast, you may have thought, between the effect produced on us by these dismal remnants of commonplace houses, which in their best days were but the sign of a sordid life, belonging in all its details to our own vulgar era; and the effect produced by those ruins on the castled Rhine, which have crumbled and mellowed into such harmony, the green and rocky steeps, that they seem to have a natural fitness, like the mountain pine: nay, even in the day when they were built they must have had this fitness, as if they had been raised by an earth-born race, who had inherited from their mighty parent a sublime instinct of form.   (*M.F.*, p. 237)

Eliot immerses us in river gloom and river glory.

The antinomy between Rhône and Rhine is that between disjunctive fragment and coherent unity. The ruins of Rhône village houses are 'dismal remnants', the ruins of Rhine castles have 'crumbled and mellowed' into such harmony with nature that they seem like trees. The castles were built by people who 'inherited' a 'sublime instinct of form', even if, as the narrator acknowledges, those people were robber-barons. Associating the fragmented ruins of the Rhône with contemporary Victorian communities, the former at best a 'sign of a sordid life' similar to that conducted by inhabitants of the present vulgar era, the passage shows that medieval France and the Victorian Midlands are governed by the rules of commonplace materialism. The people of St Ogg's, while not utterly condemned to river gloom, are certainly less than glorious. Although set back in time from the narrator's vulgar present and inhabiting a town pleasingly remarkable for its organic relationship to the landscape, they live a life whose values destroy Maggie Tulliver, the radiant antithesis of all that is connected with Rhône villages. Maggie Tulliver ambiguously belongs with the epic builders of Rhine castles. She possesses the qualities absent in St Ogg's, a place 'irradiated by no sublime principles, no romantic visions, no active, self-renouncing faith – moved by none of those wild, uncontrollable passions which create the dark shadows of misery and crime – without that primitive rough simplicity of wants, that hard submissive ill-paid toil, that childlike spelling-out of what nature has written, which gives its poetry to peasant life' (*M.F.*, p. 238).

What the Dodsons, the Pullets and the Gleggs lack is to be found in Maggie Tulliver – she signifies an active and vital transcendence of St Ogg's materialism in the way her life *is* governed by sublime principles, romantic visions and self-renouncing faith. And she, too, possesses the seemingly less heroic qualities which the narrator delineates in the above description, yet in her they are transfigured by virtue of her heroic subjugation by the debasing worldliness of her community. Her passion is wild and uncontrolled, leading her most certainly to misery and to a social 'crime' as she transgresses the sexual code; in her childhood her wants are primitive and rough, and her tragedy is that she must continue to 'spell-out' as an adult what 'nature' – in the form that her community understands as the correct expression of a 'naturally' fine intelligence – has inscribed for her. She brings poetry, if not to a peasant life, then certainly to the petit-bourgeois world of perennial stock-taking, whether it be in terms of the linens and 'chiny' cherished by her mother and her aunts or the land fiercely possessed by her father and her uncles.

The worldly lives of Maggie Tulliver's relations are, as we can see, defined in negative terms: not enlightened, not sublime, not romantic, lacking principles and visions. It is Maggie Tulliver's unhappy fate to possess qualities aligning her with the vital pre-industrial era, with the robber barons who rode away 'to die before the infidel strongholds in the sacred East', an era eradicated, in the largest historical sense, by the aggressive mercantilism of the class to which her relations belong. This is the respectable, rural, petit-bourgeoisie, whose values the narrator summarises in these terms: 'Obedience to parents, faithfulness to kindred, industry, rigid honesty, thrift, the thorough scouring of wooden and copper utensils, the hoarding of coins likely to disappear from the currency, the production of first-rate commodities for the market, and the general preference for whatever was home-made' (*M.F.*, p. 239). The positive meaning of such attributes as obedience, faithfulness, honesty, and thrift is syntactically undermined by a taxonomy that makes domestic cleanliness semantically equivalent to fidelity to one's family; such an arrangement can, of course, raise cleanliness to a high virtue, but it can also reduce all the virtues of the Dodsons to mere commodities.[6] If one considers that St Ogg's tends to commodify everything that passes along the Floss, the latter possibility is more likely. Eliot concludes that the 'vices and virtues' of the Dodson character are 'phases of a proud, honest egoism, which had a hearty dislike to whatever made against its own credit and interest'. Refusing the moral demand that she establish moral credit by marriage to Stephen Guest, Maggie Tulliver is destroyed by values expressed in mercantile language. 'Credit' and 'interest' do indeed 'make' life along the Floss and, if accumulated against the merchants of St Ogg's, would destroy their power and reputation.

Maggie Tulliver has no such power, she 'discredits' herself in the Stephen Guest episode, loses credibility in her community, and can earn no 'interest' upon herself. Her strength is in her intellect and in her aggressiveness, and her weakness is in her sex and gender. If she had been a man, if, indeed, she were Tom rather than Maggie, the intelligence would have found a place and function in the community. St Ogg's culture and society would have licensed the direction of that intelligence to social renovation, would have appropriated potentially disruptive moral interrogation for improvement of the community. Maggie's intellectual vitality, therefore, may be aligned with the male drive for self-advancement which built St Ogg's. Unhappily for her, then, she is not only associated with the epic past, but is also implicated in the aggressive, mercantile present whose values she subverts with that intelligence embodied in her stunning female form. Maggie Tulliver must eventually be destroyed by Eliot for she bears the weight of irreconcilable ideologies, so powerful in their individual autonomy that they can only lead to a self-cancellation. She is poetry, feeling, epic grandeur, aggressive intelligence, the best of the past and the hope of the future. It is her present which remains highly problematical.

What's more, Maggie Tulliver is not only the highly charged

*[handwritten: Maggie cuts her hair / sign of gender]*

metaphor for historical, cultural and political contradiction, she is also a character in a novel, possessing all the individual yearning in conflict with social authority we connect with fictive characterisation. In her association with those Rhine Castles which 'thrill' the narrator with a 'sense of poetry', those ruins which 'belong to the grand historic life of humanity', Maggie may be read as a metaphor for 'high culture' trapped in the form of the novel. She is doomed to a form of Lukácsian homelessness: in literal exile from her childhood home, in moral exile from her community, she possesses a kind of epic grandeur making her unfit for survival in the prosaic realism and historical contingency associated with the novel as a genre. As the adolescent Maggie sits by the bed of her paralysed father, looking at the 'dull walls' of the room that is the 'centre of her world', Eliot describes her as a 'creature full of eager, passionate longings . . . yearning for something that would link together the wonderful impressions of this mysterious life and give her soul a sense of home in it' (*M.F.*, p. 205). Her yearning intensified by her sex and gender, like so many of Eliot's women characters, she longs to make connections, to discover a pattern that will explain her universe, to find gratifying expression of her woman's intelligence.

That female intelligence is a burden is made clear to Maggie at the age of nine when the St Ogg's auctioneer and appraiser, Mr Riley, is appalled by the vivid acuity she displays in interpreting illustrations for Defoe's *The History of the Devil*. Her retreat from humiliation is the attic of the mill where she keeps a 'fetish', the trunk of a large wooden doll, whose most significant part is its head. Driving nails into it, grinding and beating it against the brick chimneys, the humiliated and enraged child Maggie punishes the head of the doll as she is punished for her own 'head', for her own acute intelligence. Maggie's head becomes a compelling image of female intelligence in the novel. She cuts off her luxuriant dark hair as a child, hoping that her cleverness will shine more clearly: as she stands cropped before a dazed Tom she feels 'a sense of clearness and freedom, as if she had emerged from a wood into the open plain' (*M.F.*, p. 56). Wanting to punish her own intellect and also to display it, wanting to be thought feminine by her provincial culture and also to free herself from reification into a mere object of womanly attractiveness, she is trapped in and by her conflicting desires. Cropping the extraordinary hair which is the sign of her gender, she aggressively displays her intelligence. In giving herself

*[handwritten margin note: doll's head represents her intelligence]*

*[handwritten bottom note: Wants to punish her intelligence]*

*[handwritten bottom-right note: trapped by conflicting desires]*

the appearance of being a boy, she symbolically punishes herself for being an intelligent girl, almost as if she fictively repeats Mary Ann Evans's cropping of her female identity so that she may 'appear' as 'George Eliot'.

At the end of Book 2, their father's financial failure behind them, Tom and Maggie enter 'the thorny wilderness, and the golden gates of their childhood had for ever closed behind them'.[7] Her vibrant pleasures mixed with painful humiliation, tormented by her longing for Tom's love and for familial acceptance of her acuteness, Maggie can hardly be said to have had a 'golden' childhood. Here, the Edenic image suggests that Maggie falls into a painful, developed form of the knowledge she possessed as a child: she passes into a thorny wilderness of the conflict between a desire to use her mind and the restraints of her provincial culture. Exiled at the significant age of thirteen from Eliot's ambiguously mythologised pre-lapsarian childhood, Maggie falls into full knowledge of the limitations imposed upon intelligent women in early nineteenth-century England. She passes through those 'golden gates' into a society where the one thing she possesses that might enable her to survive that passage, her moral intelligence, is the source of her eventual defeat.

Some feminist critics have tried to redeem Maggie's grief and destruction; they see the melodramatic drowning less as instance of Eliot writing herself into a corner, than as a tonic instance of the woman novelist emerging victorious through subversion in the battle for control of sexual and aesthetic ideology. A serious problem with these readings is that they tend to rehearse the Victorian dualisms of man equals rational thought and woman equals passionate feeling.

Exploring the problematic of whether the 'female self' can only be conceived in terms of resistance to plot, Gillian Beer concludes that Eliot 'rescues Maggie from the grim, cramped future that the social determinism of the plot has seemed to make inescapable'. Nancy Miller believes that as Maggie refuses Stephen Guest, so Eliot refuses plausibility: dominant ideology in the form of male fictions, in expected resolutions according to male form, is rejected for 'the peculiar shape of a heroine's destiny in novels by women'. Mary Jacobus believes that the novel's notorious ending signifies subversion of dominant discourse, a reaching beyond the analytic and realistic modes to 'metaphors of unbounded desire'.[8] Where in Miller's view dominant ideology is refused by rejection of plausibility, in Jacobus's formulations dominant ideology is refused by rejection of rational discourse. While these two readings offer suggestively fresh interpretations of Eliot's fiction, they have nagging implications: Eliot rejects plausibility and stable discourse for skittishness, flux, instability, and wanton metaphor. She may emerge as triumphant over dominant ideologies of form and imagery, but her victory is achieved through methods conventionally and negatively associated with female thought and practice.

A more particularised political reading of Maggie Tulliver is less compatible with an opposition between the female dissatisfaction of women novelists and male orders of representation. Such a reading shifts the ground from subversion of conventional modes of fictional representation to subversion of the structures of society that both produce, and are produced by, ideologies of form. Plot and metaphor, fiction itself, are elements of a discursive formation that is, in its turn, an element of a larger order of social discipline – the ideologies of the dominant middle class that constitute and are constituted by a number of modes of discourse, the novel among them. Miller and Jacobus confine their readings to what Frederic Jameson terms an 'ideologeme': as he defines it, 'the smallest intelligible unit of the essentially antagonistic collective discourses of social classes' (*The Political Unconscious*, p. 76) – or, to cast this in terms of feminist criticism, we can see the 'ideologeme' as 'the essentially antagonistic collective discourses' of women novelists and male-dominated ideologies of form.

If we argue that through the destruction of her heroine Eliot expresses her antagonism to conventional modes of fictional representation, then we must also allow that she expresses her antagonism to the social classes which authorise, by their patronage, those conventional modes. Through the destruction of Maggie, Eliot may be said to express her antagonism to two related institutions: one, the petit-bourgeois social class which has both created and rejected Maggie; and two, the form of the popular novel which as well as dictating logical resolutions of erotic confusion and female dissatisfaction, is also the favoured form of the petit-bourgeoisie. It is important to remember here that Eliot did not consider herself an 'ordinary' novelist. She worked on *The Mill on the Floss* from April to December 1859 and in the following June, before she had started *Silas Marner* and with the reception of *The Mill* fresh in her mind, she wrote to an old Swiss friend to correct Continental

confusions between Dinah Mulock and herself: 'The most ignorant
journalist in England would hardly think of calling me a rival of Miss
Mulock, a writer who is read only by novel readers, pure and
simple, never by people of high culture. A very excellent woman she
is, I believe, but we belong to an entirely different order of writers'
(*L.*, 3: 302). If Eliot writes for people of 'high culture', then St Ogg's is
a community of 'novel readers, pure and simple'.

Writing from an earlier critical perspective, Leslie Stephen also
noted disjunction in Eliot's plot: Stephen Guest is a 'provincial
narcissist' and Maggie's attraction to him 'jars upon us, because it is
not a development of her previous aspirations, but suddenly throws
a fresh and unpleasant light upon her character' (*George Eliot*, p.
103). Stephen does not develop a definition of this unpleasant light,
but what he objects to, perhaps, is the pleasure Maggie derives from
the attentions of a physically attractive and socially powerful figure.
The appeal of Stephen Guest lies in his status as the provincial and
pampered narcissist Leslie Stephen perceives him to be. The
relationship between Maggie and Stephen is a struggle for sexual
power: he masters her reluctance to get in the boat and so
compromises her that, in the view of all concerned, she must elope
with him. But she refuses in her own exercise of power, in fact in the
only means of power available to her, that of a moral superiority
expressed in Eliot's discourse of past and present: 'If the past is not
to bind us, where can duty lie? We should have no law but the
inclination of the moment' (*M.F.*, p. 417). Maggie's unhappy, even
existentialist, freedom comes from realising that she is powerless to
escape the determinants of her past life in the form of familial ties to
Tom, her cousin Lucy, and of moral ties to her community. The
dilemma in which she finds herself leads, in effect, to a privileged,
and tragic, form of consciousness. Her bitter recognition is that the
only power and freedom to be achieved comes from understanding
that neither woman nor man is free from the contingencies of
history. In this recognition she accepts the restrictions and suffering
that history places upon her and she acknowledges her burdensome
intelligence as enabling such a bittersweet understanding. The
woman intellectual who created this character in all likeli-
hood experienced another, related understanding: Eliot's acute
intelligence surely made her painfully conscious of how history both
limited other intellectual women and permitted her own dazzling
eminence.

And what Maggie understands, too, is the power of her own will and the miserably restricted opportunities she has to exercise it. Throughout her life, she has struggled to renounce that will, has spent two years of her life from the age of 17 to 19 with the mirror turned to the wall, has slept on the floor (a form of punitive self-enlightenment adopted by Dorothea Brooke after she sees Rosamund Lydgate and Will Ladislaw together), has agonised about whether she should forego the indulgent pleasure of walking in the Red Deeps. What Eliot seems to articulate through Maggie Tulliver's experience is that in the provincial society which she, as Mary Ann Evans, left behind in her journey to metropolitan celebrity, the *only* expression for an intelligent female self is renunciation of that self. Maggie's intellectual being is relegated by this strategy of containment to a topos of *moral choice*, a territory patrolled by women in the Victorian period. Actively renouncing the self, showing that renunciation is the only means of expression for a self denied any other form of activity, Maggie seems to possess an ironic understanding of what is happening to her. When she refuses Stephen's wrenching appeal, Eliot says of her, 'She had made up her mind to suffer' (*M.F.*, p. 416). What distinguishes Maggie Tulliver from all of Eliot's other women characters who experience a conflict between the drive of their own minds and the punitive governance of their fathers, husbands, brothers, indeed of their male culture, is that she consciously makes a choice – even if it is the choice to suffer.

Sadly and powerfully, then, the primary contradiction embodied in Maggie Tulliver is that between her vital intelligence and her confining gender. Because she is so splendid in so many ways, because she can symbolise that intellectual and moral progress involved in the struggle of young people 'to rise above the mental level of the generation before them', because she can metaphorically bear the weight of so much (the grand poetic past, the driving, fertile present, a morally better future) she can only die. All remains autonomous, locked in ideological contention in this character, and all seems to deny reconciliation, to demand only one strategy of containment – the relegation of Maggie to a place where intolerable history has no meaning. As Maggie Tulliver drowns in the Floss, she makes an end to ideology and she is the end of ideology. She ends ideology in her death and her death is the result of ideological conflict.

I suggested earlier that in identifying narrative paradigms or in analysing rhetorical figures, it is essential also that we identify and analyse those larger systems of signification producing the paradigms and the larger systems of social relationships reproduced in rhetorical figures. If we do that, if we identify these broader systems, we must confront, of course, the androcentric culture which enabled Eliot's success as a woman intellectual. Maggie Tulliver, then, along with all her other ideological burdens, carries the weight of Eliot's own dilemma: how to reconcile her complicity with and her resistance to patriarchal attitudes?

Eliot, as we know, does not reconcile her conservative sexual politics (primarily expressed in her letters and essays) with the desires of her female characters for cultural and social autonomy and to believe that she should have is to bring to her work those unfair expectations I spoke of at the beginning of my discussion. I submitted that Eliot's success leads us to ask more from her than we do from other Victorian women intellectuals and that we sometimes unfairly expect Eliot's intelligence, learning, and fame to have made her more strongly resistant to a male-dominated culture. I have aimed to work against such unfair expectations and have tried to elucidate in Eliot's work the conflict *inherent* in her position as iconised woman intellectual in Victorian patriarchy. Eliot's own conflicts, of course, do not give us the primary hermeneutic key to *The Mill on the Floss*. Maggie Tulliver's death is radically over-determined and Eliot's most intelligent and unhappy female character is vanquished on a number of ideological fronts. In the death that unites sister and brother, she is destroyed as an intellectually ambitious young woman and as a metaphorical representation of a way of life eradicated by the materialism of St Ogg's; she is also destroyed as a character whose consciousness is produced *by* the historical forces of St Ogg's and whose epic grandeur dislocates her from the contingent social realism of the popular novel. And, lastly, she dies, perhaps, as an emblem of irresolvable contention between the Victorian containment of woman to an undeveloped intellectual life and the elevation of one woman intellectual to iconic sagehood. For me, Maggie Tulliver embodies more movingly than any other character in Eliot's fiction the conflict felt by an intelligent woman living in an androcentric world. Feeling the sadness of *The Mill on the Floss* is tonic antidote to immersion in the myth of 'George Eliot', iconic sage. To defend itself against the anomalous conjunction of rigorous mind and female body, Victorian patriarchy created this myth, but it was also created by Mary Ann Evans – an intellectual woman who lived with the painful knowledge that to be 'George Eliot' was to *be* an anomaly.

# Afterword: 'The Authority to Speak'

I want to end this book by talking about how it began. Early in my academic career, I submitted to a scholarly journal an article about two of Joseph Conrad's short stories. After the usual long time it takes for these things to get settled, I received a letter informing me that the article would be published. This was good, but not so good was the way in which I had been addressed by the journal: Mr David Deirdre. But then again, so my thinking went at the time, this was also not so bad; the journal's assumption that I was a man could only have been derived from my prose. I wrote like a man – therefore I thought like a man. However, this was the post-women's liberation mid-1970s and to feel pleased I had been mistaken for a male critic was a rather shabby response. I then became appropriately ashamed of my pleasure, subdued my delight in passing, so to speak, in what I took to be the tough, male world of academic scholarship. What happened, of course, in this sequence of rapid reactions to being addressed as Mr David Deirdre was that I began to understand in practice what I was just beginning to read about in theory: the complex position of a woman intellectual working in a male-dominated culture.

From where does a woman intellectual derive her authority to speak in such a culture? If she writes in her best graduate school style about the most 'male' of novelists, will she always be mistaken for a male critic? And if she writes about a female rather than a male struggle for identity (about *Villette*, say, rather than *Great Expectations*), will her style, then, inevitably be different? These and other related complex issues began to come into focus for me. And what began in my critical consciousness as I thought about Mr David Deirdre was this book about the careers of three women intellectuals who felt themselves powerful by virtue of their success but uneasy as a consequence of their subjugation by Victorian patriarchy.

The central issue is one of genesis and origins; that is to say, who and what 'makes' the woman intellectual? My analysis of the careers of Martineau, Barrett Browning, and Eliot will have made it clear that I believe Victorian women intellectuals are both complicit with and resistant to the powers generating their authority to speak. I

225

also believe that women intellectuals 'make' their androcentric culture to the degree they are enabled to do by that culture (despite and because of their resistance to subjugation), and that they certainly do so to a larger degree than has been acknowledged by feminist critics working from a 'gynocritical' or 'separatist' perspective. For me, all intellectual activity is part of a complex climate of beliefs and practices, and I have tried to see the careers of Martineau, Barrett Browning, and Eliot as dynamic processes rather than as hypostatised products, as actively contributing to the formation of the culture which gives them authority and against whose patriarchal attitudes they sometimes position themselves. From this perspective, I have aimed to achieve a balance between identifying complicit ratification and resistant subversion to Victorian patriarchy.

All intellectuals of both sexes can trace their genesis, in the most general terms, to a matrix of cultural and social influences, but the woman intellectual in the Victorian period possessed a less firm sense of lineage and affiliation with a tradition than was the experience of the male intellectual, whether he was the country solicitor subscribing to the local review or the metropolitan man of letters writing for the *Leader*. Inventing or discovering intellectual ancestry was, therefore, an informing event in the careers of Martineau, Barrett Browning, and Eliot.

As we have seen, Harriet Martineau felt her genesis as an intellectual to lie in the demands which were made upon her as fluent writer in a variety of popular Victorian forms. Deciphering the social, cultural, and political signs of the time is the foundation of her career. From her initial outstanding success as populariser of Benthamite political economy to her last autobiographical writings, she performed her work of 'auxiliary usefulness' with confident vigour, never uneasy about the elaborative nature of the textual service she rendered the male, middle-class establishment of her time. Throughout her career, she retained her beliefs and her forthright crusty personality. The early Unitarianism gave way to the later Comtean positivism but the Necessarian belief in denial of an autonomous human will remained unshaken. There is a certain cheery, if occasionally irritating, aspect of her career to be found in this stability, and in her clear, and almost always correct, self-acknowledgment of what she was and what she achieved. Martineau's career almost perfectly fitted the category of intellectual practice which Gramsci termed organic. Her emergence as an intellectual accompanied the solidification of power of the English liberal middle class; she gave 'homogeneity' and 'awareness' to that class and embraced all the popularising work that came her way.

Invigorated by her belief in the subordinate nature of women's intellectual life, and relishing her duties as subaltern officer in the liberal battle for the minds of the literate lower classes, she followed the cultural and social guidelines provided for her. Yet she also unambiguously championed the rights of women for equality of opportunity, never faltered in articulation of her forthright, courageous, and life-long feminism, and her own life is a movingly splendid example of female and feminist independence. She managed to balance patriarchal attitudes and active feminism through her alignment of woman's conventional domestic acquiescence with female rational ratification of male ideas. But she was asked to pay some stiff psychological and physical prices for her independence and her contradictory politics, as the *Autobiography*, with its troubled filial narrative of the relationship with her mother and details of recurrent minor and major illnesses, reveals. However, she exhibited no timid reservation about her authority to *speak* as a woman intellectual. Perhaps because her relatively untroubled acceptance of popularising work in the service of male political ideas liberated her for a confident presentation of herself to the world, her intellectual voice resonated authoritatively throughout her texts.

Elizabeth Barrett Browning was hailed 'as the greatest female poet that England has produced' by her adoring male critics and proposed by the *Athenaeum* as the next poet laureate after the death of Wordsworth in 1850 with the judgement that there 'is no living poet of either sex who can prefer a higher claim than Mrs Barrett Browning' (as things turned out, the laureate went to Tennyson). Her woman's poetic voice penetrated the male literary establishment, and not only as the soft speaker of sonnets to her famous husband. Associated in the popular imagination with darkened rooms and a quivering sensibility, she was actually very much concerned with worldly matters in her poetry. She affiliated herself with the 'secular clerisy' and saw herself as graced to apprehend an ideal vision of society existing prior to the shifting phenomena of the material world. She was immersed in poetic tradition and highly educated from early childhood, and her precocious scholarship is evidence of the fact that not all upper-middle-class girls in the nineteenth century learned little more than music, needlework, and drawing. Very early in her writing life, she invented her own genesis, brought herself forth, so to speak, from the body of male poetic tradition; she thereby associated herself with a powerful lineage and invested herself with the authority of centuries of poetic practice.

Barrett Browning's enduring, yet narrowing, concern with the function of the poet in society tended, however, less to broaden her vital, sensitive intelligence than to concentrate it in her aesthetic and political thought. Tutored in a conventionally male classical education, feeling the absence of a sustaining female literary tradition, and barred by illness from public participation in any female or feminist community, she lived in a world of texts, ministering through her poetry to a world divided by the 'social cleft' which she read about in those texts. She implicitly dedicated her work to the healing of cultural and social wounds inflicted by vulgar materialism. Associating herself with the class and cultural interests opposed to English middle-class self-promotion, she engendered a career which places her strongly in the category of Gramsci's traditional intellectual. But despite her difference from Martineau in her denigration of English middle-class values and the manner in which she mythologised herself as a privileged poet, Barrett Browning still saw her work as performing an auxiliary function. Steeped in the poetic tradition that figures the poet as gifted witness to transcendent word and form, and influenced by the Romantic belief that the poet is redemptive mediator between ideal values and their debased realisation, her poetry is governed by the dictum issued to Aurora Leigh by Romney: 'Art's a service'.

In sometimes brutal contrast to her self-affiliation with a spiritual, philosophical tradition in poetry, she also daringly referred to rape and female sexuality, described in erotic detail the breasts of a voluptuous aristocrat, and so vividly evoked the poor in *Aurora Leigh* that she seems more like Charles Dickens than the daughter Milton should have had (which is how she was lauded by a contemporary admirer). I have argued, however, that Barrett Browning should not be regarded as a feminist poet. The sexual politics of *Aurora Leigh* are coherent with her conservative politics in general, and, moreover, finally not at odds with the firm belief expressed in her letters that women are intellectually inferior to men. For Barrett Browning, the woman poet intellectual finds her genesis and authority in androcentric tradition. Speaking patriarchal discourse without rancour and instructed by male authority, she performs as the 'enjoined' poet of 'A Curse for a Nation'.

Although George Eliot's intellectual genesis was similar to Martineau's in the sense that they both ambitiously transformed themselves from provincial young women to metropolitan celebrities, and despite the fact that Eliot was similar to Barrett Browning in her self-mythologisation as the intellectual who is witness to a morally deficient society, she did not view herself as performing work of 'auxiliary usefulness', nor as enacting a subaltern role in a patriarchal culture. The power of her intelligence, the ability to gain recognition not only as a novelist but also as a social/philosophical thinker, partly enabled her self-engenderment as an intellectual celebrity, and I would argue that she is the most thoroughly self-made of the three women writers I have studied. Eliot's intense ambition was fully realised when she became a sovereign presence in Victorian culture, the 'iconic sage' of the Priory. To the end of her writing life, she directed her expansive mind across a wide scope of cultural, social, scientific, and political thought that differentiates her career from the work of Martineau and Barrett Browning. Martineau was a political journalist and travel writer, Barrett Browning was an intellectual poet, but Eliot was *the* woman intellectual of the Victorian period. Moreover, her social and cultural thought is unambiguously opposed to that elaborated by Martineau and thereby more identifiable with Barrett Browning's ratifications of conservative values. Her essentialist views of woman's qualities, her desire to believe in an historical continuity unmolested by change, her persistent return to the past in her fiction – all these things reveal an implicit desire to cast herself in the role of a Gramscian traditional rather than organic intellectual.

I have suggested that Eliot's attitudes towards women, woman's mind, and her own women characters betray the tension to be found almost everywhere in her writings: that between a female desire for autonomy and a male governance of such desire. Perhaps as a way of dealing with this conflict, Eliot relegates most of the women she writes about in her essays and her fiction to a realm of essentialist inherency; and when she does not do that, women lurk in her texts as sabotaging figures. Arabella Transome, whose transgressive adultery disrupts male social and political order, may be said to exemplify Eliot's subversive sexual politics at their most accessible. More frequently in Eliot's career, however, indignation about woman's subjugation and unease with her own problematical position can only be traced through disjunctions in her texts. As apotheosised woman intellectual in an androcentric culture that both enables her own success *and* relegates women to lives of limited possibility, she is forced into evasion and contradiction and to the adoption of strategies of containment to manage the ideological contention in her cultural and political thought. Eliot possessed immense authority to speak, but was necessarily troubled by the genesis of that authority.

Eliot is not only the most prominent of the three intellectual women I have written about, she has also been more subject to feminist charges of patriarchal collaboration than either Martineau or Barrett Browning. If not as actively feminist as Martineau, she was certainly more sensitive to the misery of women's lives than Barrett Browning. I have tried to adjust the unfair expectations that readers bring to Eliot's texts. Her intellectual strength should not subject her to charges of insufficient resistance to patriarchal values and her collaboration with the culture that permitted her eminence is neither more nor less than that of Martineau or Barrett Browning. It is merely different by virtue of her different circumstances.

When the French socialist Flora Tristan arrived in London in 1840, she declared 'What a revolting contrast there is in England between women's abject servitude and the intellectual superiority of women writers'. Doubtless, she overstated the case – not all women lived in 'abject servitude' and certainly not all women writers displayed 'intellectual superiority'. In a way, I have aimed to revise this easy, polarised view of things, to show that although Martineau, Barrett Browning, and Eliot experienced circumscription of their intellectual talents, they were neither ideological slaves to patriarchal thought, nor distinctly separate from patriarchal culture. They were both collaborators and saboteurs in the world that enabled their very existence as women intellectuals. I selected them because their careers demonstrate three fruitful ways in which a woman could be a working intellectual in the Victorian period (as a political journalist, as a poet, and as a novelist). Making careers for themselves as professional writers, they may have been compelled (consciously or not) to cloak their intellectual ambition with the dressing of service to male authority, but they were working women, paid for their writing and judged in the literary market place. And during the years that are spanned by their writings (1832 to 1879) the woman intellectual emerged as an increasingly powerful social figure – writing novels, travel narratives, political journalism, poetry; editing, translating, teaching; agitating against unjust laws concerning women's rights (or the lack of them), working for the higher education of women, and a better life for *all* women, intellectual or not. These three women, in particular, have enabled many women to examine what it means to be an intellectual *and* a woman. And as I read their texts and wrote about their lives, I was enabled to think carefully about what it means to be addressed as Mr David Deirdre. I would like to think a male critic could have written this book, or perhaps I should say would have wanted to do so. For me, the desire of female and male critics to write from a feminist perspective about writers of both sexes signifies an end to the patriarchal attitudes resisted, in one way or another, by Martineau, Barrett Browning, and Eliot.

# Notes

## Notes to the Introduction

1. Edward Said points out that 'Well before Foucault, Gramsci had grasped the idea that culture serves authority, and ultimately the national State, not because it represses and coerces but because it is affirmative, positive and persuasive. Culture is productive, Gramsci says, and this – much more than the monopoly of coercion held by the State – is what makes a national Western society strong, difficult for the revolutionary to conquer' (*The World, the Text, and the Critic*, p. 171). Raymond Williams's recent anatomy of intellectuals in modern life (*Culture*) shows the influence of Gramsci upon his thought. Williams argues that intellectual activity must not be falsely hypostatised and that it exists in informing, inescapable relation to other cultural and social activities. Claiming that no aspect of cultural production 'is itself wholly specialized', Williams argues that 'ideas' and 'concepts' are both produced and reproduced in the whole social and cultural fabric at times directly as ideas and concepts, but also more widely in the form of shaping institutions, signified social relations, religious and cultural occasions, modes of work and performance' (p. 216). Terry Eagleton is particularly concerned with these 'modes of work and performance' as they were enacted in the coffee-houses of the eighteenth century and in the printed discourse of the journals and periodicals read in such places. According to Eagleton, eighteenth-century English intellectuals gain coherence through a belief in themselves as a group of 'discoursing subjects . . . sharing in the consensus of universal reason' (*The Function of Criticism*, p. 9). Radically seeking to dissociate its knowledge arrived at through reason from the world of politics, this group ran into trouble when the self-promoting mercantile interests of the early nineteenth century threatened the serene world of rational discourse. History in the form of political action intractable to political analysis intrudes upon this robustly male 'public sphere'. In reading Williams and Eagleton, I am struck by their unselfconscious use of the term 'man of letters'. Somewhat surprisingly for critics polemically committed to unmasking mystified relationships between dominant social classes and culture, they do not acknowledge the existence of women intellectuals. And, as I have pointed out, none of the theorists of intellectual life whom I have discussed (Benda, Mannheim, Shils, Gouldner, Gramsci) recognises the presence of thinking women in culture and society.
2. See Robert McPherson, *Theory of Higher Education in Nineteenth-Century England*, for an historical examination of the fate of the 'Classical Ideal'.
3. Martha Vicinus's study of the possibilities and achievements permitted single women between 1850 and 1920 is invaluable reading in this connection. See *Independent Women*, particularly Chapter 4, 'Women's Colleges: an Independent Intellectual Life'.

4. For useful analysis of anti-intellectual attitudes on the part of the Victorian middle class, see Walter Houghton, *The Victorian Frame of Mind, 1830–1870*, pp. 110–36. Houghton points out that this philistine way of thinking is strongly rebutted by Matthew Arnold: 'In *Culture and Anarchy* . . . Arnold set up the cultivation of the mind, including the aesthetic sensibility, to oppose the anarchical tendencies of thoughtless action, and wrote the classic protest against Victorian anti-intellectualism' (p. 118).

5. An imputation of harmful 'feminisation' also appeared in criticism of the novel during the nineteenth century. For example, in the 1860s Julia Kavanagh laments the loss of a certain manly vigour in the novel brought about by the domination of the genre by women writers: 'The character of the English novel has, for the last seventy years, been much modified by what threatens to become an overwhelming influence – that of women. It has lost its repelling coarseness – a great gain – but it is to be feared that its manliness and its truth are in peril' (*English Women of Letters*, pp. 4–5). See Elaine Showalter, *A Literature of their Own*, for a breakdown of the tradition of women writers in the nineteenth century into three phases: the 'feminine' from the 1840s to the 1880s; the 'feminist' from 1880 to 1920; and the 'female' from 1920 to the present. The novels to which Julia Kavanagh refers belong to the 'feminine' phase – damagingly 'feminine' from her perspective.

6. See Martha Vicinus, *Suffer and be Still: Women in the Victorian Age*, and its companion volume *A Widening Sphere: Changing Roles of Victorian Women*. For a forceful, ground-breaking discussion of Ruskin's sexual politics, see Kate Millet, *Sexual Politics*, pp. 88–108. Nina Auerbach makes an appealing argument for the power of Ruskin's 'queens'. Acknowledging that here 'in undiluted form are the Victorian stereotypes we love to hate', she shows the 'large visionary world', 'the commanding magic' that belong to these women. She concludes that 'Ruskin's essay reminds us of how shallow the roots of patriarchal precepts were in contrast to their rich foundation of mythic perception' (*Woman and the Demon*, p. 61). Perhaps. From my perspective of concern with woman's *mind*, Ruskin may grant women 'rule', but it is not a rule that permits the 'ruling' of their own intellect.

7. See Elizabeth Roberts, *A Woman's Place: An Oral History of Working-Class Women, 1890–1940*. The Ruskinian ideals also found their way into the Victorian novel; in Gissing's *The Odd Women* they are the subject of strong criticism. One of the most pitiable husbands in Victorian fiction, Edmund Widdowson, announces to his restless wife that she should read Ruskin 'for every word he says about women is good and true'. Mary Barfoot's beliefs are radically opposed to Widdowson's frantic desire to keep his angelic Monica in the suburban house: in her weekly lectures to aspiring women office workers, she exhorts them to feminist refutation of Ruskin's doctrines.

8. Patricia Hollis, *Women in Public, 1850–1900*, p. 134. For an excellent discussion of the teaching profession in girls' schools, see Chapter 5: 'The Reformed Boarding Schools: Personal Life and Public Duty' in Martha Vicinus, *Independent Women*. Josephine Kamm's *Hope Deferred:*

*Girls' Education in English History* presents an informed survey of the topic from the scholarly Anglo-Saxon abbess, St Hilda, to the English government recommendations of 1964 that advocated the increased teaching of science to girls. Sara Delamont's essay 'The Contradictions in Ladies' Education' also usefully discusses the central issues.

9. Quoted in Hollis, *Women in Public*, p. 144.

10. Quoted in Deborah Gorham, *The Victorian Girl and the Feminine Ideal*, p. 104.

11. A dazzling example of the 'strong-minded woman' in Victorian fiction is Marian Halcombe in Wilkie Collins's *The Woman in White*. She is described by the narrator, Walter Hartright, as possessing a 'rare beauty' of form, but to his startled horror she also possesses 'an almost swarthy complexion' and a 'dark down on her upper lip'. She is a male vision of the contradiction between intellectual adroitness and female sex and gender. Nina Auerbach analyses Marian's 'masculine' qualities and identifies her as 'fiction's first female detective (*Woman and the Demon*, pp. 137–8).

12. T. S. Clouston, *Female Education from a Medical Point of View*. Elaine Showalter observes that 'When the Victorians thought of the woman writer, they immediately thought of the female body and its presumed afflictions and liabilities. They did so, first, because the biological creativity of childbirth seemed to them directly to rival the aesthetic creativity of writing' (*A Literature of their Own*, p. 76). It is interesting to discover early anticipations of the Victorian biology-as-destiny argument in Aristotle's *Politics*. Susan Okin notes that 'In keeping with his [Aristotle's] general theory of reproduction, since the mother provides only the matter for the child and the father his rational soul, it is only the father's mental prime that is taken into account, and while the mother is advised to exercise and eat well while pregnant, since the growing foetus draws on her body, her mind should be kept idle, in order that more of her strength be preserved for the child's growth' (*Women in Western Political Thought*, p. 83).

13. In his biography of the Shirreff sisters, Edward Ellesworth observes that they 'laid the foundation of a national educational system for girls at the secondary level, a valid teacher-training pattern for that level of education, a revamped, in fact a new national system of early childhood education and the teacher-training structure to sustain it' (*Liberators of the Female Mind*, p. 4). It should be noted that Girton was not the first British institution of higher education for women. Queen's College (designed to provide governesses with sound training) and Bedford College were both founded in 1849. However, Queen's and Bedford were not residential colleges and neither did they train their students for higher degrees.

14. Deborah Gorham has also remarked that throughout the Victorian period the pioneer women educators 'cling tenaciously to the Victorian ideal of femininity' (*The Victorian Girl and the Feminine Ideal*, p. 108).

15. Lawrence Stone points out that when serious pressure for a better education for women began in the late seventeenth century, 'it was led by a group of middle-class women, with a little male help from John

Locke, William Law and Jonathan Swift addressing the gentry and from John Dunton and Daniel Defoe addressing the bourgeoisie' (*The Family, Sex and Marriage in England, 1500–1800*, p. 344). According to Hilda Smith, what emerges at the end of the seventeenth century is a feminist realisation of women's group identity; demographic and economic changes lead to a climate of change in which women intellectuals begin to inhabit a wider social circle. In the seventeenth century, too, the image of the intellectual woman changed from that prevalent in the sixteenth: where she had been perceived as a talented scholar, she now became the middle-class girl who received a genteel education. Stone believes that the changes in women's consciousness 'from a humiliating sense of their educational inferiority in 1700 to a proud claim to educational superiority in 1810 is little short of revolutionary' (ibid., p. 359).

16. In her study of the struggles of American women for intellectual autonomy, *Perish the Thought*, Susan Conrad points out that the American 'woman of letters' was perceived as a less disruptive figure than the outspoken feminist thinker. The writer of aesthetic criticism and of history 'masks' the aggressiveness of intellectual activity.

17. Matthew Arnold, 'Haworth Churchyard, April 1855' (*Poetry and Prose*, pp. 193–6). The elegy was first published in *Fraser's Magazine* in May 1855, signed 'A'. Harriet Martineau was thought to be on the verge of death after she retired to her Lake District home seriously ill with heart disease. However, she lived until 1876.

## Notes to Chapter 1: Textual Services

1. Harriet Martineau, 'Female Writers on Practical Divinity, no. I, Mrs More' (*Monthly Repository*, 17:593–6); 'Female Writers on Practical Divinity, no. II, Mrs More and Mrs Barbauld' (ibid., 17:746–50); 'Female Education' (ibid., 18:77–81). For a history of this periodical under its various editors, see Francis Mineka, *The Dissidence of Dissent: 'The Monthly Repository', 1806–1838*.

2. In this same entry for the *Dictionary of National Biography* Stephen was more charitable when it came to Martineau's moral fortitude: 'As an interpreter of a rather rigid and prosaic school of thought, and a compiler of clear compendiums of knowledge, she certainly deserves a high place, and her independence and solidity of character give a value to her more personal utterances.'

3. In her excellent analysis of Martineau's *Autobiography*, Mitzi Myers observes that the work 'is both a moving psychological study and a didactic success story, delineating in vivid detail the progress of a Victorian woman's mind from the paralysis of childhood fear to the serene freedom of full self-government' ('Harriet Martineau's *Autobiography*', p. 54). In making the useful point, however, that Martineau's philosophy is expressed through the form of autobiography itself, that is to say, belief in positive self-government

finds its formal correlative in the conventions of controlled self-analysis, Myers neglects to trace philosophy and form to an ideology that produces both the structure of thought *and* the text – an ideology of the progressivist self.

4. Rejoicing in the relief from four years of pain and enforced bed-rest, which she believed she achieved through mesmerism, she describes 'a clear twilight' closing in upon her, one picture remaining 'like a patch of phosphoric light', and 'all outlines dressed in this beautiful light' (*L.M.*, 8).

5. As Valerie Pichanick notes in her critical biography of Martineau, she was 'living at a time when principle and practice could not but be at odds; when radical theory and humanitarian sympathy were in conflict; in a paradoxical age of which she was, in a sense, a paradigm' (*Harriet Martineau: The Woman and the Work*, p. 241). Building upon Pichanick's excellent analysis of paradox in Martineau's life and career, I am more centrally concerned with the conflict between gender and intellectual activity. Martineau has long been treated as a conflictive figure by her critics: see, for example, Narola Elizabeth Rivenburgh's privately published PhD dissertation 'Harriet Martineau, an Example of Victorian Conflict', which focuses upon the opposition between Martineau's endorsement of *laissez-faire* economic systems and her humanitarian care for the poor. Vera Wheatley's *The Life and Work of Harriet Martineau* takes a less scholarly approach and derives a good deal of its style and content from Theodora Bosanquet's *Harriet Martineau: An Essay in Comprehension*. R. K. Webb's impressive intellectual biography is essential reading in all Martineau studies: *Harriet Martineau: A Radical Victorian*.

6. Martineau's move to London, the journey of the ambitious intellectual woman to the metropolis, had been undertaken by Mary Wollstonecraft when she left Ireland in 1787, bent on becoming 'The first of a new genus'. As Mary Poovey describes Wollstonecraft's plans, she was determined to become 'a self-supporting, professional woman writer' (*The Proper Lady and the Woman Writer*, p. 55). In some ways, this transition in Martineau's life also resembles a crucial turn in the plot of Barrett Browning's *Aurora Leigh*. As Aurora is trained by her aunt in the conventional female accomplishments of sewing, music, and drawing, she is at the same time devouring a rich textual feast (Aurora recalls that she 'nibbled here and there' in her father's library): the death of her aunt enables her to go to London with a small private income where she becomes a successful poet.

## Notes to Chapter 2: Political Economy and Feminist Politics

1. Smiles's two-part study of the various means available to the working man for saving his money, *Workmen's Earnings, Strikes and Savings*, teaches many of the lessons set forth by Martineau. Sensible economy 'is the representative of patient industry, and untiring effort, of

temptation resisted, and hope rewarded; and rightly used, it affords indications of prudence, fore-thought, and self-denial – the true basis of manly character' (p. 63). In much the same way that Martineau makes capital the hero of her *Illustrations*, Smiles celebrates its origins in the heroic labour of the working man: 'Capital flies turbulence and strife, and thrives only in security and freedom. Though senselessly denounced for the tyranny it exercises over labour, it is really its motive power. It is also the result of labour, and represents the self-denial, the providence, and the enterprise of the past. The most successful accumulations of capital have in all times risen from the ranks of labour itself; they are working men who have shot ahead of their fellows' (p. 158).

2. The criticism was savagely sexist. The *Quarterly Review* was appalled by 'dull didactic dialogues' and 'unfeminine and mischievous doctrines' and labelled Martineau 'a *female Malthusian*. A *woman* who thinks child-bearing a *crime against society*! An *unmarried woman* who declaims against *marriage*!!' (49:97). *Fraser's Magazine* adopted a ridiculing anti-feminist approach, employing low references to Martineau's reliance on 'Mother Wollstonecraft' and considering it 'disgusting' that the 'more mystical topics of generation' were discussed by a woman writer (3:42). Carlyle objected strongly to the latter review, writing to Mill that he found Martineau 'the most intelligible of women; also the most measurable. There was the abominable tirade against her in *Fraser*; which you I suppose were happy enough not to see' (*Letters of Thomas Carlyle to John Stuart Mill, John Sterling, and Robert Browning*, p. 90, 24 December 1833).

3. In her memoir/obituary, Martineau declares that *Society in America* is 'not a favourable specimen of Harriet Martineau's writings, either in regard to moral or artistic taste. It is full of affectations and preachments, and it marks the highest point of the metaphysical period of her mind' (*A.*, 3:464). She preferred *Retrospect of Western Travel*, which is a trimmer work of sociological analysis and travel narrative and less interfused with the political digressions that make *Society in America*, in my view, the richer and denser text.

4. As Margaret Walters cogently observes in a comparison of Wollstonecraft and Martineau, 'The fact that she [Martineau] was so successful in an exclusively male province led her to minimise the depth of sexual distinctions. She refuses to confront the fact that inequality is one of the bases of bourgeois society' ('The Rights and Wrongs of Women', pp. 304–78). Mary Wollstonecraft was a heroine for Elizabeth Barrett Browning: she confided to Mary Russell Mitford that she first read Wollstonecraft when she was twelve years old, 'and, through the whole course of my childhood, I had a steady indignation against Nature who made me a Woman, and a determinate resolution to dress up in men's clothes as soon as even I was free of the nursery, and go into the world "to seek my fortune" ' (*The Letters of Elizabeth Barrett Browning to Mary Russell Mitford*, 2:7). For a lively discussion of the historical context of women's feminist writing in the 1830s, see Janet Courtney's *The Adventurous Thirties: A Chapter in the Women's Movement*. Grouping

writers according to particular affiliations, Courtney places Martineau with 'Critics of America'.

5. Alice Rossi has made a fine, condensed argument for Martineau's status as founding mother of the discipline of sociology, noting that 'her mode of analysis is very close to what is now known as the comparative analysis of social structures' ('The First Woman Sociologist: Harriet Martineau (1801–1876)', p. 118). Rossi believes that Martineau 'paved the way for the emerging field by the care with which she handled her observations of social behavior and the terms in which she analysed them. What makes her work even more outstanding is the self-consciousness with which she advocated the view that the study of societies constitutes a separate scientific discipline' (p. 119). R. K. Webb's view of *Society in America* is much less positive. While praising the 'keenness of observation' and 'incisive portraiture', he considers the view of society that Martineau imposed upon America in order to fulfil certain abstract propositions, 'limited, naive, even at times embarrassing' (*Harriet Martineau: A Radical Victorian*, p. 172). For a popular, chatty account of Martineau's travels, see Una Pope-Hennessy's *Three English Women in America*.

6. In pointing to Victorian womanhood as a 'literary idea in perpetual incarnation', Nina Auerbach examines the demonic, disruptive energy that is disguised by myths of woman as transcendent saviour of race and culture: while Martineau never figures woman as the awesome icon we encounter in the novels and paintings of Auerbach's study, the disjunctions of her feminist writings verify the mythologisations which structure those works. While I admire Auerbach's reconstruction of central paradigms in the mythologisation of Victorian womanhood (the angel/demon, the old maid, and the fallen woman), I think we differ in the degree of importance we attach to the political determinants of cultural icons. For a more generalised, but still stimulating, analysis of the mythologisation of women which moves beyond specific analysis of literature and painting to make broad interpretations of Western culture, see Dorothy Dinnerstein's *The Mermaid and the Minotaur*. Dinnerstein links male legends of women, the sort Auerbach identifies in Victorian literature and art, to a Western distaste for female flesh rooted in a desire for immortality (obviously common to both sexes) which takes woman as the fearful, literal embodiment of the inescapable, paradoxical facts of birth, decay, and death.

7. Most of Martineau's essay 'Criticism on Women' is reprinted in Gayle Graham Yates's intelligently assembled anthology of Martineau's feminist writings, *Harriet Martineau on Women* (pp. 66–74).

### Notes to Chapter 3: The Social Parent

1. The setting and tone of Elizabeth Barrett Browning's Abolitionist poem, 'The Runaway Slave at Pilgrim's Point', composed in 1848 for a Boston anti-slavery bazaar, bear strong resemblance to Martineau's accounts of

slave experience, accounts which, of course, were common in the literature of the abolitionist campaigns.

2.  *A History of the Thirty Years' Peace, 1816–1848* was initially published in six monthly instalments during 1848–9, the first written by Charles Knight and the rest by Martineau. A two-volume edition was published in 1849–50. In 1858 Martineau revised and expanded these two volumes, and in 1864 the final and most complete version of the work was published in America in four volumes under the title *The History of England from the Commencement of the XIXth Century to the Crimean War.*

3.  In contrast to Webb's justified criticism of Martineau's *History* as not an extensively researched study, her less-scholarly readers have always responded to its lively accessibility. Writing in 1936, Sir Edward Boyle, for example, declares that 'The reader who to-day takes up this handsome work with its maps and its steel-engraved portraits will find it a readable record of the period with which it deals, written in a flowing and unmannered style which is at the same time never slipshod or lacking in dignity' (*Biographical Essays*, p. 183). The 'flowing and unmannered style' is partly derived from the source of some of the economically vivid portraits which punctuate the historical analysis – Martineau's obituary writing for the *Daily News*. That Martineau was so prolific is certainly attributable to her indefatigability. She was not reluctant, however, to recycle material when it seemed appropriate.

4.  Martineau, in her own popularising and non-theoretical manner, anticipates Walter Benjamin in her understanding that in this way art loses its sanctified meaning: it becomes politicised in its very availability to the viewer. See Benjamin's essay 'The Work of Art in the Age of Mechanical Reproduction'.

5.  An invaluable account of Peel's career and achievements may be found in Asa Briggs, *The Making of Modern England 1783–1867: The Age of Improvement*, pp. 325–43. Peel was not as heroic to others as he was to Martineau. Robert Browning wrote to Elizabeth Barrett that his head was 'dizzy' with reading Peel's Corn law speeches, and that despite the fact it would be a 'measure after Miss Martineau's own heart', he would not like to see women in Parliament, emotionally and physically ill-equipped as he considered them for political life (*The Letters of Robert Browning and Elizabeth Barrett Barrett*, 2:280). Browning's low estimation of woman's physical endurance may have originated in his fifteen-month-long observation of Elizabeth Barrett's seclusion in Wimpole Street: he certainly had little sympathy for Martineau's feminist politics, and he and his wife had none at all for her laudations of the rapid social alterations engineered by an aggressive mercantile class. As a woman sympathetic to enforced retirement from the world, Elizabeth Barrett Browning, however, admired Martineau's fortitude in illness ('a very noble woman' was how she described Martineau): she was also impressed by Martineau's skilful imagination, so much so, in fact, that she considered the writing of nineteenth-century history unworthy of her talents. She wrote to Mary Russell Mitford, 'Do you know that Miss Martineau takes up the "History of England" under Charles Knight, in the continuation of a popular work? I regret her fine

imagination being so wasted' (*The Letters of Elizabeth Barrett Browning to Mary Russell Mitford*, 3:256–7).

6. For a commanding examination of the influence of German biblical scholarship on English Romanticism, see E. S. Shaffer's *'Kubla Khan' and the Fall of Jerusalem*.

### Notes to Chapter 4: A Novel Liberty: 'Deerbrook'

1. Martineau was the least self-effacing of women and exhibited a confidence characterised as vanity by many of her acquaintances. For example, after Martineau left America, Catherine Sedgwick contrasted her behaviour with that of another recent visitor, Anna Jameson, in a letter to a close friend written in February 1838: 'I could not but contrast her feelings with Harriet Martineau's. *She* has enough, but they circulate around herself. . . . With all Miss Martineau's ascetic disclaimure [*sic*] about flattery, no one ever seemed better to relish the clouds of incense while they were floating about her nor did she ever imply a doubt of her divine right to them' (*Life and Letters of Catherine M. Sedgwick*, quoted in Bertha-Monica Stearns, 'Miss Sedgwick Observers Harriet Martineau').

2. George Levine, *The Realistic Imagination*, p. 12. Martineau's ideal relationship between language and reality is somewhat similar to her ideal relationship between language and ideas: just as digressive attempts to trace the antecedents of every action in a novel will result in an imperfect plot, so the words wasted by those 'charming discourses', de Quincey and Coleridge, defy an economical model and result in 'barren eloquence'.

3. She followed the advice of the male member of her family who had the most influence upon her and with whom she had the most difficult of sibling relationships. In her *Autobiography* she refers discreetly to a person who interfered with her brief engagement; most of Martineau's biographers and critics conclude that this was James Martineau. In discussing her feelings for James, she says, 'All who have ever known me are aware that the strongest passion I have ever entertained was in regard to my youngest brother, who has certainly filled the largest space in the life of my affections of any person whatever' (1:99). Harriet and James Martineau severed their relationship entirely in 1851 when James reviewed *Letters on the Laws of Man's Nature and Development* under the caustic title 'Mesmeric Atheism' in the *Prospective Review*. This work contains the correspondence exchanged between Martineau and George Henry Atkinson, a mesmerist and amateur philosopher. As Valerie Pichanick observes, the correspondence is 'long winded, often illogical, and sometimes even arrant nonsense but it is noteworthy for what it reveals about Martineau's "conversion" from theism' (*Harriet Martineau: The Woman and the Work*, p. 187). James Martineau's review, written from the perspective of restoration of belief in prayer and divine powers after a faith shared with his sister in Unitarianism and

Necessarianism, is virulently personal. In her explanation of the rift between James and herself, written a few years later, Martineau strives for a charitable objectivity, but the account is so tentatively and ambiguously worded, so fearful still of offending the brother she never ceased to love, that it is difficult to sort out who is to blame for what (see the *Autobiography*, 1:99–100).

4. Vineta Colby values *Deerbrook* as a pioneering work in the history of the nineteenth-century novel. Its focus on domestic middle-class life makes for 'the emergence of a new and powerful shaping influence. . . . In the next quarter century, the English novel followed a course that this novel set.' Colby sees *Deerbrook*'s emphasis on the 'Christian-evangelical imperatives of duty, submission of the individual will, self-sacrifice, and endurance' giving shape to the novel of community. In emphasising these undeniably present aspects of *Deerbrook*, however, Colby rather over-states the case and neglects the omnipresent technical flaws which Martineau herself was the first to identify and acknowledge (*Yesterday's Woman: Domestic Realism in the English Novel*, pp. 211–12).

5. Robert Lee Wolff, 'The Novel and the Neurosis', in *Strange Stories and Other Explorations in Victorian Fiction*, pp. 69–141. Gaby Weiner, in her introduction to the Virago edition of *Deerbrook*, tends to a biographical reading: she believes that Martineau took the opportunity 'of using it [*Deerbrook*] as a vehicle for the expression of private feelings and experiences, through the mouths of her characters' (p. xi), and that the 'similarities between Maria and her creator, i.e. both poor in health and both observers of the social scene, are too coincidental to have other than biographical implications' (p. xiv). For evidence of the feminist recovery of Martineau, instigated in part by the Virago editions of *Deerbrook* and the *Autobiography*, see Leah Fritz's review essay, 'Eminent Victorian', in *The Women's Review of Books*, 1:10.

6. See Martineau's essay 'The Governess' in *Health, Husbandry and Handicraft*. She was consistently critical of the working conditions of governesses describing their status as anomalous, unnatural, and depressed, and called for 'an awakening of society to the inquiry why this class is one which suffers so bitterly, and whether it can be justifiable to have among us a class so indispensable, and yet so unhappy' (*H.*, 4:362–3). The causes of this unhappiness have been thoroughly documented by M. Jeanne Peterson: a high availability of single women with no private income, a wretched wage justified by the offering of a comfortable home to women who had no other, the peculiar class position of a woman who is neither servant nor lady, her potentially disruptive sexual presence in the family ('The Victorian Governess: Status Incongruence in Family and Society'). In November 1860 *The English Woman's Journal* issued a serious plea to financially straitened middle-class parents of prospective governesses: 'We earnestly entreat parents not to doom their daughters to the wretched life of governesses. Give them a trade. Do not be led away by insane ideas of silly pride.'

7. 'Essays on the Art of Thinking' (*MS.*, 1). In these two essays she

addresses herself to those who wish to improve their habits of thinking, and looks into the causes of the evils of 'deficient observation, perverted judgment, unchastened imagination, indolent attention, treacherous memory'.

8. According to some Victorian readers such passages weakened the work, and, significantly, were considered signs of female weakness in an otherwise 'male' text. Edward R. Russell, for example, declared in 1877 that 'one is haunted by a conspicuous disparity between the greatness and excellence of a noble woman's work and the fretful fussiness of a weak woman's fancies . . . a woman who has got rid of the customary mental sterility of her sex ought to make short work of its frailties of mood and temper' (*The Autobiography and Memorials of Miss Harriet Martineau*, a Paper read before the Literary and Philosophical Society of Liverpool, 16 April, 1877).

9. Pichanick, *Harriet Martineau: The Woman and the Work*, p. 121. See Webb's biography and Cecil Woodham-Smith, 'They Stayed in Bed', *Listener*, 16 February 1956. For a professional account of Martineau's illness, see Thomas M. Greenhow, 'Termination of the Case of Miss Harriet Martineau', *The British Medical Journal*, 14 April 1877: 449–50. It is worth noting that Martineau's verifiable illness continues to be treated rather lightly by her readers: Richard Shannon, for example, in reviewing the Virago edition of the *Autobiography* in the *Times Literary Supplement*, describes Martineau's enforced seclusion as 'five years prostrate on sofas in Tynemouth' and labels her 'a specialist in invalidism' – all true, but Shannon neglects to add that an autopsy disclosed more serious illness than his wry tone allows.

10. *Letters of Thomas Carlyle to John Stuart Mill, John Sterling and Robert Browning*, p. 284, 23 June 1847.

### Notes to Chapter 5: A Clerisy of Poets and the Softer Sex

1. Barrett Browning makes this significant distinction between Wordsworth and Byron: 'Wordsworth is a philosophical and Christian poet with depths in his soul to which poor Byron could never reach.' The Byronic poet of 'The Poet's Vow' cannot learn the message of 'Lines Left upon a Seat in a Yew-Tree' (*L.*EBB, 1:110).

2. Sandra M. Gilbert has recently argued that Barrett Browning's intense emotional and poetic involvement with Italy's Risorgimento is closely connected with her own personal and artistic struggles for identity. Gilbert also makes an astute analysis of the figure of the wounded woman in Barrett Browning's poetry and shows that 'by using metaphors of the healing and making whole of a wounded woman to articulate both the reality and fantasy of her own female/poetic revitalisation, Barrett Browning figuratively located herself in a re-creative female poetic tradition' ('From *Patria* to *Matria*: Elizabeth Barrett Browning's Risorgimento').

3. *Blackwoods Magazine*, 56:621–39. Sandra M. Gilbert and Susan Gubar

believe that Barrett Browning's 'skill as a classicist . . . was barely noticed in her own day and has been almost completely forgotten in ours' (*The Madwoman in the Attic*, p. 547). Actually, Barrett Browning's Classical learning was frequently noted by contemporary reviewers of her poetry, although today she is certainly more remembered as the author of love poems to her husband than as an amateur classicist. Elizabeth Barrett's account of her girlhood reading indicates her precociousness: she notes that at age eight, 'I perused the History of Greece and it was at this age that I first found real delight in poetry. "The Minstrel", Popes [sic] "Iliad", some parts of the "Odyssey", passages from "Paradise Lost" selected by my dearest Mama and some of Shakespeares [sic] plays among which were, "The Tempest", "Othello" and a few historical dramatic pieces constituted my studies. . . . At eleven I wished to be considered an authoress. Novels were thrown aside. Poetry and Essays were my studies and I felt the most ardent desire to understand the learned languages. . . . At twelve I enjoyed a literary life in all its pleasures. Metaphysics were my highest delight and after having read a page from Locke my mind not only felt edified but exalted . . . I read Homer in the original with delight inexpressible, together with Virgil' ('Glimpses', pp. 124–7).

4. In her analysis of the influence of a restricted life upon women writers in the nineteenth century, Ellen Moers plausibly argues that 'All writers are limited in experience. . . . It is true that the invalid Miss Barrett never worked in a factory – she hardly left her bedroom – but to write "The Cry of the Children" she need only read R. H. Horne's official report on child labor in the factories' (*Literary Women*, p. 83). This is true enough, but Barrett Browning's unusually secluded life was an extreme instance of the limited experience of all writers to which Moers refers. Moreover, Barrett Browning's employment of metaphors which link the life with a text tends to emphasise the ways in which her own texts were almost exclusively generated by other texts, rather than by even the most restricted experience outside her world of reading and writing. The two most thorough guides to Barrett Browning's life are Dorothy Hewlett's *Elizabeth Barrett Browning: A Life*, and Gardiner B. Taplin's *The Life of Elizabeth Barrett Browning*. Hewlett's study, for the most part undocumented, takes a quasi-popular psychological approach to the richly suggestive material of Barrett Browning's relationship to her father, whereas Taplin's study is more concerned with intellectual influences upon Barrett Browning, and is, therefore, the more scholarly biography. Cora Kaplan has made a biographical reading of *Aurora Leigh* in which she suggests that Barrett Browning 'memorialised her own troubled history and the men who figured in it, in a pattern which very closely follows that of family romance' ('Wicked Fathers', p. 130).

5. *Shakespeare's Sisters: Feminist Essays on Women Poets* is but one example of the critical attention which has been paid to the poetic 'grandmothers' Barrett Browning looked for but could not find. Barrett Browning herself became, if not a poetic grandmother, then certainly a sororal inspiration for Emily Dickinson. John Walsh examines this

relationship in great detail, going so far as to provide a book by book/
poem by poem table of Dickinson's 'borrowings' from *Aurora Leigh*.
Walsh claims that Dickinson's reaction to *Aurora Leigh* 'as a source of
inspiration has scarcely a parallel in the lives of other writers' (*The
Hidden Life of Emily Dickinson*, p. 97). His tabulated evidence is
interesting but his palpably untrue claim for *Aurora Leigh* that 'Few
literary works have set sail so gloriously as this peculiar novel-in-verse'
(p. 92) must call into question his many assertions.

6. As Margaret Homans, among others, has observed, 'the novel was
more available to women because those portions of society that women
experienced formed appropriate subjects for prose fiction' (*Women
Writers and Poetic Identity*, p. 7). See Dorothy Mermin, 'Genre and
Gender in *Aurora Leigh*' for an interesting discussion of how Barrett
Browning remakes inherited formal structures in the poem.

7. For reviews of *Aurora Leigh*, see *Westminster Review*, 68:399–415;
*Blackwood's Magazine*, 81:23–41; *The Spectator*, 29:1239–40. The following
reviews of *Aurora Leigh* are also of particular interest: *Saturday Review*,
2:776–8; *Dublin University Magazine*, 49:460–70; *National Quarterly
Review*, 5:134–48. When the poem was first published, *Blackwood's*
adopted a thoroughly offended stance, finding 'the extreme
independence' of Aurora detracting from the paucity of 'feminine'
charm she might possess and marring all interest that the reader might
have in 'so intellectual a heroine'. Barrett Browning is accused of
indelicately affecting 'masculine' language, of becoming 'coarse' in her
desire not to be squeamish. If there is one critical thread that holds the
negative reviews of the poem together, it is an accusation of coarseness
of language and of theme. Propriety and good taste are particularly
called into question in discussion of what *The Spectator* called 'the
"Clarissa Harlowe" calamity': 'The bar of the Old Bailey is the only
place where we wish to hear of such things!' The violence in *Aurora
Leigh* has been interpreted in a number of different and differing ways:
writing in 1881, Peter Bayne, for example, attributed Barrett Browning's
demonic vision of the poor to her lack of experience. Bayne finds it
totally implausible that Aurora Leigh would have been as insulted as
she was when she visits Marian's working-class neighbourhood in
London: 'It cannot be said of the English poor that they are slow to
recognise the wish to do them good, or to reciprocate kindly feeling'
(*Two Great Englishwomen*, p. 148). Alice Meynell traces Barrett
Browning's use of violent imagery to a fervent religiosity: 'Mrs.
Browning's morality was positive. The kingdom of heaven suffereth
violence, and her poetry was almost always violent. . . . The blank
verse of "Aurora Leigh" is defiant almost throughout, and the phrase
has a turn of assertion and of menace' ('Elizabeth Barrett Browning',
pp. 161–3). See Kay Moser, 'The Victorian Critics' Dilemma', for
detailed discussion of contemporary responses to Barrett Browning.

8. Both Cora Kaplan and Ellen Moers have analysed the literary influences
upon *Aurora Leigh*, principally those of the work of Madame de Staël
and George Sand. Ellen Moers, in particular, makes an invaluable
analysis of the significance of *Corinne* in the work of nineteenth-century

women writers. In terms of the intense meaning of reading and writing in Barrett Browning's life, it is interesting to note her feelings on meeting Robert Browning after some four months of almost daily correspondence: 'The writer of the letters seemed nearer to me . . . than did the personal visitor who confounded me' (*L*.RB/EBB, 1:372). Understandably, those of Barrett Browning's acquaintances familiar with the details of her secluded life made connections between her poetry and her experience. Harriet Martineau, for example, found the poetry 'wonderfully beautiful' in its way, but wished Barrett Browning were 'more familiar with the external realities which are needed to balance her ideal conceptions' (*Autobiography*, 1:418).

9. Ben Knights's description of the 'central assertion' of the 'clerisy' argument in the nineteenth century usefully defines Barrett Browning's poetic and intellectual work. Knights observes that the most important members of the secular clerisy (in his study, Coleridge, Carlyle, Arnold, and Mill) believed that there 'historically has been or that there ought to be a group in society which sees more clearly, describes the permanent and truly important behind the ever-shifting, untrustworthy phenomena, and consequently knows society's needs better than its ostensible rulers' (*The Idea of the Clerisy in the Nineteenth Century*, p. 6). Knights describes a self-created ideology of the intellectual that is primarily derived from the influence of German thought upon British culture; a new epistemology emerges which presents a challenge to the materialist enlightenment, and the intellectual is graced to participate in the apprehension of ideal forms which exist prior to shifting phenomena of the material world (p. 20).

10. A friend from the Italian years, Mrs David Ogilvy, rather acidly summed up the Brownings' sense of themselves as follows: 'Their idea of Poetry was to be written for the Higher Intellect, the Lords of Mind, and they were to interpret it to the common herd. As for being "understanded of the people", they as little thought Poetry should be so, than did the Peers and Bishops of the middle ages think the Bible should be comprehensible to the masses' (*L*.EBB/DO, p. xxviii). As a scholarly poet intellectual, Barrett Browning certainly wrote for the 'Higher Intellect', but it must also be acknowedged that if not exactly writing for the 'masses', she did intend much of her poetry as instructional – in the 'highest' sense, that is.

11. See 'Milton's Bogey: Patriarchal Poetry and Woman Readers', in Gilbert and Gubar, *The Madwoman in the Attic*, pp. 187–212.

12. George Landow observes that the aesthetic views set forth by Aurora in this section of the poem demonstrate Barrett Browning's Victorian interest in typology; Aurora's exhortation that the poet must link 'natural things / And spiritual' shows that Barrett Browning 'founds a theory of the arts upon typology' (*Victorian Types, Victorian Shadows*, p. 6). The poet is graced to see the 'type' and the 'antetype' and is made witness to a work superior to his own, a work complete and unified.

**Notes to Chapter 6: The Social Wound and the Poetics of Healing**

1. In her sensitive reading of Marian Erle's relationship to mothers and the meaning of Marian's own motherhood, Sandra M. Gilbert makes the point that Marian bears a likeness 'not only to the fallen woman Mary Magdalen but also the blessed Virgin Mary, whose immaculate conception was the sign of a divine annunciation' ('From *Patria* to *Matria*', p. 204).

2. For closely related interpretations of the imagery of motherhood and suckling in *Aurora Leigh*, see Sandra Donaldson, Barbara Charlesworth Gelpi, and Virginia V. Steinmetz. Donaldson postulates a link between Barrett Browning's own motherhood and a more powerful poetry than that she had produced in her childless days: by the time of *Aurora Leigh* she uses the 'metaphor of breasts boldly as a symbol of activity and vitality' ('Motherhood's Advent in Power', p. 59). Focusing upon Aurora's ambivalent attitude towards her mother's portrait, Gelpi argues that Aurora finally trusts her own womanhood by the end of the poem. Steinmetz's reading discusses the maternal images less positively and more psychoanalytically, and sees them as 'negative symbols reinforcing the theme of deprivation and representing the poet's need to bring obsessive infantile desires into light where they could serve rather than dominate her' ('Images of "Mother-Want" in Elizabeth Barrett Browning's *Aurora Leigh*', p. 351).

3. Sandra M. Gilbert and Susan Gubar observe, correctly in my view, that Aurora is 'neither a glittering and inspired figure nor a passionately self-assertive Jane Eyre' (*The Madwoman in the Attic*, p. 578). I am less in agreement, however, with their suggestion that Aurora ends up labouring for her 'blind master', ministering as 'submissive helpmate' to Romney who plays the role of Victorian sage (p. 579). At the end of the poem, Romney and Aurora relinquish their ideologies to each other in an equality of confessed intellectual and moral wrong.

4. Gilbert and Gubar see these forms in the portrait as 'melodramatic, gothic, the moral extremes of angel and monster characteristic of male-defined masks and costumes' (ibid, p. 19). In a recent essay, Dolores Rosenblum argues that when Aurora sees Marian's face in Paris, she *re*-sees the iconised female face of nineteenth-century poetry, and is thereby liberated to a full expression of her art: 'The poet who imagines this recognition and the persona who finds the living woman symbolically recover their mothers, lost not only through death, but also through the repudiation of the mother that is the "natural" course of a daughter's development' ('Face to Face' p. 231). Nina Auerbach forcefully dissects the contradictory 'faces' of Victorian woman in *Woman and the Demon* (passim.)

5. E. Royston Pike's *Human Documents of the Industrial Revolution in Britain* offers a harrowing selection from the Parliamentary Papers from the first half of the nineteenth century and indicates some of the material Barrett Browning surely encountered in her extensive newspaper and periodical reading. In the second half of the nineteenth century, the infernal topos continued to be a favoured image for writers

investigating living and working conditions of the poor. Peter Keating (ed.), *Into Unknown England, 1855–1913: Selections from the Social Explorers* contains many instances of such representation.

### Notes to Chapter 7: Defiled Text and Political Poetry

1. Elizabeth Barrett and Robert Browning were impelled to live abroad after their marriage. For a number of reasons, their life together would have been unmanageable in England. With Barrett Browning's limited private income which, until it was supplemented with a hundred pounds annuity from Frederic Kenyon on the birth of her son, constituted the Brownings' principal financial support, it was cheaper to live in Italy. It was also better for Barrett Browning's health. And lastly, her father having forbidden any of his children to marry, it was probably easier for his daughter to bear his absolute rejection from a distance, a rejection which lasted until Edward Barrett's death.

2. The most extensive discussion of the influence of the early Victorian Spasmodics upon Barrett Browning is that of Jerome Buckley. Buckley suggests that *Aurora Leigh* 'throbbed with a Spasmodic faith in the poet's mission', and that until the end of her life Barrett Browning 'retained the highly emotional attitude towards aesthetic and religious problems which characterized the work of the many younger Spasmodics' (*The Victorian Temper*, pp. 61–2).

3. The Moulton Barrett family fortunes, founded in the eighteenth century, were based on the possession of Jamaican estates. Barrett Browning's father's maternal grandfather was the original patriarch, the owner of extensive plantation and slave holdings; her mother's family owned sugar plantations and a shipping company which plied the West Indian trade.

4. While Gardiner Taplin may be correct in judging the poem 'too blunt and shocking to have any enduring artistic worth' (*The Life of Elizabeth Barrett Browning*, p. 194), its very violence contributes to Barrett Browning's dramatisation of what was, in actuality, a commonplace event. As Barbara Omolade has pointed out, the sexual exploitation of black female slaves by white male owners was an 'accepted burden of the slave community'. Omolade's carefully documented essay, an historical collage of events, personal accounts documenting the black woman's subjugation, testifies to Barrett Browning's dramatic distortion of what was established practice – male sexual domination and exploitation ('Hearts of Darkness', in Ann Snitow *et al.* (eds), *Powers of Desire: The Politics of Sexuality*, pp. 350–67).

## Notes to Chapter 8: Women's Art as Servant of Patriarchy

1. For discussion of the problematical issue of women and language and of important issues in feminist literary criticism at the present time, see Elaine Showalter's essay, 'Feminist Criticism in the Wilderness', which appeared in the 'Writing and Sexual Difference' issue of *Critical Inquiry*, 8:2. *New French Feminisms*, edited by Elaine Marks and Isabelle de Courtivron, is a comprehensive selection from the recent writings of French feminists who are particularly concerned with the relationship between women's experience and women's language. The essay which most notably expounds a theory of women's 'writing from the body', Helene Cixous's 'The Laugh of the Medusa', is to be found in this collection: it first appeared in *Signs*, 1 (Summer 1976) 878. For further analysis of women's language, see McConnell-Ginet *et al.*, 'Linguistics and the Feminist Challenge', in *Women and Language in Literature and Society*. Toril Mois's recent exposition of the major issues in feminist critical theory, *Sexual/Textual Politics*, pays detailed attention to the issue of 'women's language'. I find that we are in strong agreement in rejection of an 'autonomous' and 'separatist' tradition for women.

2. The alliance of patriarchal formations and bourgeois ideology is examined in great detail by Michèle Barrett in her attempt to isolate the multiple and related determinants of women's oppression: she analyses nineteenth-century relationships between existing structures of control over women's lives and the emergence of new structures of economic organisation which both altered and reinforced the established social and cultural subjugation of women (see *Women's Oppression Today: Problems in Marxist Feminist Analysis*).

3. One of Barrett Browning's critics, Alethea Hayter, appears to concur in her anti-feminist views. Employing a language that buttresses, even echoes, the opinions of her subject, she makes it difficult for the reader to distinguish accurate paraphrase from the paraphraser's opinion in such comments as the following: 'She [E.B.B.] did not think that a rabid feminist movement was the best way to combat this foolish idea [that women need male protection]; the rights of women would not be won by raucous prophetesses' (*Mrs Browning: A Poet's Work and its Setting*, p. 185). Hayter seems to betray her own anti-feminism throughout her study.

4. The most important and extensive discussion of the influence of Sand upon Barrett Browning is to be found in Patricia Thomson's *George Sand and the Victorians*: Thomson labels the strong identification Barrett Browning felt with Sand 'a love affair . . . as intense, as liberating' as her romance with Browning, and she points to the strong similarities between the two women: 'Both were warm impulsive, emotional; both were romantics, Byron-worshippers in their youth, radicals, moderate feminists; both were genuinely and effortlessly creative, enthusiastic reformers; and for both, literary creation came first' (p. 46).

5. See John D. Rosenberg's *The Fall of Camelot: A Study of Tennyson's 'The Idylls of the King'* for a close reading of the poem as apocalyptic vision and also for Rosenberg's detailed examination of the *Idylls'* contribution

to the Victorian literary concern with clearing the wasteland. The exhortation to 'Workers' at the end of Carlyle's *Past and Present* should also be noted: 'Subdue mutiny, discord, widespread despair, by manfulness, justice, mercy and wisdom. Chaos is dark, deep as Hell; let light be, and there is instead a green flowery world' (pp. 293–4).

## Notes to Chapter 9: Iconic Sage

1. Quoted in Redinger, *George Eliot: The Emergent Self*, p. 292.
2. David Carroll (ed.), *The Critical Heritage*, p. 292.
3. The major intellectual influences upon Eliot's work have been so extensively identified and are so much a diffused part of Eliot criticism, that detailed reference to particular studies would be redundant here. However, Gordon Haight's commanding biography of Eliot must be mentioned: it is indispensable for any study of Eliot's life, career, and intellectual experience.
4. For Jameson's dismantling of 'strategies of containment' in the work of writers such as Balzac, Conrad, and Gissing, see Chapters 3, 4, and 5 of *The Political Unconscious*.
5. In February 1857 Mary Ann (christened Mary Anne) Evans became 'George Eliot', and in May of the same year (almost three years after beginning to live with Lewes) she began to designate herself Marian Lewes. Encouraged by Lewes, she invented herself as novelist and as the wife she could not become in legal actuality. Alexander Welsh perceives a connection between the secrecy of Mary Ann Evans's authorship and Lewes's troubled family experience, and argues that they both resulted in the changing of names to George Eliot and Marian Evans ('The Secrets of George Eliot'). George Eliot's various forms and informal nominations should be noted: Mary Ann Evans, Mary Anne Evans, Marian Evans, Mrs Lewes, Mrs John Cross, 'Pollian', and 'the Mutter'. See Elaine Showalter's essay, 'Women Writers and the Double Standard' for discussion of the significance of pseudonyms for Victorian women novelists. Phyllis Rose has recently interpreted the 'birth' of 'George Eliot' as 'moving testimony to the connection there may be between creativity and sexuality' (*Parallel Lives*, p. 212). In Rose's reading, the sexual union with Lewes liberates Eliot from 'meager, virginal equanimity' to her orgasmic fulfilment as 'George Eliot', creative novelist. I am uncomfortable with this view as it tends to suggest that Eliot only needed a man to blossom forth as intellectual novelist.
6. *The Critical Heritage*, pp. 114–15, 143, 150, 165, 277.
7. Ibid., Introduction, p. 40.
8. Ibid., p. 502.
9. Ibid., Introduction, p. 42.
10. Quoted in David Willians, *Mr George Eliot*, pp. 285–6. To Charles Eliot Norton, Eliot was no monster but she was certainly the source of disappointment. He reported that over a two to three hour Sunday

lunch conversation with her in January 1869, her talk was 'by no means brilliant' and her manner that 'of a woman who feels herself to be of mark and is accustomed, as she is, to the adoring flattery of a coterie of not undistinguished admirers'. Struggling to be gallant and tending finally to cherish the memory of Eliot's essentialist 'womanly' qualities rather than her acquired 'masculine' ones, Norton concludes his reminiscences by chivalrously emphasising her sympathetic eye and her warm attention to his remarks (*Letters of Charles Eliot Norton*, 1:319).

11. See Q. D. Leavis's interpretations of Eliot as a social thinker in the Introduction to *Silas Marner* (Penguin edn).

12. The Oxford English Dictionary recognises no such thing as a female sage: while the adjective definition neutrally refers to the 'wise, discreet, judicious' qualities of 'a wise person', the noun definition refers to 'a man of profound wisdom'.

13. See Hardy's *Particularities*. In one of the essays, 'The Reticient Narrator', Hardy does discuss the gender-specific nature of Eliot's narrators. But while she makes a strong argument for two developments in the stories and novels ('a gradual diminution of autobiographical anecdote' and 'gradual disappearance of the masculine allusions which identify the early narrators; they drop from explicit detail into implication, into a form of androgynous address, with occasional female markings, and finally into an attempt to speak carefully and comprehensively not for men or for women, but for human nature' – p. 128), she does not investigate the conditions which might have led Eliot to adopt such strategies and to write in such a way that Hardy can actually talk about 'development' from masculine to androgynous. It should be noted that Hardy's readings of *Middlemarch* certainly refer to the 'author's sharply feminist consciousness', making the point that Dorothea's non-internalisation of this attitude reflects Eliot's 'care to avoid anachronisms in political consciousness' (p. 123). U. C. Knoepflmacher has recently correlated two divisions in Eliot's work, one formal the other psychological: a 'split between history and romance' and a 'psychic split between male and female aspects that her powerful hermaphroditic imagination tried to overcome' ('Genre and the Integration of Gender', p. 96). He sees Eliot 'triangulating them into a higher fused self', and argues that Eliot attempts a unification of contrary genres and gender divisions.

14. Thomas Pinney, 'The Authority of the Past in George Eliot's Novels'. Pinney's essay first appeared in *Nineteenth-Century Fiction*, 21:131–47. Margaret Homan's reading of the Eliot/Wordsworth relationship, perceived in terms of Harold Bloom's paradigm of Oedipal rebellion and guilt on the part of poetic sons and refined by a feminist recognition of Eliot as woman writer, establishes Eliot as both deferential and rebellious in relation to Wordsworth. Resenting her subordinate relationship to the male poet she admires, Eliot creates devastatingly practical, anti-Wordsworthian figures such as Tom Tulliver. Wordsworth is revered, resented, and rejected in a dialectics of poetic influence. Homan's reading is tonic after the evasion of Eliot's sex and gender, but subject, perhaps, to one revision: Daniel Deronda is a

Wordsworthian and anti-Wordsworthian brother to Gwendolen Harleth, despite her desire that he be otherwise. Deronda is imaginative and practical, inspirational without being oppressively authoritative, a figure who may be said to dissolve the contradiction Homans adroitly identifies. Wordsworth's poetic presence in Eliot's fiction has been the subject of many essays. For representative discussion of this relationship, see Henry Auster, 'George Eliot and the Modern Temper'; Deborah H. Roazen, '*Middlemarch* and the Wordsworthian Imagination'; Jay Clayton, 'Visionary Power and Narrative Form: Wordsworth and *Adam Bede*'.

15. Raymond Williams, *The Country and the City*, pp. 170–1. *George Eliot: A Collection of Critical Essays* (ed. George Creeger, 1970) appeared just as the women's movement was beginning to find its scholarly correlative in feminist literary criticism, but it is still remarkable that Eliot floats through the essays as disembodied 'mind'. George Creeger, in his introduction to these essays, does refer to Eliot as the 'Wise Woman'. This designation, however, makes Eliot sound like some witch-like creature dispensing oracular advice from The Priory.

### Notes to Chapter 10: Instructed Women and 'Romola'

1. George Eliot, *Letters*, 2:227. The petition was presented to Parliament on 14 March 1856 with more than 3000 signatures.
2. See *Letters*, 5:58. Lewes recorded in his journal that this was 'the most magnificent offer yet made for a novel; and Polly, as usual, was disinclined to accept it, on the ground that her work would not be worth the sum!' (*Letters*, 4:17–18). See *Letters*, 7: Appendix I for records of Eliot's literary earnings and Lewes's literary receipts.
3. Nicholas McGuinn has made a valiant effort to read Eliot's review essay as a defiance of patriarchy. He claims she has no reason to include Wollstonecraft and that she does so 'to advance the idea of a growing tradition of feminist theory', bringing Wollstonecraft's ideas 'covertly' into the review. I find his claim for Eliot's interest in feminist theory unsupported by evidence from other sources, and to describe Eliot as 'proudly independent, exceptionally emancipated and actively feminist' is just plain wrong. Independent and emancipated she may have been, but actively feminist she was not.
4. Eliot evoked this language in writing to Emily Davies some fourteen years later. She observes that in the higher education of women 'woman's peculiar constitution for a special moral influence' must be preserved – 'that exquisite type of gentleness, tenderness, possible maternity suffusing a woman's being with affectionateness, which makes what we mean by the feminine character' must be guarded against contamination by over-zealous intellectual activity (*Letters*, 4:467). Eliot expresses the common Victorian fear that over-stimulation of a woman's brain depleted energy from her reproductive organs, a fear

unconsciously articulated by Harriet Martineau in describing the origins of her illness.

5. Arnold Bennett found Eliot's style anything but masculine: 'It is downright, aggressive, sometimes rude, but genuinely masculine never. On the contrary, it is transparently feminine – feminine in its lack of restraint, its wordiness, and the utter absence of feeling for form that characterises it' (*Journals*, 1:7–8).

6. Eliot, *Letters*, 1:124. This view of Hannah More, here expressed to John Sibree in February 1848, differs from that expressed to Maria Lewis some ten years earlier when Eliot was still strongly under the Evangelical influence of her teacher. She wrote to Maria Lewis, 'I have highly enjoyed Hannah More's letters; the contemplation of so blessed a character as hers is very salutary' (*Letters*, 1:7).

7. Nina Auerbach observes that this passage from the 'Silly Novels' essay utilises 'a pervasive nineteenth-century stereotype . . . silly women are exhorted to rise to generalities' (*Woman and the Demon*, p. 54).

8. The essays are typical of the nineteenth-century quarterlies and representative of what Walter Bagehot termed 'the review-like essay and essay-like review', when he analysed the function of the Victorian essayist in his own 1855 essay, 'The First Edinburgh Reviewers'. Bagehot identifies as a 'peculiarity' of the times the imperative to 'instruct so many persons', and that function was, of course, performed by the social group of intellectuals to which Eliot belonged (*Walter Bagehot*, 1:146–7).

9. Hugh Witemeyer points out that Eliot was in Florence in the spring of 1861 to do research for *Romola*. He notes, 'She kept no journal of this visit, but we know from her correspondence and from *Romola* itself that she was particularly concerned with paintings of late-fifteenth-century faces and costumes such as Ghirlandaio's frescoes in the choice of Santa Maria Novella' (*George Eliot and the Visual Arts*, p. 13).

10. Auerbach, *Woman and the Demon*, pp. 48–52.

11. Felicia Bonaparte observes that Eliot copied into her *Quarry* certain notes about Fedele from William Roscoe's *Life of Lorenzo de' Medici*. Bonaparte believes that Eliot's 'chief point' about Romola's desire to emulate Cassandra Fedele is that in her, 'classicism does not . . . become scholarship, it becomes something far more important, a clear critical intelligence. . . . For it was that critical intelligence, in all its many forms, that, in Eliot's view, the highest gift of the ancients' (*The Triptych and the Cross*, p. 42). In a revisionist reading, Bonaparte sees the novel more as an epic poem than a work of realistic fiction, finding in it 'the full range of Eliot's poetic imagination, and a quarry of all the myths that were the central poetic images of her fiction' (p. 33). For a useful list of the books Eliot consulted for the writing of *Romola* see Bonaparte (p. 35).

12. As Sandra Gilbert and Susan Gubar cogently observe, Romola discovers that 'she resembles the Ariadne abandoned by Theseus far more than the Ariadne crowned by Bacchus' (*The Madwoman in the Attic*, p. 527).

13. Felicia Bonaparte reads this baptismal sequence in Romola's life as 'her

last sacrament' in the novel, a moment of rebirth into a life 'to which the Christ child symbolically awakens her'. Romola is re-christened after completing 'the largest historical and mythological circle of the book' (*The Triptych and the Cross*, pp. 236–8).

14. Other critics, of course, read Savonarola in more positive ways than I have done here. I have necessarily emphasised his discipline (negative in my view) of Romola. Karen Mann, in discussing the 'language of sound' in Eliot's fiction, interprets Romola's 'hearing' of the Frate's voice in positive terms (*The Language that Makes George Eliot's Fiction*, p. 78). After Eliot describes the suffering of Savonarola at the hands of his torturers, Mann believes that 'Eliot hopes to console us, in the face of Savonarola's inability to renovate the church and the state, by emphasizing the real effect he has had on Romola individually and on various Florentine citizens collectively' (ibid., pp. 82–3). Where Mann sees this 'effect' in positive terms, I see it as negative. Andrew Sanders believes that if 'we balk at the nineteenth-century ideal, we ought to see that she [Romola] remains something of a feminist and humanist ideal' (Introduction to *Romola* (Penguin edn), p. 28). Romola is certainly a humanist ideal, but hardly a feminist one.

### Notes to Chapter 11: Subversive Sexual Politics

1. Harold's sensuous vitality, combined with the trembling bitterness of his mother, stand in significant contrast to the failure that is Felix Holt. As George Levine succinctly observes, Felix is 'wooden, priggish, and asexual', where Mrs Transome is 'not wish but vision, and her part of the story is a stunning and moving psychological drama totally removed from Felix's didacticism and moralism, though tied to it brilliantly in the surface thematic and formal structure of the novel' (Introduction to *Felix Holt* (Norton edn), p. xiv). F. R. Leavis, writing in the mid-1940s makes an interesting reading of Mrs Transome, suggesting that Eliot does not have in this character 'a heroine with whom she can be tempted to identify herself' and that we see Mrs Transome 'with complete objectivity . . . poignant sympathy' (*The Great Tradition*, p. 55). Leavis believes that in her characterisation of Mrs Transome we are privileged to see that 'George Eliot brought a magnificent intelligence, functioning here as mature understanding' to the character' (p. 54).

2. Robin Sheets observes that in *Felix Holt* 'women have little opportunity to participate in religious and political discourse. . . . Frustrated by their powerlessness and by the absence of a sympathetic audience, they never acquire the art of communication' ('*Felix Holt*: Language, the Bible, and the Problematic of Meaning', p. 160). I would only add to this that Mrs Transome has almost made an ironic art out of silence itself. From the perspective of Eliot's interest in nineteenth-century science, Sally Shuttleworth argues, as I do, that Mrs Transome is a disruptive figure: Mrs Transome 'stands as a challenge to all ideals of unity,

continuity, and organic harmony'. The Comtean 'organicist ideal' is irreparably undermined by her defiance. See pp. 115–141 of Shuttleworth, *George Eliot and Nineteenth-Century Science*, for a reading of social and sexual politics in *Felix Holt*. William Myers believes that all of Eliot's women characters are based upon Comte's 'assertion that women had "a more lively moral and physical sensibility" ' (*The Teaching of George Eliot*, p. 49). Myers also believes that 'a principal concern' of *Felix Holt* is the 'problem of what it means to be a woman from a baby' (ibid., p. 169).

3. See Chapter 2, 'Language of Nature: Production and Consumption' for Karen Mann's discussion of animal imagery in Eliot's novels. Mann suggests that 'the language of animals – unlike the language of plants – seems in her novels to have a validity both literary and literal' (*The Language that Makes George Eliot's Fiction*, p. 17).

4. J. Hillis Miller, *The Form of Victorian Fiction*, p. 30.

### Notes to Chapter 12: Maggie Tulliver's Desire

1. Laslett argues that the source of our 'feeling that there is a world which once we all possessed, a world now passed away, is the fact of the transformation of the family life of everyone which industrialism brought with it (*The World We Have Lost*, p. 19). His perception is born out by Eliot's invitation to the Victorian reader to peep in at the windows of the Hall Farm as it looked in 1799 and to witness the strong familial and communal ties that bind the Poysers to each other and to their community of farmhands.

2. Martineau, *History of England*, 4:450. Eliot's attitudes towards the railway altered somewhat and by the time of *Middlemarch* and she has Caleb Garth articulate a more accommodating view of technological progress in his mollification of the farm labourers who attack the railway surveyors with their pitchforks: 'Now my lads, you can't hinder the railroad: it will be made whether you like it or not. . . . Somebody told you the railroad was a bad thing. That was a lie. It may do a bit of harm here and there, to this and to that, and so does the sun in heaven. But the railway's a good thing' (p. 408).

3. Barry Qualls draws many illuminating parallels between the thought of Eliot and that of Carlyle. For discussion of *Adam Bede* in particular see *The Secular Pilgrims of Victorian Fiction*, pp. 143–6. Eliot wanted Carlyle to read *Adam Bede* in order that the 'philosopher' might derive some 'pleasure' from it (*Letters*, 3:23).

4. William Wordsworth, *Selected Poems and Prefaces*, p. 449. See Raymond Williams, *The Country and the City* for extensive analysis of the literary responses to industrialism.

5. A. J. Cockshut makes this point, observing that the 'signs are that men of his [Adam Bede's] stamp will become heads of regular business organisations in the next generation' (*The Unbelievers*, p. 46).

6. Barry Qualls's observation that Eliot is 'unsure about the Dodsons'

points to the contradictions I am concerned with here (*The Secular Pilgrims of Victorian Fiction*, p. 158).

7. In a reading that combines structuralist and psychoanalytic approaches, Diane F. Sadoff argues that Eliot punishes deficient fathers in the process of assuming narrative authority. See *Monsters of Affection*.

8. See Gillian Beer, 'Beyond Determinism: George Eliot and Virginia Woolf'; Nancy K. Miller, 'Emphasis Added: Plots and Plausibilities in Women's Fiction'; Mary Jacobus, 'The Question of Language: Men of Maxims and *The Mill on the Floss*'. William Myers interprets the ending as a conflict between 'meliorist' and 'realistic' perspectives. His study, in general, insists that we always comprehend what Eliot 'intends' in her fiction. Nowhere, however, does he refer to what Eliot may have 'intended' about Maggie's problems with sex and gender (*The Teaching of George Eliot*).

# Works Cited

Adamson, Walter L., *Hegemony and Revolution: A Study of Antonio Gramsci's Political and Cultural Theory* (Berkeley and Los Angeles: University of California Press, 1980).

Annan, Noel, *Leslie Stephen: The Godless Victorian* (New York: Random House, 1984).

Arnold, Matthew, *Poetry and Prose*, ed. John Bryson (Cambridge, Mass.: Harvard University Press, 1963).

Auerbach, Nina, *Communities of Women: An Idea in Fiction* (Cambridge, Mass.: Harvard University Press, 1978).

——, Nina, *Woman and the Demon: The Life of a Victorian Myth* (Cambridge, Mass.: Harvard University Press, 1982).

Auster, Henry, 'George Eliot and the Modern Temper', *The Worlds of Victorian Fiction*, ed. Jerome H. Buckley (Cambridge, Mass.: Harvard University Press, 1975).

Bagehot, Walter, 'The First Edinburgh Reviewers', in *Walter Bagehot: Literary Studies*, 2 vols (London: J. M. Dent, 1932).

Banks, J. A. and Olive, *Feminism and Family Planning in Victorian England* (New York: Schocken Books, 1964).

Barrett, Michèle, *Women's Oppression Today: Problems in Marxist Feminist Analysis* (London: Verso Editions, 1980).

Barrett, Elizabeth Barrett, *The Letters of Robert Browning and Elizabeth Barrett Barrett 1845–1846*, 2 vols (New York: Harper, 1899). (Abbreviated in the text as *L.RB/EBB*.)

Barrett Browning, Elizabeth, *The Letters of Elizabeth Barrett Browning*, ed. with biographical additions by Frederic G. Kenyon, 2 vols (London: Macmillan, 1897). (Abbreviated in the text as *L.EBB*.)

——, *Letters of Elizabeth Barrett Browning to Richard Hengist Horne*, with a preface and memoir by Richard Henry Stoddard (New York: Worthington, 1889). (Abbreviated in the text as *L.EBB/RHH*.)

——, *The Letters of Elizabeth Barrett Browning to Mary Russell Mitford, 1836–1854*, ed. Meredith B. Raymond and Mary Rose Sullivan, 3 vols (Winfield, Kan.: Armstrong Browning Library of Baylor University, The Browning Institute, Wedgestone Press and Wellesley College, 1983). (Abbreviated in the text as *L.EBB/M*.)

——, *Elizabeth Barrett Browning's Letters to Mrs David Ogilvy, 1849–1861*, with recollections by Mrs Ogilvy, ed. Peter N. Heydon and Philip Kelley (New York: Quadrangle/The New York Times Book Co. and the Browning Institute, 1973). (Abbreviated in the text as *L.EBB/DO*.)

——, *The Complete Works of Mrs Elizabeth Barrett Browning*, ed. Charlotte Porter and Helen A. Clarke, 6 vols (New York: George D. Sproul, 1901). (All references to the work of Elizabeth Barrett Browning are to this edition; citations are by volume and page or line number(s), except in the case of *Aurora Leigh* where citations are by book and line number(s), and book numbers are indicated by roman numerals.)

——, 'Glimpses into My Own Life and Literary Character', ed. William S. Peterson, *Browning Institute Studies*, 2 (1974) 121–34.

Bayne, Peter, *Two Great Englishwomen: Mrs Browning and Charlotte Brontë* (London: James Clarke, 1881).

Beer, Gillian, 'Beyond Determinism: George Eliot and Virginia Woolf', in *Women Writing and Writing about Women*, ed. Mary Jacobus (New York: Barnes and Noble Books, 1979).

Benda, Julien, *The Treason of the Intellectuals*, trans. Richard Aldington (1928; rprt. New York: W. W. Norton, 1969).

Benjamin, Walter, 'The Work of Art in the Age of Mechanical Reproduction', in *Illuminations* (New York: Schocken Books, 1969).

Bennett, Arnold, *The Journal of Arnold Bennett*, 3 vols (New York: Viking Press, 1932).

Bonaparte, Felicia, *The Triptych and the Cross: The Central Myths of George Eliot's Poetic Imagination* (New York: New York University Press, 1979).

Bosanquet Theodora, *Harriet Martineau: An Essay in Comprehension* (London: Frederick Etchels and Hugh Macdonald, 1927).

Boyle, Sir Edward, 'Harriet Martineau', in *Biographical Essays: 1790–1890* (London: Oxford University Press, 1936).

Briggs, Asa, *The Making of Modern England 1783–1867: The Age of Improvement* (New York: Harper and Row, 1965).

Brontë, Charlotte, *Shirley* (London: J. M. Dent, 1908).

Browning, Robert, Prefatory Note to *Poems by Elizabeth Barrett Browning* (London: Smith, Elder, 1899).

Buckley, Jerome Hamilton, *The Victorian Temper: A Study in Literary Culture* (New York: Vintage Books, 1951).

Burne-Jones, Georgianna, *Memorials of Edward Burne-Jones*, 2 vols (New York and London: Macmillan, 1904).

Carlyle, Thomas, *Letters of Thomas Carlyle to John Stuart Mill, John Sterling and Robert Browning*, ed. Alexander Carlyle (1923; rprt. New York: Haskell House, 1970).

——, *Past and Present*, ed. Richard D. Altick (Boston, Mass.: Houghton Mifflin, 1965).

——, 'Signs of the Times', in *A Carlyle Reader: Selections from the Writings of Thomas Carlyle*, ed. G. B. Tennyson (New York: Random House, 1969).

Carroll, David (ed.), *George Eliot: The Critical Heritage* (London: Routledge and Kegan Paul, 1971). (Abbreviated as *C.H.* in the text).

Chodorow, Nancy, *The Reproduction of Mothering: Psychoanalysis and the Sociology of Gender* (Berkeley and Los Angeles: University of California Press, 1978).

Cixous, Helene, 'The Laugh of the Medusa', trs. Keith and Paula Cohen, *Signs*, 1 (1976) 875–99.

Clayton, Jay, 'Visionary Power and Narrative Form: Wordsworth and *Adam Bede*', *English Literary History*, 46 (1979) 645–72.

Clouston, T. S., *Female Education from a Medical Point of View* (Edinburgh, 1982).

Cockshut, A. J., *The Unbelievers: English Agnostic Thought 1840–1890* (London: Collins, 1964).

Colby, Vineta, *Yesterday's Woman: Domestic Realism in the English Novel* (Princeton: Princeton University Press, 1974).

Coleridge, Sara, *Memoir and Letters of Sara Coleridge*, ed. by her daughter (New York: Harper, 1974).

Collins, Wilkie, *The Woman in White* (London: J. M. Dent, 1910).

Conrad, Peter, *The Victorian Treasure-House* (London: Collins, 1973).

Conrad, Susan Phinney, *Perish the Thought: Intellectual Women in Romantic America, 1830–1860* (New York: Oxford University Press, 1976).

Courtney, Janet E., *The Adventurous Thirties: A Chapter in the Women's Movement* (London: Oxford University Press, 1933).

Craik, Dinah Mulock, *A Woman's Thoughts about Women* (London: Hurst and Blackett, 1958).

Creeger, George R. (ed.), *George Eliot: A Collection of Critical Essays* (Englewood Cliffs, N.J.: Prentice Hall, 1970).

Cross, J. W., *George Eliot's Life; As Related in Her Letters and Journals* (New York: Harper, 1899).

Delamont, Sara, 'The Contradictions in Ladies' Education', in Sara Delamont and Lorna Duffin (eds), *The Nineteenth-Century Woman: Her Cultural and Physical World* (London: Croom Helm, 1978).

Dickens, Charles, *Dombey ad Son*, ed. H. W. Garrod (London: Oxford University Press, 1950).

Dinnerstein, Dorothy, *The Mermaid and the Minotaur: Sexual Arrangements and Human Malaise* (New York: Harper and Row, 1976).

Disraeli, Benjamin, 'Society in America', *The Times*, 30 May, 1837.

Donaldson, Sandra, 'Motherhood's Advent in Power: Elizabeth Barrett Browning's Poems about Motherhood', *Victorian Poetry*, 18 (1980) 51–60.

Dowling, William C., *Jameson, Althusser, Marx: An Introduction to 'The Political Unconscious'* (Ithaca, N.Y.: Cornell University Press, 1984).

Eagleton, Terry, *Criticism and Ideology: A Study in Marxist Literary Theory* (London: Verso Editions, 1978).

——, *The Function of Criticism: From 'The Spectator' to Post-Structuralism* (London: Verso Editions, 1984).

Eliot, George, *Adam Bede* (New York: New American Library, 1961). (Abbreviated in the text as *A.B.*)

——, *Complete Poems* (Boston, Mass.: Estes and Lauriat, n.d.) (Abbreviated in the text as *C.P.*)

——, *Essays of George Eliot*, ed. Thomas Pinney (New York: Columbia University Press, 1963). (Abbreviated in the text as *E.*)

——, *Felix Holt, the Radical*, ed. Fred C. Thomson (Oxford: Clarendon Press, 1980). (Abbreviated in the text as *F.H.*)

——, *The George Eliot Letters*, ed. Gordon S. Haight, 9 vols (New Haven, Conn: Yale University Press, 1954–1978). (Abbreviated in the text as *L.*)

——, *Middlemarch*, ed. Gordon S. Haight (Boston, Mass.: Houghton Mifflin, 1956). (Abbreviated in the text as *M.*)

——, *The Mill on the Floss*, ed. Gordon S. Haight (Oxford: Clarendon Press, 1980). (Abbreviated in the text as *M.F.*)

——, *Romola*, ed. Andrew Sanders (Harmondsworth, Middx: Penguin Books, 1980). (Abbreviated in the text as *R.*)

——, *Scenes of Clerical Life*, ed. David Lodge (Harmondsworth, Middx: Penguin Books, 1973). (Abbreviated in the text as *S.C.L.*)

——, *Silas Marner*, ed. Q. D. Leavis (Harmondsworth, Middx: Penguin Books, 1967). (Abbreviated in the text as *S.M.*)

Ellmann, Mary, *Thinking about Women* (New York: Harcourt Brace Jovanovich, 1968).

Ellsworth, Edward W., *Liberators of the Female Mind: The Shirreff Sisters, Educational Reform, and the Women's Movement* (Westport, Conn.: Greenwood Press, 1979).

Fisher, Philip, *Making up Society: The Novels of George Eliot* (Pittsburgh, Penn.: University of Pittsburgh Press, 1981).

Fritz, Leah, 'Eminent Victorian', *The Women's Review of Books*, 1 (1984) 10.

Gaskell, Elizabeth Cleghorn, *The Life of Charlotte Brontë* (London: J. M. Dent, 1908).

Gelpi, Barbara Charlesworth, 'Aurora Leigh: the Vocation of the Woman Poet', *Victorian Poetry*, 19 (1981) 35–48.

Gilbert, Sandra M., 'From *Patria* to *Matria*: Elizabeth Barrett Browning's Risorgimento', *PMLA* 99.1 (1984) 194–211.

——, and Susan Gubar, *The Madwoman in the Attic: The Woman Writer and the Nineteenth-Century Literary Imagination* (New Haven, Conn.: Yale University Press, 1979).

—— (eds), *Shakespeare's Sisters: Feminist Essays on Women Poets* (Bloomington, Ind.: Indiana University Press, 1979).

Gissing, George, *The Odd Women* (1893; rprt. New York: W. W. Norton, 1977).

Gorham, Deborah, *The Victorian Girl and the Feminine Ideal* (Bloomington, Ind.: Indiana University Press, 1982).

Gouldner, Alvin W., *The Future of Intellectuals and the Rise of the New Class* (London: Macmillan, 1979).

Gramsci, Antonio, 'The Intellectuals', in *Selections from the Prison Notebooks of Antonio Gramsci*, ed. and trs. Quintin Hoare and Geoffrey Nowell Smith (New York: International Publishers, 1971).

Greenhow, Thomas M., 'Termination of the Case of Miss Harriet Martineau', *British Medical Journal*, 8 July 1876, p. 64; 14 April 1877, p. 449–50; 21 April 1877, p. 496; 5 May 1877, pp. 543–50.

Haight, Gordon S., *George Eliot: A Biography* (New York: Oxford University Press, 1968).

Hamerton, Philip Gilbert, *The Intellectual Life* (Boston, Mass.: Roberts, 1891).

Hardy, Barbara, *Particularities: Readings in George Eliot* (Athens, Ohio: Ohio University Press, 1982).

Hayter, Alethea, *Mrs Browning: A Poet's Work and its Setting* (London: Faber and Faber, 1962).

Hewlett, Dorothy, *Elizabeth Barrett Browning: A Life* (New York: Alfred A. Knopf, 1952).

Heyck, T. W., *The Transformation of Intellectual Life in Victorian England* (New York: St Martin's Press, 1982).

Himmelfarb, Gertrude, *Victorian Minds* (New York: Alfred A. Knopf, 1968).

Hobsbawm, E. J., *The Pelican Economic History of Britain*, vol. 3: *From 1750 to the Present Day: Industry and Empire* (Harmondsworth, Middx: Penguin Books, 1969).

Hollis, Patricia, *Women in Public, 1850–1900: Documents of the Victorian Women's Movement* (London: George Allen and Unwin, 1979).

Holloway, John, *The Victorian Sage: Studies in Argument* (New York: W. W. Norton, 1965).

Homans, Margaret, 'Eliot, Wordsworth, and the Scenes of the Sisters' Instruction', *Critical Inquiry*, 8 (1981) 223–241.

——, *Women Writers and Poetic Identity: Dorothy Wordsworth, Emily Brontë, and Emily Dickinson* (Princeton, N.J.: Princeton University Press, 1980).

Horne, R. H. (ed.), *A New Spirit of the Age* (London: Saunders and Otley, 1844).

Houghton, Walter E., *The Victorian Frame of Mind, 1830–1870* (New Haven, Conn.: Yale University Press, 1957).

Jacobus, Mary, 'The Question of Language: Men of Maxims and *The Mill on the Floss*', *Critical Inquiry*, 8 (1981) 207–22.

Jameson, Fredric, *The Political Unconscious: Narrative as Socially Symbolic Act* (Ithaca, N.Y.: Cornell University Press, 1981).

Kamm, Josephine, *Hope Deferred: Girls' Education in English History* (London: Methuen, 1965).

Kaplan, Cora, Introduction to *'Aurora Leigh' with Other Poems* (London: The Women's Press, 1978).

——, 'Wicked Fathers: a Family Romance', in Ursula Owen (ed.), *Fathers: Reflections by Daughters* (New York: Pantheon Books, 1985).

Kavanagh, Julia, *English Women of Letters: Biographical Sketches*, 2 vols (London: Hurst and Blackett, 1863).

Keating, Peter (ed.), *Into Unknown England, 1866–1913: Selections from the Social Explorers* (Manchester: Manchester University Press, 1976).

King, Margaret L., 'Book-Lined Cells: Women and Humanism in the Early Italian Renaissance', in Patricia A. Labalme (ed.), *Beyond Their Sex: Learned Women of the European Past* (New York: New York University Press, 1980).

Kingsley, Charles, 'Literary and General Lectures and Essays', in *The Works of Charles Kingsley*, 20 vols (London: Macmillan, 1880).

Knights, Ben, *The Idea of the Clerisy in the Nineteenth Century* (Cambridge: Cambridge University Press, 1978).

Knoepflmacher, U. C., 'Genre and the Integration of Gender: from Wordsworth to Virginia Woolf', in James R. Kincaid and Albert J. Kuhn (eds), *Victorian Literature and Society: Essays Presented to Richard D. Altick* (Columbus, Ohio: Ohio State University Press, 1984).

Landow, George P., *Victorian Types, Victorian Shadows: Biblical Typology in Victorian Literature, Art and Thought* (Boston, Mass.: Routledge and Kegan Paul, 1980).

Laslett, Peter, *The World We Have Lost* (New York: Charles Scribner's Sons, 1973).

Leavis, F. R., *The Great Tradition: George Eliot, Henry James, Joseph Conrad* (1948; New York: New York University Press, 1969).

Levine, George, Introduction to George Eliot, *Felix Holt, the Radical* (New York: W. W. Norton, 1970).

——, *The Realistic Imagination: English Fiction from Frankenstein to Lady Chatterley* (Chicago: University of Chicago Press, 1981).

Linton, Eliza Lynn, *My Literary Life* (London: Hodder and Stoughton, 1899).

Lukács, Georg, *The Theory of the Novel*, trs. Anna Bostock (Cambridge, Mass.: MIT Press, 1971; first published Berlin, 1920).

McConnell-Ginet, Sally, Ruth Borker and Nelly Furman, *Women and Language in Literature and Society* (New York: Praeger, 1980).

McGuinn, Nicholas, 'George Eliot and Mary Wollstonecraft', in Sara Delamont and Lorna Duffin (eds), *The Nineteenth-Century Woman: Her Cultural and Physical World* (London: Croom Helm, 1978).

McPherson, Robert, *Theory of Higher Education in Nineteenth-Century England* (Athens, Georgia: University of Georgia Press, 1959).

Mann, Karen, *The Language that Makes George Eliot's Fiction* (Baltimore, Md: Johns Hopkins University Press, 1983).

Mannheim, Karl, *Ideology and Utopia: An Introduction to the Sociology of Knowledge*, trs. Louis Wirth and Edward Shils (New York: Harcourt Brace, 1954).

Marcet, Mrs Jane, *Conversations on Political Economy: In which the Elements of that Science are Familiarly Explained* (Boston, Mass.: Bowles and Dearborn, 1828).

Marcus, Steven, 'Literature and Social Theory: Starting in with George Eliot', in his *Representations: Essays on Literature and Society* (New York: Random House, 1975).

Marks, Elaine, and Isabelle de Courtivron (eds), *New French Feminisms* (Amherst, Mass.: University of Massachusetts Press, 1980).

Martin, Wendy, *An American Triptych: Anne Bradstreet, Emily Dickinson, Adrienne Rich* (Chapel Hill, N.C.: University of North Carolina Press, 1984).

Martineau, Harriet, *Autobiography*, with Memorials by Maria Weston Chapman, 3 vols (London: Smith, Elder, 1877). (Abbreviated in the text as *A*.)

——, *Biographical Sketches* (New York: Leypoldt and Holt, 1869). (Abbreviated in the text as *B.S.*)

——, *British Rule in India: A Historical Sketch* (London: Smith, Elder, 1857). (Abbreviated in the text as *B.R.*)

——, *Deerbrook*, 3 vols (London: Edward Moxon, 1839). (Abbreviated in the text as *D*.)

——, *Eastern Life, Present and Past*, 3 vols (London: Edward Moxon, 1848). (Abbreviated in the text as *E.L.*)

——, 'Female Writers on Practical Divinity, no. 1, Mrs More', *Monthly Review*, 17 (1822) 593–96.

——, 'Female Writers on Practical Divinity, no. 2, Mrs More and Mrs Barbauld', *Monthly Review*, 17 (1822) 746–50.

——, 'Female Education', *Monthly Review*, 18 (1823) 77–81.

——, *Health, Husbandry, and Handicraft* (London: Bradbury and Evans, 1861). (Abbreviated in the text as *H.H.H.*)

——, *The History of England from the Commencement of the XIXth Century to the Crimean War*, 4 vols (Philadelphia: Porter and Coates, 1864). (Abbreviated in the text as *H*.)

——, *Household Education* (Philadelphia, Penn.: Lea and Blanchard, 1849). (Abbreviated in the text as *H.E.*)

——, *How to Observe Manners and Morals* (New York: Harper, 1838). (Abbreviated in the text as *H.O.*)

——, *Illustrations of Political Economy*, 9 vols (London: Charles Fox, 1832). (Abbreviated in the text as *P.E.*)

——, *Letters on Mesmerism* (London: Edward Moxon, 1845). (Abbreviated in the text as *L.M.*)

——, 'Life in the Sick-Room', in *Essays* (Boston, Mass.: William Crosly, 1845). (Abbreviated in the text as *L.S.*)

——, 'Middle-Class Education in England: Girls', *Cornhill Magazine*, 10 (1864) 549–68.

——, *Miscellanies*, 2 vols (Boston, Mass.: Hilliard, Gray, 1836). (Abbreviated in the text as *MS.*)

——, *Retrospect of Western Travel* (London: Saunders and Otley, 1838).

——, *Society in America*, 3 vols (London: Saunders and Otley, 1839). (Abbreviated in the text as *S.A.*)

Mermin, Dorothy, 'Genre and Gender in *Aurora Leigh*', *The Victorian Newsletter*, 69 (1986) 7–11.

Meynell, Alice, 'Elizabeth Barrett Browning', in P. M. Fraser (ed.), *Selected Literary Essays of Alice Meynell* (London: Oxford University Press, 1965).

Mill, James, *Elements of Political Economy* (London: Baldwin, Cradock and Joy, 1821).

Miller, J. Hillis, *The Form of Victorian Fiction: Thackeray, Dickens, Trollope, George Eliot, Meredith, and Hardy* (Notre Dame, Ind.: University of Notre Dame Press, 1968).

Miller, Nancy K., 'Emphasis Added: Plots and Plausibilities in Women's Fiction', *PMLA*, 96 (1981) 36–47.

Millet, Kate, *Sexual Politics* (New York: Avon, 1971).

Mineka, Francis Edward, *The Dissidence of Dissent: The Monthly Repository 1806–1838* (Chapel Hill, N.C.: University of North Carolina Press, 1944).

Mitford, Mary Russell, *Recollections of a Literary Life; or, Books, Places, and People*, 3 vols (London: Richard Bentley, 1852).

*Modern Women and What is Said of Them; A Reprint of a Series of Articles in the 'Saturday Review'*, with an introduction by Mrs Lucia Gilbert Calhoun (New York: J. S. Redfield, 1868).

Moers, Ellen, *Literary Women* (New York: Doubleday, 1976).

Moi, Toril, *Sexual/Textual Politics: Feminist Literary Theory* (London: Methuen, 1985).

Moser, Kay, 'The Victorian Critics' Dilemma: What to Do with a Talented Poetess?', *Victorians Institute Journal*, 13 (1985) 59–66.

Myers, Mitzi, 'Harriet Martineau's *Autobiography*: the Making of a Female Philosopher', in Estelle C. Jelinek (ed.), *Women's Autobiography: Essays in Criticism* (Bloomington, Ind.: Indiana University Press, 1980).

Myers, William, *The Teaching of George Eliot* (Leicester: Leicester University Press, 1984).

Norton, Charles Eliot, *Letters of Charles Eliot Norton*, ed. Sara Norton and M. A. DeWolfe Howe, 2 vols (London: Constable, 1913).

Okin, Susan Moller, *Women in Western Political Thought* (London: Virago, 1980).

Omolade, Barbara, 'Hearts of Darkness', in Ann Snitow, Christine Stansell and Sharon Thomson (eds), *Powers of Desire: The Politics of Sexuality* (New York: Monthly Review Press, 1983).

Peterson, M. Jeanne, 'The Victorian Governess: Status Incongruence in Family and Society', in Martha Vicinus (ed.), *Suffer and Be Still: Women in the Victorian Age* (Bloomington, Ind.: Indiana University Press, 1972).

Pichanick, Valerie Kessew, *Harriet Martineau: The Woman and the Work 1802–1876* (Ann Arbor, Mich.: University of Michigan Press, 1980).

Pike, E. Royston, *Human Documents of the Industrial Revolution in Britain* (London: George Allen and Unwin, 1966).

Pinney, Thomas, 'The Authority of the Past in George Eliot's Novels', *Nineteenth-Century Fiction*, 21 (1966) 131–47.

Ponsonby, Mary, *A Memoir, Some Letters and a Journal*, ed. by her daughter Magdalen Ponsonby (London: John Murray, 1927).

Poovey, Mary, *The Proper Lady and the Woman Writer: Ideology as Style in the Works of Mary Wollstonecraft, Mary Shelley, and Jane Austen* (Chicago: University of Chicago Press, 1984).

Pope-Hennessy, Una, *Three English Women in America* (London: Ernest Benn, 1929).

Qualls, Barry, *The Secular Pilgrims of Victorian Fiction: The Novel as Book of Life* (New York: Cambridge University Press, 1982).

Redinger, Ruby V., *George Eliot: The Emergent Self* (New York: Alfred A. Knopf, 1975).

Rivenburgh, Narola Elizabeth, 'Harriet Martineau: an Example of Victorian Conflict', PhD dissertation (New York: Columbia University, 1932).

Roazen, Deborah H., '*Middlemarch* and the Wordsworthian Imagination', *English Studies*, 58 (1977) 411–25.

Roberts, Elizabeth, *A Woman's Place: An Oral History of Working-Class Women, 1890–1940* (Oxford: Basil Blackwell, 1984).

Rose, Phyllis, *Parallel Lives: Five Victorian Marriages* (New York: Alfred A. Knopf, 1983).

Rosenberg, John D., *The Fall of Camelot: A Study of Tennyson's 'Idylls of the King'* (Cambridge, Mass.: Belknap Press of Harvard University Press, 1973).

Rosenblum, Dolores, 'Face to Face: Elizabeth Barrett Browning's *Aurora Leigh* and Nineteenth-Century Poetry', *Victorian Studies*, 26.3 (1983) 321–38.

Rossi, Alice S. 'The First Woman Sociologist: Harriet Martineau (1801–1876)', in Alice S. Rossi (ed.), *The Feminist Papers: From Adams to de Beauvoir* (New York: Columbia University Press, 1973).

Ruskin, John, 'Of Queens' Gardens', in *Sesame and Lilies: Two Lectures delivered at Manchester in 1864* (London: Smith, Elder, 1865).

Russell, Edward R., *The Autobiography and Memorial of Miss Harriet Martineau*, a Paper read before the Literary and Philosophical Society of Liverpool, 16 April 1877.

Sadoff, Dianne M., *Monsters of Affection: Dickens, Eliot, and Brontë on Fatherhood* (Baltimore, Md: Johns Hopkins University Press, 1982).

Said, Edward W., *Orientalism* (New York: Pantheon Books, 1978).

——, *The World, the Text, and the Critic* (Cambridge, Mass.: Harvard University Press, 1983).

Shaffer, E. S., *'Kubla Khan' and the Fall of Jerusalem: The Mythological School in Biblical Criticism and Secular Literature, 1770–1880* (Cambridge: Cambridge University Press, 1975).

Shannon, Richard, 'The Consolations of Omniscience', *The Times Literary Supplement*, 1 July 1983, pp. 687–8.

Sheets, Robin, '*Felix Holt*: Language, the Bible, and the Problematic of Meaning', *Nineteenth-Century Fiction*, 37 (1982) 146–69.

Shelley, Mary, *Frankenstein*, in Peter Fairclough (ed.), *Three Gothic Novels* (Harmondsworth, Middx: Penguin Books, 1968).

Shils, Edward, 'The Intellectuals and the Powers: Some Perspectives for Comparative Analysis', in *'The Intellectuals and the Powers' and Other Essays* (Chicago: University of Chicago Press, 1972).

Shirreff, Emily, *Intellectual Education and its Influence on the Character and Happiness of Women* (London, 1858).

Showalter, Elaine, *A Literature of Their Own: British Women Novelists from Brontë to Lessing* (Princeton, N.J.: Princeton University Press, 1977).

——, 'Feminist Criticism in the Wilderness', *Critical Inquiry*, 8.2 (1981) 179–205.

——, 'Towards a Feminist Poetics', in Mary Jacobus (ed.), *Women Writing and Writing about Women* (New York: Barnes and Noble Books, 1979).

——, 'Women Writers and the Double Standard', in Vivian Gornick and Barbara K. Moran (eds), *Woman in Sexist Society* (New York: New American Library, 1972).

Shuttleworth, Sally, *George Eliot and Nineteenth-Century Science: The Make-Believe of a Beginning* (Cambridge: Cambridge University Press, 1984).

Sidgwick, Mrs Henry, 'University Education of Women', a Lecture delivered at University College, Liverpool, May 1876.

Smiles, Samuel, *Workmen's Earnings, Strikes and Savings* (London: John Murray, 1862).

Smith, Adam, *An Inquiry into the Nature and Causes of the Wealth of Nations* (1775–76), 2 vols (London: Oxford University Press, 1904).

Smith, Hilda, *Reason's Disciplines: Seventeenth-Century English Feminists* (Urbana, Chicago, and London: University of Illinois Press, 1982).

Stearns, Bertha-Monica, 'Miss Sedgwick Observes Harriet Martineau', *New England Quarterly*, 25 (1934) 533–541.

Steinmetz, Virginia V., 'Images of "Mother-Want" in Elizabeth Barrett Browning's *Aurora Leigh*', *Victorian Poetry*, 21 (1983) 351–67.

Stephen, Leslie, *George Eliot* (London; Macmillan, 1902).

S[tephen], L[eslie], 'Martineau, Harriet', in *Dictionary of National Biography*, xxxvi: 309–14 (London: Smith Elder, 1893).

Stone, Lawrence, *The Family, Sex and Marriage in England 1500–1800* (New York: Harper and Row, 1977).

Taplin, Gardner B., *The Life of Elizabeth Barrett Browning* (New Haven, Conn.: Yale University Press, 1957).

Tennyson, Alfred, *Poems of Tennyson*, selected with an Introduction and

Notes by Jerome Hamilton Buckley (Boston, Mass.: Houghton Mifflin, 1958).

Thomson, J. Arthur and Patrick Geddes, *Problems of Sex* (London: National Council for Public Morals, 1912).

Thomson, Patricia, *George Sand and the Victorians: Her Influence and Reputation in Nineteenth-Century England* (New York: Columbia University Press, 1977).

Vicinus, Martha, *Independent Women: Work and Community for Single Women 1850–1920* (London: Virago Press, 1985).

——, (ed.), *Suffer and Be Still: Women in the Victorian Age* (Bloomington, Ind.: Indiana University Press, 1973).

——, (ed.), *A Widening Sphere: Changing Roles of Victorian Women* (Bloomington, Ind.: Indiana University Press, 1980).

Walsh, John Evangelist, *The Hidden Life of Emily Dickinson* (New York: Simon and Schuster, 1971).

Walters, Margaret, 'The Rights and Wrongs of Women: Mary Wollstonecraft, Harriet Martineau, Simone de Beauvoir', in Juliet Mitchell and Ann Oakley (eds), *The Rights and Wrongs of Women* (Harmondsworth, Middx: Penguin Books, 1976).

Webb, R. K., *Harriet Martineau: A Radical Victorian* (New York: Columbia University Press, 1960).

Weiner, Gaby, Introduction to Harriet Martineau, *Deerbrook* (London: Virago Press, 1983).

Welsh, Alexander, 'The Secrets of George Eliot', *Yale Review*, 68 (1978–9) 589–97.

Wheatley, Vera, *The Life and Work of Harriet Martineau* (London; Secker and Warburg, 1957).

Williams, David, *Mr George Eliot: A Biography of George Henry Lewes* (London: Hodder and Stoughton, 1983).

Williams, Raymond, *The Country and the City* (London: Chatto and Windus, 1973).

——, *Culture* (Glasgow: William Collins, 1981).

Witemeyer, Hugh, *George Eliot and the Visual Arts* (New Heaven, Conn.: Yale University Press, 1979).

Wolff, Robert Lee, 'The Novel and the Neurosis', in *Strange Stories and Other Explorations in Victorian Fiction* (Boston, Mass.: Gambit, 1971).

Woodham-Smith, Cecil, 'They Stayed in Bed', *Listener*, no. 55, 16 February 1956.

Woolf, Virginia, '*Aurora Leigh*', in Michèle Barrett (ed.), *Virginia Woolf: Women and Writing* (New York: Harcourt Brace Jovanovich, 1980).

——, *Moments of Being: Unpublished Autobiographical Writings*, ed. Jeanne Schulkind (New York: Harcourt Brace Jovanovich, 1976).

Wordsworth, William, *Selected Poems and Prefaces*, ed. Jack Stillinger (Boston, Mass.: Houghton Mifflin, 1965).

Young, G. M., *Portrait of an Age* (Oxford: Oxford University Press, 1936; rprt. 1971).

# Index